FROM CLEMENT TO ORIGEN

From Clement to Origen addresses the engagement of a number of pre-Nicene Church Fathers with the surrounding culture. David Rankin considers the historical and social context of the Fathers, grouped in cities and regions, their writings and theological reflections, and discusses how the particular engagement of each with major aspects of the surrounding culture influences, informs and shapes their thought and the articulation of that thought.

The social and historical context of the Church Fathers is explored with respect to the Roman state, the imperial office and imperial cult, Greco-Roman class structures and the patron-client system, issues of wealth production and other commercial activity, the major philosophical thinkers in antiquity, and to rhetorical theory and practice and the higher learning of the day.

To the memory of my dear wife Julie (1961-2002) and in honour of my parents, Leatha Dawn Rankin and Hugh Douglas Rankin

From Clement to Origen

The Social and Historical Context of the Church Fathers

DAVID IVAN RANKIN
Trinity Theological College, Brisbane, Australia
and
Griffith University, Brisbane, Australia

ASHGATE

Published by

Ashgate Publishing Limited
Gower House
Croft Road
Aldershot
Hampshire GU11 3HR
England

Ashgate Publishing Company
Suite 420
101 Cherry Street
Burlington, VT 05401-4405
USA

Ashgate website: http://www.ashgate.com

British Library Cataloguing in Publication Data
Rankin, David (David Ivan), 1952–
From Clement to Origen : the social and historical context of the Church Fathers
1.Fathers of the church 2.Church history – Primitive and early church, ca. 30-600 3.Civilization, Classical 4.Rome – Social conditions 5.Rome – Civilization – Christian influences
I.Title
270.1'0922

Library of Congress Cataloging-in-Publication Data
Rankin, David (David Ivan), 1952-
From Clement to Origen : the social and historical context of the church fathers / David Ivan Rankin.
p. cm.
Includes bibliographical references and index.
ISBN 0-7546-5716-7 (hardback : alk. paper)
1. Fathers of the church. 2. Church history – Primitive and early church, ca. 30-600. I. Title.

BR67.R25 2006
270.1–dc22

2005037731

ISBN-10: 0-7546-5716-7
ISBN-13: 978-0-7546-5716-3

Printed and bound in Great Britain by MPG Books Ltd. Bodmin, Cornwall.

Contents

Acknowledgements

I would like to thank, as always, my teacher, mentor and friend, the Revd Prof. Eric Osborn of Latrobe University, Melbourne, for his advice and support over many years. My colleagues at Trinity Theological College in Brisbane, and those within the Brisbane College of Theology and the School of Theology at Griffith University have been great sources of encouragement. The untiring support of my secretaries at Trinity as Academic Dean and now as Principal of the College during this time, Mrs Astrid Hill and Mrs Alice Foo, cannot go unremarked. I would also like to thank Dr Graeme Clarke of the Australian National University and Dr John Patterson of Magdalane College, Cambridge, for their comments on earlier drafts of portions of this work. My appreciation goes also to my publisher at Ashgate, Sarah Lloyd, for her encouragement and to the anonymous reviewer who read my manuscript and made many helpful suggestions. I am in debt also to my children, Nicole and Michael, and to my parents, Lea and Doug. To my dear wife Julie (1961-2002), who sadly died during my engagement in this project, I give my eternal love and gratitude for her unfailing and unconditional support and encouragement. To her most precious memory I dedicate this work.

List of Abbreviations

ACW	Ancient Christian Writers
A-NCL	Ante-Nicene Christian Library
BJRL	Bulletin of the John Rylands Library
CCL	Corpus Christianorum, Series Latina
CH	Church History
HTR	Harvard Theological Review
JECS	Journal of Early Christian Studies
JEH	Journal of Ecclesiastical History
JRH	Journal of Religious History
JRS	Journal of Roman Studies
JTS	Journal of Theological Studies
LCC	Library of Christian Classics
LCL	Loeb Classical Library
PBSR	Papers of the British School at Athens
RAC	Reallexikon für Antike und Christentum
REAug	Revue des études Augustiniennes
SC	Sources Chrétiennes
SJTh	Scottish Journal of Theology
SP	Studia Patristica
TheolStuds	Theological Studies
VC	Vigiliae Christianae

Chapter 1

Introduction

> '[Christians] dwell in their own fatherlands, but as if sojourners in them; they share all things as citizens, and suffer all things as strangers. Every foreign country is their fatherland, and every fatherland is a foreign country. ... They pass their time upon the earth, but they have their citizenship in heaven.' (*Epistle to Diognetus* 5,5f.)

It would seem that only a few scholarly writings on the Fathers have included in their bibliographies significant numbers of monographs or journal articles either on the world - as a particular socio-cultural entity in which those Fathers lived and wrote - or on the particular engagement or interface of those Fathers with that world. Few patristic scholars evidence much conspicuous interest in the secular world of antiquity, and the compliment is largely repaid by historians of that ancient world.[1] The only major exception to this would seem to be the attention given by some scholars to the philosophical background of or influences upon a particular Father or group of Fathers. There are, of course, those who do give some attention to social and cultural matters, but more often than not scholars who employ sociological models, for example, do so to better understand the nature of the particular Christian community from which an individual Father emerges than particularly to place that community in a wider socio-cultural context. Yet the early Church Fathers did live, work, think and engage - consciously or unconsciously, explicitly or implicitly - in particular social, political, historical, religious, economic and cultural contexts. Clement of Rome writes from Rome at the end of the rule of Domitian, Theophilus from Antioch during the reign of Commodus. Irenaeus, a bishop of Gaul but in all probability Smyrnaean in origin, cannot have been untouched by the fact that he was leader of a religious community which only very recently had come into violent and bloody conflict with both the power of Rome itself and a hostile and suspicious local population.

The world into which the Christian Gospel came - the world of the Roman Empire and of Greco-Roman culture and society - was one which had only recently emerged from a long series of civil wars - those between Marius and Sulla, Caesar and Pompey, and Octavius and Mark Anthony in particular. This was an empire which stretched at the time of Octavian/Augustus' establishment of the Principate around 27 BCE from Armenia in the East to Lusitania in the West, and from Germania Inferior in the north to Egypt in the south. Over the next two or three centuries it knew at least two further major periods of civil war - from 68-69 CE

1 There are, of course, exceptions to this, of whom an obvious one is Timothy Barnes.

following the death of Nero and the end of the Julio-Claudian dynasty and from 193-197 CE following that of the Commodus and the Antonines - and increasing persecution of Christians - in Rome under Nero in 64, occasionally under Marcus Aurelius (see Lyons in 177), in Alexandria and Carthage under Septimius Severus in 202-203, the first truly universal persecutions under Decius in 250-1 and Valerian in 257-8, and finally the Great Persecution under Diocletian and others from around 297 until before the first edict of toleration in 311. The early empire saw a mix of absolute rule and constitutionalism, the latter a mere shadow of the old Republic. The Augustan settlement actually provided no new office of emperor formally established and consequently there was no particular legal basis for the selection of an emperor, that is, as distinct from the powers formally granted an emperor on his accession by the Senate (see the *lex de imperio*). It also saw the growth of the cult of the emperor (which involved not worship but homage and prayers for the safety of the emperor and the imperial house), quite naturally in the East, but by way of governmental determination in the new Roman colonies of the West (though not in Rome itself). It was a world in which, though emperors were not normally deified until after death, it became common from the early second century CE (Vespasian in the 1st century CE had represented himself as the elect of Serapis, and Domitian Isis), and increasingly so from the early third, to regard the emperor as the elect of God (Jupiter). The Greco-Roman world was deeply disturbed, even terrified, by the prospect of civil strife, disorder and anarchy, and accorded a high value to the qualities of peace, order and harmony (*homonoia/concordia*). Society was divided by clear class boundaries (the 'orders' were those social categories defined through statute or custom) - senatorial, equestrian, provincial decurian, the humble free (freeborn and freedperson), and the slave, patrician and plebeian, citizen and non-citizen. This last distinction, however, lost significance throughout the course of the Principate and was effectively replaced in time (emerging principally during the reign of Hadrian) by that between *honestior* (comprising the three elite classes, senatorial, equestrian and decurion, and army veterans) and *humilior* (the remainder of the free). [2] This latter distinction was most obvious in the treatment of parties before the courts, where the advantages enjoyed by one class and the disadvantages endured by the other were first a matter of convention and finally of legislation. Such social structures reinforced the commitment of many to the maintenance of order and harmony.

Brown declares that 'what makes the second century significant is the frequency with which the domestic concord associated with the nuclear family was played up symbolically, as part of a public desire to emphasise the effortless harmony of the Roman order'. [3] Examples of this may be found in the emphasis given on coins of the period to the *concordia* evident in relations between emperor and spouse and the

---

2 See P. Garnsey, *Social Status and Legal Privilege in the Roman Empire*. (Oxford, 1970).

3 P. Brown, *The Body and Society: Men, Women and Sexual Renunciation in Early Christianity*. (London, 1988), p. 16.

notion of the settled married state as a paradigm for social order. Plutarch declared that 'a man who had "harmonised" his domestic life with such elegance and authority could be trusted to harmonise state, forum and friends'.[4]

It was a world in which some ex-slaves (freedmen) accumulated great wealth - four of the ten richest individuals known from the Principate were from this class - as well as considerable political influence if not outright power. It was a world in which systems of patronage (reaching all the way to the emperor himself) - Seneca described the exchange of favours and services which constituted this patronage system as that which 'most especially binds together human society'[5] - dominated relationships between people of different class levels as patrons and clients.[6] It was a world in which wealth and the pursuit of material possessions and the concomitant status of having accumulated these counted for much. It was a world in which piety (*pietas*) comprised loyalty to family, to class, to city and to emperor and was demonstrated, by way of example, by a loyalty to the old ways of religious ritual in which patriality, territoriality and mutual (but not absolute) tolerance were highly regarded.

It was a world in which education, particularly higher education, was directed towards 'the achievement of the fullest and most perfect development of the personality'.[7] It was a world where *paideia* was understood as not only education in the conventional sense but also as 'culture' in the modern.[8] In this Greco-Roman classical culture, but particularly in the specifically Greek, Homer was the dominating figure - he was, for Plato, the 'educator of Greece' - and with Euripides, Menander and Demosthenes its main pillars. The seven liberal arts of late antiquity - the so-called 'encyclical *paideia*' - were grammar, rhetoric, dialectic, geometry, arithmetic, astronomy and music theory, but rhetoric was queen and the particular focus of Greco-Roman education and of the highest notions of culture. In both Greek and Roman society and education rhetoric generally triumphed in a broad contest with philosophy for the most desirable intellectual pursuit (much as today many parents may prefer schooling in information technology than the humanities for their children).

There was no strictly autonomous Roman education, though there were distinct Latin characteristics within the broader Greco-Roman context. Roman education was for the most part derivative, an adaptation of Hellenistic education to Latin circumstances. While there was some opposition[9] to Greek scholarship from 'old Romans' like Cato the Censor, ambitious Roman parents enthusiastically sought a

---

4 Plutarch, *Praecept. Conjug*. 43.144c. p.333.

5 *De Beneficiis* 1.4.2.

6 See R.P. Saller, *Personal Patronage under the Early Empire*. (Cambridge, 1982) for the most comprehensive treatment of this subject.

7 H.I.Marrou, *A History of Education in Antiquity*. tr. G.Lamb. (Madison, 1956), p. 98.

8 It is noteworthy that this Greek word *paideia* was often translated by Latins (see Varro and Cicero) as *humanitas*, with its meaning as civilisation, cultivation and refinement.

9 See the expulsions of philosophers from Rome in 173 and 154 BCE and the attacks of Juvenal on philosophy in *Satire* 3, 60-108.

Greek education for their children. Even in Latin-speaking districts of the empire the educated person was understood to be the one who knew Homer and Menander. Cicero was himself a Latin hellenist, proficient in both the Greek language and Greek learning. Yet after him the knowledge of Greek in Rome went into decline as a specifically Latin culture developed and the educated Latin emerges who knows also his Cicero and Virgil. [10] This trend can be observed in the writings of the rhetorician Quintilian at the end of the first century CE, and by the time of the Late Empire a common Greco-Roman culture had largely disappeared and been replaced by two distinct cultures, a Latin one in the West and a Greek in the East. In Rome Augustus set up public libraries and Vespasian funded chairs in rhetoric both Latin and Greek, and Marcus Aurelius chairs for each of the major philosophical schools in Athens. A Latin *quadriga* emerged[11] comprising Virgil, the poet Terence, the historian Sallust and Cicero, the 'Roman Demosthenes'. As with its Greek counterpart Latin rhetoric, which was itself a mere derivative of the Greek, dominated grammar and philosophy. Within Roman higher education the teaching of law was alone the one original feature.

Much of ancient discourse, particularly in the Greek and Roman worlds, was shaped by the demands of rhetorical forms and structures. Training in rhetoric provided the basic core of ancient education and even when political and judicial life no longer in any real sense provided the context for the formal exercise of these skills it remained at the centre of a quality education. In the Greek world Aristotle's rhetorical writings, particularly his *Rhetoric*, formed the basis for Greek practice and while Plato was often heard to challenge its value, seeing it at its lowest as sophistry, even his writings, or at least the constructed speeches within them, were themselves often shaped by the demands of rhetoric. [12]

Around 330 BCE Aristotle composed his *Rhetoric* in three books, what George Kennedy calls 'the most admired monument of ancient rhetoric'. [13] In books 1 and 2 he deals with the matter of 'invention' (Lat. *inventio* or Gk. *euresis*), establishing the subject matter of the speech, the question (the *status* or *stasiṣ* and the arguments for proof or refutation. He identifies at 1356a the possible means of persuasion

---

10 Note, however, the comment of P. Garnsey and R.P.Saller, *The Roman Empire: Economy, Society and Culture*. (London, 1987), p. 180, that 'it is arguable that Latin literature had no distinguished representative (with the possible exception of Apuleius) between the first quarter of the second century and the last quarter of the fourth'.

11 See Arusianus Messius, *Gell.* 15.24.

12 See, for example, his *Phaedrus* where Socrates' speech from 237a-241c is shaped by the classic rhetorical model: 237a7f. constitutes the introduction or *exordium*, 237b2f. the background to the case or *narratio*, 237b7f. the argument-by-proofs or *probatio*, and 241c6f. the conclusion or *peroratio*. Yet in the same dialogue Plato makes clear that true rhetoric is best exemplified in the dialectic which persuades and ennobles. From 257b7 to the end of the dialogue Plato offers a theoretical discussion of rhetoric. At 260e Socrates declares that 'a real art of speaking…which does not seize hold of the truth, does not exist and never will'. For Plato, rhetoric served truth or it had no independent value.

13 G.Kennedy, *The art of persuasion in Greece*. (Princeton, 1963), p. 81.

(remembering that normally the formal audience is a jury or magistrate or political assembly):

- the ethical (or character of the speaker)
- the pathetical (or state of mind of the hearer)
- the logical (or rational argument)

At 1358a he identifies three particular kinds of oratory:

- the deliberative (exhortatory/symbouleutic or dissuasive)
- the forensic or judicial (for accusation or for defence)
- the epideictic (for praise or for blame)

In book 3 Aristotle discusses issues of style (*elocutio* or *lexis*) and arrangement (*disposition* or *taxis*). His rhetorical structure - its arrangement - provides for four parts:

- the introduction (*exordium* or *prooimion*) in which the speaker seeks the interest and the goodwill of the audience;
- the statement (*prothesis*) or narration (*narratio* or *diēgēsis*) which provides an exposition of the background to the case and its factual details (it should be clear, brief and persuasive); [14]
- the proof/s (*probatio* or *pistis*), always the longest part of a speech, in which arguments are led for the confirmation of one's own case and/or the refutation of one's opponent's; [15]
- the conclusion (*peroratio* or *epilogos*) in which the speaker recapitulates his key arguments and makes a final, often emotional appeal to his audience.

The later Platonists were not greatly interested in rhetoric and the Epicureans were utterly hostile. In the second century BCE the professional teacher Hermagoras of Temnos emphasised invention (discovery of the subject matter); arrangement (*oikonomia*) and style (*elocutio* or *lexis*), for which the four recognised virtues were correctness, clarity, ornamentation and the use of figures; memory (*memoria* or *mnēmē*) or the use of mnemonic devices; and delivery (*actio* or *hupokrisis*) which gave particular attention to voice, stance and gesture.

In the emerging Roman world rhetoric reflected its Greek origins but also developed its own distinctive features. In the first century BCE 'Atticism' referred to the imitation of the old Attic orators and 'Asianism' was a pejorative term which suggested excesses of ornamentation in delivery. Around 88 BCE the young Cicero produced his famous *De Inventione* in two books (incomplete) in which he identifies the main parts of a speech and the different kinds of oratory. He identifies four basic

---

14 Note that the deliberative form rarely employs a narrative.

15 Proofs might include topics such as expediency, possibility, justice, or honour.

issues of a speech (*constitutiones* or *staseis*): [16] the question of fact; the question of law; the question of the nature of a particular act at issue; and the question of legal procedure. In book 2 he deals with the three kinds of rhetoric - judicial (forensic); deliberative; and epideictic - which mirror those identified by Aristotle. [17] To the Aristotelian arrangement of the speech were added the partition (*partitio*) before the proof[18] - in which the speaker identifies particular issues agreed upon by both parties as constituting the main point of contention - and a formal refutation after it. [19] Later Quintilian (c.35-100 CE), perhaps the greatest teacher of Latin oratory, produced his *Institutes* in 12 books, perhaps 'the finest statement of ancient rhetorical theory'. [20] In the Augustan age, though oratory no longer had any real judicial or political significance, it remained a highly prized skill and declamations or exercises in rhetorical skill on set topics remained the mainstay of Greco-Roman education.

In antiquity the principal modes of philosophical and intellectual discourse included the apologetic (defence and explicatory), the protreptic (exhortatory), and the didactic (teaching).That these influenced the shape of Christian discourse from the very beginning is beyond doubt. Those which we consider as examples here include the *Euthydemus* of Plato (428-348 BCE), the re-constructed *Protrepticus* of Aristotle (384-322 BCE), and *Epistle 90* of the Stoic Seneca (4 BCE-65 CE).

Edwards and others in their introduction to *Apologetics in the Roman Empire* describe *apologetic* as 'the defence of a cause or party supposed to be of paramount importance to the speaker'[21] and Grant declares that '[a]pologetic literature emerges from minority groups that are trying to come to terms with the larger culture in which they live'. [22] Price points out that '[i]n the Hellenistic and Roman periods *apologoumai* means "to render an account or explanation", without any forensic or defensive overtones'. [23] *Protreptic*, on the other hand, is to be distinguished from apologetic though they have much in common. Where the former seeks to convert through explanation and exhortation, the latter seeks only to explain; the former seeks to convince, preferably through being understood, the latter only to be understood. [24] Bergian declares that the aim of the protreptic genre 'is to induce

---

16 1.8.10f..

17 2.4.12f.. See also 1.5.7.

18 1.22.31.

19 1.42.78.

20 G.Kennedy, *The art of rhetoric in the Roman world, 300 B.C. – A.D. 300*. (Princeton, 1972), p. 496.

21 M.Edwards and others, 'Introduction: Apologetics in the Roman World', in *idem.* (eds), in M.Edwards and others, *Apologetics in the Roman Empire*, (Oxford, 1999),p. 1.

22 R.M.Grant, *Greek Apologists of the Second Century*. (Philadelphia, 1988), p. 9.

23 S.Price, 'Latin Christian Apologists: Minucius Felix, Tertullian, and Cyprian', in Edwards, *Apologetics*, p. 116.

24 Some Christian apologetic – see, for example, Tertullian's *Apologeticum* - seeks to convince the authorities to treat the believers in a more just manner but it does not seek the actual conversion of those to whom it is addressed.

choice'.[25] Jordan argues in a perceptive article that '[t]he protreptic has as its explicit aim the winning of a student for philosophy'[26] though '[t]he philosopher's protreptic is one among many'.[27] He later adds, '[t]he end of the protreptic [sc. he speaks here of Socrates' second interlude in the *Euthydemus*: see below] is to point beyond itself towards an enactment; that is clear enough in the nature of an exhortation'.[28] He also, however, points out that '[i]t is plain that protreptic cannot be a genre in the ordinary poetic sense, that is, as dictating a certain combination of form, diction, and subject-matter'.[29] He concludes,

> 'The unity of the protreptic genre could be provided, then, by the recurring situation of trying to produce a certain volitional or cognitive state in the hearer at the moment of decision about a way-of-life'.[30]

Aune describes the *logos protreptikos* as

> 'a lecture intended to win converts and attract young people to a particular way of life. The primary *Sitz im Leben* of the *logos protreptikos* was the philosophical schools where it was used to attract potential adherents by exposing the errors of alternative ways of living by demonstrating the truth claims of a particular philosophical tradition over its competitors'.[31]

Epictetus, in a discussion of philosophical protreptic, says that *protreptic* is

> 'the ability to show to the individual, as well as to the crowd, the warring inconsistency in which they are floundering about, and show they are paying attention to anything rather than what they truly want' (3.23-33-35).

Aune says that *protreptic* 'refers to a single method comprised of both encouragement and rebuke intended to bring a person to the truth', 'encouraging conversion'.[32] Aristotle divided deliberative rhetoric into two types, the hortatory (*protropē*) and the dissuasive (*apotropē*) (*Rhet.* 1358b). Thus the two forms of deliberative rhetoric are normally referred to as the *protreptic* and the *apotreptic*. Thus *protreptic* will include both itself and the *apotreptic* since it must first draw a person away from past (present) beliefs and practices before leading them to the new truth.

---

25 S-P.Bergian, 'How to speak about early Christian apologetic literature? Comments on the recent debate', *Studia Patristica* 36 (2001), 177.

26 M.D.Jordan, 'Ancient Philosophic Protreptic and the Problem of Persuasive Genres', *Rhetorica* 4 (1986): 309.

27 Ibid., 312.

28 Ibid., 322.

29 Ibid., 328.

30 Ibid., 331.

31 D.E.Aune, 'Romans as a Logos Protreptikos in the Context of Ancient Religious and Philosophical Propaganda' in M.Hengel and U.Heckel (eds), *Paulus und das antike Judentum.* (Tübingen, 1991), p. 91.

32 Ibid., 95.

Apologetic is then generally easy to identify but it is the distinction between it and protreptic which is the more difficult. Often what is acknowledged as apologetic is actually protreptic and often, though admittedly less so, what is identified as protreptic - because it, perhaps, displays the odd hortatory subjunctive - is actually apologetic. If we identify apologetic as that form of discourse which seeks to explicate or to articulate a given position - to either believers or non-believers – without any intention, explicit or implicit, to seek the conversion of its addressees, and protreptic as that which seeks explicitly to convert by exhortation non-believers (*paraenetics* is exhortation to believers), then we will not be far from the truth. Below we consider some examples of classic protreptic literature.

Plato: *Euthydemus*

Socrates' first major speech in Plato's *Euthydemus* is a particularly good example of ancient protreptic (278e-282e). In this brief set-piece Socrates argues for the main contention of the dialogue, that the young must be persuaded that they ought to be philosophers and to study virtue (275a). Socrates first establishes that everybody desires happiness. He then asks his principal dialogue partner, Crito, what are the goods which lead to happiness and then himself lists these as wealth, health, beauty, good birth, power, honours in one's own land, temperance, justice, courage, wisdom and good fortune, the last the greatest of all goods (279a). He then suggests that in fact good fortune is nothing but wisdom and wisdom always makes men fortunate (280a). But, he says, in order for goods to lead to fortune and happiness it is not enough that they be possessed but that they be used (280b-c) and used rightly (280e). It is the knowledge of the artisan, he says, that allows something to be used rightly (281a) so that goods are not actually goods *in se* but only so under the guidance of knowledge used rightly (281d). Further, both he and Crito agree that wisdom can be taught and that philosophy is the acquisition of such knowledge and wisdom (288d). Jordan comments at this point that

> 'First, the protreptic does not seek so much to arouse a desire as to connect an admitted desire with its object…second, the aim of the protreptic is to produce a choice, an action.. the argument relies, third, on showing that access to the desired objects is provided only by a master-good, by wisdom'.[33]

The second Socratic interlude in the *Euthydemus* begins at 288c and follows on from the first. Socrates and Crito agree that philosophy is the acquisition of knowledge and that such knowledge is one which will do them good (288e). They explore, albeit briefly, what kind of knowledge they should seek and reject, in turn, the rhetorical arts - where Plato takes a further opportunity to raise his concerns about rhetoric-as-sophistry (289e) - military skill, political skill, and others, and Socrates declares that 'we are just as far as ever, if not farther, from the knowledge of the art or science

33 Ibid., 320.

of happiness' (292e). This discussion is continued at 304c when Socrates suggests that those who seek to combine philosophy and politics fail in their endeavour. He finishes with the protreptic exhortation:

> 'Do not mind [Crito] whether those who pursue philosophy are good or bad, but think only of philosophy herself. Test her well and truly, … if she be what I believe she is [sc. good], then follow her and serve her, you and your house, as the saying is, and be of good cheer' (307b-c).

Aristotle: *Protrepticus*

The following discussion is based on Düring's celebrated 'reconstruction' of Aristotle's otherwise lost work.[34] In section 2 (B2) Aristotle declares that 'if the soul is educated, such a soul and such a person must be called happy'. In B5 he continues that philosophy should be pursued, for all 'would agree that wisdom comes from learning and from seeking the things that philosophy enables us to seek'. He then goes on to state that we must become philosophers if 'we are to govern the state rightly and lead useful lives' (B8). In philosophy alone lies right judgement and wisdom which does not err (B9). In B20, having argued that wisdom is the natural end of man, he declares that 'the exercise of wisdom must be the best of all things' and wisdom 'the supreme end' (B21). From B22 to B30 he argues that of all the levels of thought the highest level is that which exists for its own sake and that 'the good and the honourable [are to be] found above all in philosophical speculation' (B27). Deprived of reason a person becomes a brute; deprived of irrationality and abiding by reason he becomes like God (B28). From B38 to B44 Aristotle argues that wisdom is the greatest good even though it be not practical and that 'it is chiefly through philosophical reflection [that] we reach a clear opinion of these matters' (B41). In B45 he maintains that 'the exercise of wisdom is a good in itself, even if it should contribute nothing that is useful for human life'. In B49 he states that 'it is clear that to the philosopher alone among craftsmen belong laws that are stable and actions that are right and noble'. Philosophy is the acquisition and exercise of wisdom (B53). Truth is the supreme work of the rational part of the soul (B65) and the supreme end of this is philosophical thinking (B66). Indeed, 'philosophical thinking and contemplation are the proper work of the soul' (B70). It is 'to those who think and to those who possess philosophical insight' that the 'perfect life' must be ascribed (B85). 'All who can should practise philosophy, for this is either complete good life, or of all single things most truly the cause of good life for souls' (B96). Aristotle concludes protreptically,

> 'Humanity has nothing worthy of consideration as being divine or blessed, except what there is in us of reason and wisdom; this alone of our possessions seems to be immortal, this alone to be divine..(B110). We ought, therefore, either to pursue philosophy or to say

---

34 I.Düring, *Aristotle's Protrepticus: An Attempt at Reconstruction*. (Stockholm, 1961).

> farewell to life and to depart hence, since all other things seem to be great nonsense and folly' (B108 and B110).

Seneca: *Epistle 90*

Stoic philosophy, quite dominant in the Rome of the second century CE, argued, unlike with Platonism where the highest end of human life was to become 'like the gods' (see *Theaetetus* 176c), that the highest end was to live 'in accordance with nature'. Seneca, Stoic philosopher (4 BCE-65 CE) and one-time mentor to the emperor Nero, addressed this letter to his friend Lucilius Junior, a native of Pompeii and procurator of the province of Sicily, and argued there the case of the Stoic ideal. He argued that 'living well is the gift of philosophy' and that philosophy itself 'was something bestowed by the gods'. It is not itself given naturally or automatically but merely the means to acquire it. Philosophy, for Seneca, 'has the single task of discovering the truth about the divine and human worlds'. Religion, piety, justice and all the interdependent goods rest beside her. She teaches people to worship the divine, to love what is human, and argues for the authority of the gods and the fellowship of humankind. Seneca speaks of the so-called primitive Golden Age, before the advent of technological advance and avarice, when people lived in harmony together and wanted for nothing needful because they lived in accord with nature. The wise man then, he maintains, followed a simple way of life. Follow nature, he declares, and you will feel no need for craftsmen (and their technological advances). Nature has equipped us for everything she requires us to contend with. 'Nature demanded nothing hard from us, and nothing needs painful contriving to enable life to be kept going. We were born into a world in which things were ready to our hands.' 'Nature suffices for all she asks of us, luxury has turned her back on nature.' But now, through greed and possessiveness, 'the bounds of nature, which set a limit to man's wants by relieving them only where there is necessity for such relief, have been lost sight of'. But 'philosophy is far above all this [sc. technological advances]. She does not train men's hands: she is the instructress of men's minds'. Philosophy's 'voice is for peace, calling all humanity to live in harmony'. Philosophy 'takes as her aim the state of happiness… she opens routes and guides us'. 'She shows us what are real and what are only apparent evils.' 'She imparts a knowledge of the whole of nature, as well as of herself. She explains what the gods are, and what they are like.' Seneca attributes to philosophy a complete and certain knowledge of religious truth (28-30). Philosophy has brought to life truth and nature, in the first place, and then a rule of life which brings life into line with things universal. She teaches not only how to recognise the gods but to obey them; she teaches a calm acceptance of all that happens in life. Seneca repudiates Epicureanism with its placement of citizens beyond the pale of public life and gods beyond any care for the world. But the primitive life of the Golden Age was not perfect. The people of that time were wonderful and guileless but not particularly wise. Their personalities fell short of perfection for nature does not give virtue. To become virtuous is an art.

The innocence of the primitive was owed to ignorance. 'Virtue' rather 'only comes to a character which has been thoroughly schooled and trained and brought to a pitch of perfection by unremitting practice'. We are born for virtue but not with it. Even in the best of people there is the material for virtue but not virtue itself. Thus does Seneca argue for conversion to the Stoic view of life and for the truly virtuous and perfect human being as that one who lives in perfect accord with nature.

The world into which the Gospel came was a world in which questions of ultimate meaning were determined and reflected, not primarily in religious rituals, but in the great schools of philosophy, in (Middle) Platonism, Aristotelianism, Stoicism (particularly in the West), Epicureanism, Cynicism, Neopythagoreanism, and so on. There were generally three main parts to philosophical training, these being ethics, physics and logic, and while early teachers of philosophy were concerned as much as anything with matters of political and social theory and practice the Hellenistic philosophers were more personalist in their interests. In the Rome of the first and second centuries CE, though not elsewhere in the Greco-Roman world, Stoicism clearly dominated among the major philosophical schools. The eclecticism of the age, however, also meant that the forms of Stoicism followed also contained elements of (Middle) Platonism, Epicureanism and Aristotelianism. The history of Stoicism[35] is normally divided into three periods: Early Stoicism dominated by its traditional founder Zeno of Citium (c. 333-262 BCE), Cleanthes (d. 232 BCE) and Chrysippus (c.280-c.206 BCE); Middle Stoicism by Panaetius of Rhodes (c.185-c.110 BCE) and Posidonius of Apamea (c.135-c.55 BCE); and Late Stoicism in Rome by Seneca (1-65 CE), a native of Spain, Epictetus (fl. 89 CE), Musonius (fl. 65-89 CE), Hierocles (fl. 100 CE), and Marcus Aurelius the emperor (121-180 CE). Seneca, perhaps the best known and most influential of those from the last period, taught that given that the world of nature is planned and consistent, providence must purpose the end of man (*De Providentia*). In his *Naturales Quaestiones* he speaks of a God who controls all that is as the Mind of the universe. In his tragedies he speaks, as did most Stoics, of the dangers of wealth and luxury to the proper living of life and upheld the benefits of the simple life (no matter how much this did not actually mirror his own life!). While there were significant variations in thought between Early and Late Stoicism the school in general held to a monistic cosmology and a materialist monism, promoted the notion of the highest virtue being to conform oneself to an agreement with nature, one's own and that of the world - Zeno spoke of true happiness being a 'good flow of life lived harmoniously' and his immediate followers added that this was 'agreement with nature'[36] - and that it was reason (*logos*) which joined man to God; Cicero (106-43 BCE), who did most to introduce Latin speakers to the treasures of Greek thought, at *De Natura Deorum* 1.39 reports Chrysippus as saying that the divine power resides in reason and in the mind and intellect of universal nature. Stoics spoke of achieving agreement with nature by

---

35 For much of this section I am indebted to F.H.Sandbach, *The Stoics*. 2nd edition. (London, 1989) and A.A.Long, *Stoic Studies*. (Cambridge, 1996).

36 Stobaeus 2.77, 16-27.

conforming oneself to the system devised by the God who governs the universe by rational principles, and by behaving as members of societies governed by the rule of law of the world exhibiting a structure and pattern which is both intelligent and prescriptive for man, who is not simply to model himself on this structure and pattern but to see himself as an integral part of it (Cicero, *De Finibus* 3.21). Stoics maintained both a determinism (*heimarmene*) in which there is an inevitable order of things - one scholar has identified this as nature for the Stoics being 'the way things are'[37] - and the notion of a divine providence in which the deity demonstrates a benevolent purpose for creation - Epictetus speaks of a God who cares for us and protects us like a father (3,24.3). Not all Stoics, however, maintained such a notion of a personalised god and none particularly understood God as creator. For some God was identified simply with nature or the world.

Platonism, however, remained the philosophy of choice whatever the time or place. The history of Platonism normally divides into a number of recognisable periods: that of Plato (427-347 BCE) himself; that of the so-called Old Academy with Speusippus (407-339 BCE), Xenocrates (396-314 BCE), and Polemon (c. 350-267 BCE); the so-called 'sceptical' period of the Academy with its leading figures Arcesilaus (316-241 BCE) and Carneades (c. 213-129 BCE); Middle Platonism, with which movement we are mostly concerned in this work, with leading figures Antiochus of Ascalon (130-c.68), Eudorus (1st century BCE) and Philo of Alexandria (30 BCE-45 CE), Plutarch of Chaeroneia (c.45CE-c.125), Nicostratus, Calvenus Taurus (fl/ pre-145 CE), Atticus (fl. 176 CE) and Harpocration of Argos (of the 2nd century CE), Gaius (fl. 145 CE), Albinus (fl. 149-57 CE), Apuleius of Madaura (b. c.123 CE), Galen the physician (129-c.200 CE) and Neopythagoreans like Moderatus of Gades, Nicomachus of Gerasa and Numenius of Apamea; and the Neoplatonic period beginning with Plotinus (207-270 CE) which lies outside our immediate field of enquiry. While Plato himself and his actual works, principally the *Timaeus* along with the *Republic, Phaedrus, Theaetetus, Phaedo, Philebus* and the *Laws*, are important for our period, it is more the principles enunciated by the Middle Platonists themselves and their reading of Plato which are crucially important for us. The areas of ethics and physics most concern us here. The primary issue with the Middle Platonists in ethics was the question of the purpose of life or 'the end of goods'. While the last Head of the Old Academy, Polemon, saw this in Stoic-like terms as 'life in accordance with nature' and in this was followed by the alleged founder of Middle Platonism, Antiochus, later Middle Platonism, particularly in Alexandria (one of the major centres to which Platonic studies principally moved after Antiochus)[38], embraced the notion of 'likeness to God' derived from the famous passage in the *Theaetetus* (176B) as the ultimate end or purpose of human life. The other ethical issue which much exercised the Middle Platonists, as it had their forebears, was that of freewill and necessity. Plato himself had clearly maintained a

37 Long, *Stoic Studies*, pp. 192f..

38 Alexandria did not, however, again become the centre stage for Platonist studies until the early third century CE.

belief in personal freedom of choice[39] and the Middle Platonists struggled with the competing claims of freewill and fate within the context of a clear commitment to the notion of the governance of divine providence. Ultimately the Middle Platonists asserted both freewill and providence, whatever the logical problems, against the Stoic commitment to fate (*heimarmene*).

The Middle Platonists of the first and second centuries CE,[40] though not a school in any formal sense, provide 'a reasonably unified picture' in the area of metaphysics. [41] After Antiochus, says Dillon, Alexandrian Platonists proposed two distinct entities, the Demiurge of *Timaeus* 28c - an active figure - and the Good of the *Republic* 6.508-9/One of the First Hypothesis of the *Parmenides* 138-142 [42] - a completely transcendent, self-intelligising figure. Their theology is characterised by a notion of a highest god as a transcendent *nous* who creates only indirectly through a second god, thus dividing the Platonic Demiurge in two. [43] Their system[44] explains the structure of reality in a creationist manner even while some Middle Platonists deny a literal creation. [45] There are also echoes of Plato's *Republic* books VI and VII where God is alone proposed as true being (*to ontōs on*). Eudorus is reported by Simplicius (*In Phys.* 181.10ff.) as presenting a doctrine of divine being comprising a Supreme Principle - The One - and two inferior figures - the Monad (comprising Form) and the Dyad (Matter). In this he would appear to reflect something of *Philebus* 26e-30e, where monad is 'limit' and dyad 'limitlessness', though here the Cause above these two entities is not called the One but is recognised as possessing a unifying purpose and is identified with Mind and God. Eudorus thereby postulates a supreme, utterly transcendent First Principle which transcends both limit and limitlessness. This One is the ground of all existence and the causal principle of Matter and in this Eudorus clearly reflects a monism more extreme than that favoured by later Middle Platonists and contradicts both the Old Pythagoreanism and a strict Platonism. [46]

Philo's extant works, strangely, contain no overt references to *Timaeus* 28c[47] - a favourite text for both Middle Platonists and many of the Church Fathers - though there may be some allusions to it. [48] His main concern was to make a distinction

---

39 See, for example, *Republic* 10.617e and *Laws* 10.904c.

40 I draw very heavily on the work of J.Dillon, *The Middle Platonists: 80 BC to AD 220.* (London, 1996) here.

41 D.T. Runia, *Philo of Alexandria and the Timaeus of Plato*. Philosophia Antiqua 44 (Leiden, 1986), p. 50.

42 Dillon, *The Middle Platonists*, p. 46. Dillon, ibid.,p. 61, also points out that around the middle of the first century BCE the centre of Platonism moved from Athens to Alexandria.

43 Ibid., p. 53.

44 It is probably unhelpful to speak of a Middle Platonist 'system' but I could not think of a better word here!

45 Dillon, *The Middle Platonists*, p. 54.

46 Ibid., 128.

47 'Now to discover the Maker and Father of all were a task indeed; and having discovered him, to declare him to all persons were a thing impossible'.

48 D.Runia, *Philo of Alexandria and the Timaeus of Plato*, p. 111.

between God's existence (as evident) and God's essence (as incomprehensible). He speaks of a supreme principle as the One and as, above all, the personal God of Judaism. He is the One, the Monad, the Really Existent (*to ontōs on*). In *Opif.* 100 Philo supports the fourth century BCE figure Philolaus who says that 'there is a ruler and sovereign of all things, God, ever One, abiding, unmoved, like only to himself, different from all else'. At *Leg.* 6 Philo speaks of God as 'totally untouchable and unattainable'. At *Creation* 7-9, and probably alluding to *Timaeus* 28c, he declares that 'we ought to be struck with wonder at the powers of the Maker and Father' and speaks of two elements, an active causal principle (=Mind) who is the 'perfectly pure and unsullied Mind of the universe, transcending knowledge, the Good itself and the Beautiful itself', and a passive element (matter). He thus places God above the Good (*Republic* 6.508-9) and the Beautiful (*Symposium* 211d) which Dillon describes as a 'conscious improvement' on these two passages where these two entities are paraded as being themselves, in each case, the supreme principle.[49]

Plutarch, in his *Quaestionum convivialum libri ix*, declares that

> 'I am reassured when I hear Plato himself naming the uncreated and eternal god as the father and maker of the cosmos [sc. in *Timaeus* 28c] and of other created things' (1.718a).

Runia suggests 'that the philosophical intention of this double description [of 'Maker and Father'] was a burning interpretative issue in Middle Platonism is shown by Plutarch' who dedicated one of his *Platonic Questions* to it. There the latter asks 'Why did [Plato] call the supreme god father and maker of all things?'.[50] He suggests three options: 1) that he is father of gods and of men; b) that Plato is using a metaphor; c) that there is a difference between father and maker and between birth (*gennēsis*) and coming to be (*genesis*). Plutarch concludes that 'it is reasonable that, since the universe has come into being a living thing, god be named at the same time father of it and maker' and that this 'most nearly coincides with Plato's opinion'. According to Plutarch God is Real Being (*to ontōs on*), eternal, unchanging, non-composite, uncontaminated by Matter (*De E* 393e ff.), the Good (*Def. Or.* 423d) and the One (*De E* 393b-c). At *De Is.* 373a-b he speaks of 'what truly exists and is intelligible and is good'. The supreme Principles are the One and the Indefinite Dyad (*Def. Or.* 428f.), the latter being matter but yet more than matter; it is indeed limitlessness, the element underlying all formlessness and disorder.

Apuleius posits three first Principles, God, Matter and Ideas,[51] Atticus makes the Demiurge his Supreme God, the Good and the Intellect (*Nous*), and Alcinous[52]

---

49 Dillon, *The Middle Platonists*, p. 158.

50 *Platonic Questions* 2.1000e-1001c; note the inversion of the order of 'Maker and Father' from the original.

51 In *de Platone* 1.5 he says that God is 'one, immeasurable, father and creator of all things' [*Timaeus* 28c], blessed…heavenly, unspeakable, unnameable, invisible..unconquerable'.

52 It is now generally agreed that the author of the *Didaskalikos* is Alcinous. See the discussion on authorship in J. Dillon, *Alcinous: The Handbook of Platonism*. Introduction,

maintains that the Demiurge/God in the heavens/Mind of the World is the Second God. Alcinous describes God as eternal and indescribable, and declares that 'the Father … is cause of all things and orders the heavenly Mind and the Soul of the World in accordance with himself and his thoughts … [which] itself sets in order the whole of Nature within this world' (*Didaskalikos* 164.28ff.). Here, says Dillon, Albinus combines the Demiurge of *Timaeus* 28c, the Logos (though not himself employing this term), and the World Soul in its rational aspect. [53] For Alcinous the Good of Plato's *Republic* is the Supreme God, while God 'in the heavens' is the Demiurge/Mind of the World, the Second God. It is worth noting that for Alcinous the God of *Theaetetus* 176b, to whom likeness is to be sought, is this Second God. Harpocration, Dillon suggests,[54] follows Numenius in positing three gods of whom the first is the Father - indeed the 'charioteer Zeus' of *Phaedrus* 246e who is not the son of Cronus[55] - while the second is the Creator, the Archon – Zeus, again, but this time he of *Cratylus* 396a.

Moderatus of Gades, Nicomachus, and Numenius of Apamea are strictly Neopythagoreans but consideration of their work, given their significant influence on Middle Platonist thought, is indispensable. Moderatus, as reported by Simplicius, recognised three Ones: the First, above Being and all essence – Dillon identifies this One with the Good of the *Republic* 6.508f.[56] - the Second, 'truly existent (*ontōs on*)', the object of intellection (*noēton*) (thereby the First One is supranoetic) and the Forms, while the Third is the soul realm and participates in the (First) One and the Forms (the Second One). The Second is also, according to Dillon, the Paradigm of the *Timaeus*, possibly the Logos, the Demiurge, and certainly the Second One of Eudorus and the Second God of Numenius (see below). Numenius clearly distinguishes the First God and the Demiurge of *Timaeus* 28c when he declares that the Creator (Demiurge) and the Father (Supreme God) of *Timaeus* 28c are different entities (fr. 11) and that the First God exists in one place, is simple, alone and indivisible, says that 'it is necessary to regard the First God as the father of the Demiurge God' (fr. 12), and calls the First God 'Father' and the Second 'Maker (*poiētēs*)', thus dividing the Platonic Demiurge. In fr. 15 he says that the First God is at rest and the Second in motion, that the First is concerned with the intelligible realm only, while the Second is concerned with both intelligible and sensible worlds. In fr. 16 he says that the Father is the Good (the Demiurge is good only by participation in the Father and not so by nature), in fr. 19 One (but does not specify *the* One), and in fr. 26 he speaks of the Demiurge as the Second God (known to man) and of the *autoon* as the First (unknown).

Translation and Commentary. (Oxford, 1993), pp. ix-xiii.

53 Dillon, *The Middle Platonists*, p. 284.

54 Ibid., 260.

55 See Athenagoras, *Legatio* 23.9 who also claims that the Zeus the charioteer is the true God and not the Olympian son of Cronus.

56 Dillon, *The Middle Platonists*, 348.

Whatever their differences all Middle Platonists maintained a common belief in the need for a host of intermediaries between God and humankind - brought about essentially by the elevation of the first principle - so that the former would not be contaminated by too close a contact with matter. Platonism, even in its later forms like Middle Platonism, was identified by its consistent commitment to the notions of an immaterial and transcendent supreme reality and a perfect world of Ideas which acts as paradigm for the imperfect forms of this one, of the immortality of the soul, of the moral life as a struggle to detach oneself from the world of becoming and to be like unto God, of a tendency towards monism and the divinisation of the cosmos, and of a general disregard of the world of becoming in favour of that of pure being.

Aristotle (384-322 BCE), a native of Stagira, travelled to Athens in 367 and became a pupil in the Academy of Plato. On the death of his master he left Athens and eventually became the tutor to the young Alexander of Macedon. In 335 he returned to Athens and established his own school in the Lyceum. While faithful to the memory of his revered teacher he taught many things inconsistent with and even opposed to his mentor's teaching. While he himself was the major figure on the intellectual stage of his time Aristotelianism (or Peripateticism) declined in the third century BCE, and while it re-emerged as influential in some quarters in the opening centuries of the Common Era - many commentaries on his writings were produced in the patristic period - it was not until the late Middle Ages that it again took centre stage. Like most philosophers of his time Aristotle understood happiness (*eudaimonia*) as that state in which humankind realises itself and flourishes. Aristotle, above all, promoted the notion of the pursuit of human excellence in all things as the true goal of human existence. He was a philosopher, natural scientist, zoologist, biologist and logician; he can properly be said to have established both biology and logic as proper sciences. He maintained that metaphysics was the primary philosophy, with the latter understood as the pursuit of knowledge above all, not only in the theoretical realm but very much in terms of its practical applications. He was an empiricist in that he believed that the ultimate source of knowledge lay in perception (as fact) and in this opposed the primacy given by Plato to the intellect over the senses. In the seventh chapter of his *Physics* he suggests the existence of a changeless source of change in the universe, an existence which lay apart from the universe itself, his 'unmoved mover'. Yet Aristotle's concept of deity - and his inconsistency in this has led some to posit that he did not actually believe in the gods' existence - was simply too abstract and impersonal to encourage any sense of reverence by way of devotion or worship. Again, against Plato, he maintained that the human soul cannot survive the demise of the body. He divided the universe into the sublunar realm of things subject to generation and corruption and a superlunar realm of eternally rotating heavenly spheres and excluded the concept of providence from the former.

Epicureanism produced only a few key figures in its history apart from its founder himself, Epicurus of Athens (341-270), a disciple of Socrates. These included the poet Lucretius (c.100-c.55 BCE), best known for his *On the Nature of the Universe*, Philodemos of Gadara, active in the age of Cicero, and Diogenes of Oenoanda, a second century CE figure. All were known for the reverence in which they held their founder and his writings. The school is mostly associated with the famous Garden in Athens. Epicurus argued that a happy society essentially rests upon personal friendships - 'Of the things wisdom acquires for the blessedness of life as a whole, far the greatest is the possession of friendship',[57] he wrote - and forbade the participation of his followers in public life and affairs - 'We must liberate ourselves from the prison of routine business and politics'. [58] Political life, he believed, was destructive of friendship. 'The primary entities', Epicurus said, 'must be atomic kinds of bodies'. [59] In opposing the creationist argument of the Platonists in particular,[60] he described our world as an accidental and transient product of complex, random atomic collisions with no purposive origin, or structure, or controlling or even interested deity.[61] For the last Lucretius said that 'it is essential to the very nature of deity that it should enjoy immortal existence in utter tranquillity, aloof and detached from our affairs'. [62] For the Epicureans what was important was the interiorisation of the moral law. We are genuinely autonomous agents capable in and of ourselves of structuring our own lives in accordance with the one primary, natural good, pleasure. In opposition to Stoic determinism, which was shared by Democritus, the Epicureans argued for the absolute freewill of the human person, introducing the notion of the atomic 'swerve', unpredictable in its movements, to combat the natural determinism of atomism itself. They argued that the soul perishes with the body and that the human is free of the fear of divine retribution in this life or the next. Developed by Epicurus in the midst of a fear of social collapse in the later 4th century BCE his teachings suggest in sum a philosophy of the simple life. Athenaeus quotes Epicurus saying to a friend, 'I congratulate you, Apelles, for embarking on philosophy while still untainted by any culture'.[63] The Epicureans in our period contributed to contemporary thought their concern for self-sufficiency (*autarkeia*) and the control of unnecessary desire. While it has been common in some circles to consistently charge them with atheism it is a fact rather that they simply, for the most part, declared that the gods, though they existed, had no interest in human affairs. It was this denial of divine providence and the essential atomic nature of human existence that caused them to argue that each person must then look to his or her own end and his or her own good, or 'pleasure'.

All of us live in a particular time and place and as part of a particular culture, no matter how that culture is perceived. What we are and who we are and how we live and articulate our attitudes and beliefs is affected in some way, both negatively and positively, by our necessary (inevitable) participation within that particular culture.

---

57 *Key doctrines* 27.

58 *Vatican sayings* 58.

59 *Letter to Herodotus* 41.

60 Epicurus particularly challenged the cosmology of the *Timaeus*.

61 Epicureanism was essentially at its base an adaptation of the atomism of Democritus. Atomism maintained that the only thing that has independent, autonomous, existence is body which itself consists of an infinity of atomic particles and infinite space, much of the latter sheer void.

62 *On the nature of the universe*, 2.646f..

63 *Deipnosophistai* 588A.

A culture in this sense may be understood as a complex interweaving, integration or interaction of a variety of transmitted or developed customs, social practices, ideas and symbols which are present within boundaries which are at the very least flexible and probably porous. Tanner describes a modern anthropological understanding of culture as 'some sort of social transmission of heritage, characteristic spiritual affinity, or ruled patterns of behaviour'.[64] Malinowski describes culture as the '"artificial, secondary environment" which man superimposes on the natural world and which 'comprises language, habits, ideas, beliefs, customs, social organisation, inherited artifacts, technical processes, and values'.[65] Culture, then, is that socio-political setting in which particular individuals are formed for living and for comprehending and articulating their place in the world as they experience it. This is, in my view, a useful starting point although it is important to make clear that in any given time or place there cannot be what we might regard as *the* culture but at best a series of connected and/or interrelated cultures and that even when we can recognise or identify a particular, dominant culture in a particular time and place this cannot be regarded as an easily definable or quantifiable commodity.

Niebuhr[66] provides what has become perhaps the classic description of gospel-culture engagement when he speaks of the five models or paradigms for how the Gospel reacts to or interacts with the dominant or host culture: rejectionist (Christ Against Culture); accommodationist (Christ and Culture); fulfilment (Christ Above Culture); co-existent (Christ and Culture in Paradox); transformational-conversionary (Christ the Transformer of Culture).[67] De Vogel, in her exploration of the relationship between early Christianity and Platonism,[68] presents five paradigms almost identical with those of Niebuhr for gospel and culture: rejectionist, assimiliationist, critical-receptionist; acceptance-syncretistic; transformational. These categorisations by both Niebuhr and de Vogel carry with them the notions - potentially fatal, in my view, to their respective arguments - both that the concept of culture carries within itself the sense of a quantifiable 'whole package' and that Christianity can thus be identified as such as itself a whole socio-cultural package which stands over against, alongside, within or above or beyond - utterly distinguishable from - that whole package which is its host culture.

Tanner offers a different paradigm which in my view provides another way of looking at the relationship or engagement of the pre-Nicene Fathers with their host cultures and which sees them as essentially a part of that culture, even if on the fringe, rather than essentially separate from it. She speaks of Christian social practices 'incorporating institutional forms from elsewhere', describes Christian

---

64 K.Tanner, *Theories of Culture: A New Agenda for Theology*. (Minneapolis, 1997), p. 62.

65 B. Malinowski, 'Culture', in *Encyclopedia of Social Sciences*. Vol. IV, 621ff., quoted in R. Niebuhr, *Christ and Culture*. (New York), 1951, p. 46.

66 Niebuhr, *Christ and Culture*.

67 Tanner, *Theories of Culture*, says that in this typology of Niebhur 'culture' stands in for 'world' (p. 61).

68 C.J. de Vogel, 'Platonism and Christianity: a mere antagonism or a profound common ground?', *VC* 39 (1985): 1-62.

identity as 'essentially relational', and declares that even in conscious opposition the shaping or forming of one's identity must take into account what one opposes. She maintains that it is not 'so much what cultural materials you use as what you do with them that establishes identity'.[69] 'Christians', she declares, 'do not construct out of whole cloth' but 'use in odd ways whatever language-games they already happen to speak'.[70] 'Christian practices', she says, 'are always the practices of others made odd'.[71] Christian identity is established from the outset through the use of 'borrowed materials'.[72] Christianity is a 'hybrid formation through and through'. In two key passage she says that

> '[t]he distinctiveness of a way of life emerges out of tension-filled relations with what other ways of life do with much the same cultural stuff'[73], and'the distinctiveness of a Christian way of life is not so much formed *by* the boundary as *at* it; Christian distinctiveness is something that emerges in the very cultural processes occurring at the boundary, processes that construct a distinctive identity for Christian social practices through the distinctive use of cultural materials shared with others'.[74]

Christian engagement, she maintains, with other ways of life rarely involves a face-off between distinct wholes. This last, if true, is fatal to the schemas of both Niebuhr and de Vogel.

I have chosen to look at the four great cities of the Roman world before the fourth century Council of Nicaea (325 CE): Rome itself, Carthage, Antioch (along with Smyrna and Sardis) and Alexandria. I have chosen to document and to examine the engagement and interaction of a number of pre-Nicene Fathers, associated in some way or other with one or other of those cities, with the history, society and culture of that city (or cities) and, where appropriate, with the Roman world in general. For Rome, I will look at Clement, Hermas, Minucius Felix, the North African living and working in the city, and Hippolytus. Carthage in the second and third centuries is represented by Tertullian and Cyprian. For Antioch and Asia Minor I will look at Ignatius and Theophilus of Antioch, Polycarp of Smyrna, Melito of Sardis, Justin, Tatian and Irenaeus, bishop of the Smyrnaean-founded church at Lugdunum (Lyons) in Gaul. For Alexandria I will look at the *Epistle to Diognetus*, the *Epistle of Barnabas*, Clement of Alexandria, the Athenian Athenagoras, possibly the most eloquent of second century Apologists, and, of course, most famous of that city's Christian sons, Origen. My decision to divide the study between these four cities in particular is done mainly for the sake of convenience, given that apart from Carthage and Alexandria I would not expect to find a particularly coherent story related to each locale. It is, for example, only in the broadest sense that one might name the

---

69 Tanner, *Theories of Culture*, p. 112.
70 Ibid., p. 113.
71 Ibid.
72 Ibid., p. 114.
73 Ibid., p. 112.
74 Ibid., p. 115.

Fathers listed under Rome as representing together a particularly 'Roman' view or attitude (though individuals may) on or to any particular matter. I do not, of course, claim to offer a comprehensive treatment of the writings and theology of each of the Fathers discussed.

In each main chapter (2-5) I will first offer a brief overview of the particular city (and, where appropriate, province or region) - its history, social structures, and so on. I next consider the career and writings of each Father in turn, giving attention to a number of issues, mostly as they arise from the various texts rather than being imposed artificially. These issues might include references, explicit or implicit, to matters such as the history of the particular city and region, the emperor or emperors of the time, the imperial house and the imperial cult, learning (focusing principally on the influence of the philosophers and the philosophical schools of the day and also on the use of rhetorical structures and styles), literature (with particular reference to genre and the standard literary figures, ancient and contemporary, of the day - poets, historians, medical writers, epigrammists, and so on), social and other cultural issues such as individual wealth, class structures, and the system of patronage. I have sought to allow the texts themselves to throw up these issues - and not myself to impose them on the texts - but the reader will have to judge how successful I have been in this endeavour.

(Note: I have particularly chosen not to focus on the Fathers' attitude towards Greco-Roman religion which was invariably and uniformly hostile and derisory. This can be taken for granted. The only discernible influence of pagan religion on the Fathers was their unconditional and uncompromising rejection of it as incompatible with Christian teaching.)

All this will then be analysed to see to what extent these Fathers, both individually and, where appropriate, as a group engage and interact - and in what manner - with the societies and cultures in which they lived and worked. How do they view the emperor and the whole imperial system, especially the imperial cult? How do they view the activities of their fellow citizens, their neighbours, those amongst whom they lived and worked and for whose salvation they at least in principle pray? How do they regard themselves as citizens in a world, in a time and culture that often acted with such hostility and suspicion towards them and which could, at any time, turn and visit the most appalling violence and brutality upon them? How do they engage with and react to the standard philosophical and literary texts of the day and with what constitutes the most sophisticated higher learning of their time? How do they engage with what might be characterised as popular and upper class prejudices? To what extent are they persons of their place and time rather than people who successfully or otherwise seek to stand above and apart from that place and time? What does it mean, for them, in the words of the writer of the *Epistle to Diognetus*, to be simultaneously both sojourners and citizens, both at home in their respective fatherlands and yet as utterly alien there? How are they in this world but not of this world, and to what extent does that notion actually make sense *in concreto*? When a Church Father like Tertullian, for example, appears to so stridently condemn contemporary philosophy and learning and yet his personal engagement with this leaps at the reader from nearly every page of his writings, how seriously must we take his railing against such learning, or is all for show?

A note on further reading

More specialised reading on some of the issues raised in this book may be found in a number of places.[75] On Rome and Roman administration in particular see Goodman's *The Roman World: 44BC-AD180*, on the emperors Millar's *The Emperor in the Roman World*, on the imperial cult both Fishwick's *The Imperial Cult in the Latin West: Studies in the Ruler Cult of the Western Provinces of the Roman Empire* and Price's *Rituals and Power: the Roman Imperial Cult in Asia Minor*, on Roman religion Beard's *Religion of Rome*, on rhetoric Sider's *Ancient Rhetoric and the art of Tertullian*, on Stoicism Rist's *Stoic Philosophy*, on Middle Platonism Dillon's *The Middle Platonists*, on Epicureanism Farrington's *The Faith of Epicurus* and on Aristotle Barnes' *The Cambridge companion to Aristotle*. Daniélou's three volume *A History of early Christian doctrine before the Council of Nicaea* can not be ignored in any consideration of the engagement of early Christian thought with the thought of the Greco-Roman world. Kennedy's *The Art of Persuasion in Greece* and *The Art of Rhetoric in the Roman world* are indispensable guides to the place of rhetoric in that world.

75 For full publication details see the Bibliography.

Chapter 2

Rome and the Fathers

> 'Rome, goddess of continents and peoples, to whom there is no equal and nothing approaching.' (Martial, *Epigrams* 12, 8, 1-2)

> 'The woman dressed in purple and scarlet ... Great Babylon, the mother of all the prostitutes and perversions in the world.' (*Revelation* 17, 4-5)

> 'Squalor and isolation are minor evils compared to this endless nightmare of fires and collapsing houses, the cruel city's myriad perils - and poets reciting their work in August!' (Juvenal, *Satires*, III,6-9)

Thomas Africa describes Rome in the first two centuries CE as 'the brain and stomach of a vast organism, the Roman Empire'. [1] Estimates of her population in our period vary greatly though no-one puts it much above 1,000,000 and no-one below 500,000. At least one third, and possibly more, were slaves and by the second century CE perhaps 90 per cent were of foreign extraction. Africa describes Rome as essentially a great slum, congested, foul-smelling and noisy, above all noisy. Complaining of the noise of wagons being driven at night through the narrow, winding streets of the poorer quarters of the city - as they were by law required to do - Juvenal asks plaintively, 'Who but the wealthy get sleep in the city?' Rome proper (within the *pomerium*) was only about 15 square kilometres in area, comprised mainly of 6- and 7-story tenements (the grand buildings were only its acceptable facade), had very narrow streets, and was prone to fire.

Veyne maintains that under the emperors Rome became a royal capital and was no longer a city-state. [2] She was a sovereign's court, a royal city. And this being the case the Emperor increasingly reserved for his own patronage the monopoly on benefactions in the city. The relationship of Emperor to the Roman people was likened to that of a father to his family. The term '*urba sacra*' became current under Hadrian and was later formalised under Septimius Severus; Rome was the *urbs sua*, the Emperor's, and his alone. The Senate,[3] while under the Principate, was increasingly impotent, yet continued to embody the (Republican) traditions of the Roman State. Indeed, its prestige increased, O'Rourke maintains, while 'its actual

---

1 T. Africa, *Rome of the Caesars*. (New York), 1965, p. 5.

2 P.Veyne, *Bread and Circuses: Historical Sociology and Political Pluralism*. (London, 1990), p. 384.

3 I am largely indebted for this discussion of the role of the senate in Rome to R.J.A. Talbert's fine book, *The Senate of Imperial Rome*. (Princeton, 1984).

power ... suffered a gradual erosion'. [4] Yet, equally, no emperor could seriously alienate this class and survive. The senate was the body which formally invested an incoming emperor with *imperium*, could condemn an emperor's memory and (in theory) annul a condemned emperor's acts, but the fact that after Vitellius all emperors dated their reign from the army's recognition rather than the senate's investiture of them speaks volumes to the actual *locus* of power.

The imperial cult was not officially practised in Rome except insofar as it concerned deceased emperors. Yet the cult of the *genius Augusti*, established by Octavian, in practice more than made up for this. The power of the emperor in Rome itself was, thereby, no less real but it does underline the fact that many among the traditional ruling class in Rome never actually came to terms with the idea of a Principate or a *princeps*. Charlesworth even asserts that there was actually no such thing as the 'Emperor', merely a citizen entrusted with great powers[5] and that this reflected the reluctance of Romans traditionally to accept the worship of a living person. The traditional imperial refusal of divine honours, then, and particularly so in Rome, demonstrated a measure of sensitivity on the part of some emperors to the feelings of the Roman populace, and its reverse an act of simple insensitivity to such feelings.

Juvenal expresses disgust at the fact that wealth had become the measure of the person in the city. At Rome a witness will first be asked, he declares, how many slaves he owns and how many acres of land and how big and how many his crockery. [6] In Rome 'a man's word is believed in exact proportion to the amount of cash which he keeps in his strong-box'.[7] The word of the poor man, though he be pious and attentive towards the gods, will count for nothing. 'Everything in Rome has its price', he said.[8] The wealthy of Rome, with interests mainly in land - senators were officially legally barred from commercial activity, though this may not have always stopped them - were obscenely so and a person like Pliny the Younger had to amass a fortune of at least 20 million sesterces before he could be considered rich. Juvenal speaks of the popular desire for, and the official provision of, 'bread and circuses'[9] - what Fronto calls 'the corn-dole and shows'[10] - in reference to the monthly grain dole distributed to some 200,000 Romans as a supplement only, it must be said, to their meagre livings. Yet even this corn dole was given only to the 'respectable' *plebs* of moderate means for it was more a political than a charitable gesture. The city of Rome was a consumer, a consumer of all that its Empire could furnish. It was not,

---

4 J.J.O'Rourke, 'Roman Law and the Early Church', in Benko, S., and O'Rourke, J.J., (eds), *Early Church History: The Roman Empire in the Setting of Primitive Christianity*. (London, 1972), p. 167.

5 M.P. Charlesworth, 'The Refusal of Divine Honours: an Augustan Formula', *PBSR* 15 (1939): 1.

6 *Satire* 3,141-2.

7 Ibid., 3,143.

8 Ibid., 3,183.

9 *Satire* 10, 81.

10 *Princ. Hist.* 17.

however, a free ride for the destitute but only perhaps for the generally comfortable who would be expected thereby to support the *status quo* and the cause of social order.

Juvenal speaks of the impoverished person in Rome hurrying along in his toga before dawn to his benefactor's house. [11] He speaks bitterly, too, of the fact that he and his fellow *clientes* are forced by circumstances into accepting a cake at a dinner party given by their patron and being thereby 'compelled to pay a tip [sc. to a slave] and add to a well-dressed servant's property'. [12] He paints a picture of clients rushing to a patron's home to collect a hand-out meal which must then be kept warm on the way home by their own slave![13] As Southern maintains, patronage and clientship were ingrained in the Roman way of life from earliest times. [14] For Saller, patronage in imperial Rome was a relationship between two unequal persons (in social status) which set it off from friendship between equals.[15] The pursuit of patronage, particularly from the point of view of the client, while necessary often simply to survive, was a form of self-abasement and personal humiliation which few Romans with any self respect enjoyed. 'Romans', says Saller, 'applied the language of patronage to a range of relationships, with both humble dependants and their junior aristocratic colleagues labelled *clientes*: usage was more fluid than usually supposed, and the connotations of *amicus*, *cliens* and *patronus* were subtly and variously manipulated in different circumstances'. [16] The enduring image of the Roman patronal system and of its ritual humiliation of the clientele was the *salutatio*, yet the patron-client relationship actually had no formal status at law and was therefore not subject to juridical regulation.

The constant fear of ancient urban was of riot and disorder. Thus, Order and Concord (*Concordia* had of course been a widely recognised Republican virtue) were promoted as particular Augustan virtues. [17] The relationship between the urban masses and the Imperial authority was a political relationship, impersonal and unilateral; the inhabitants of Rome - no longer citizens of a great city-state, but mere residents of the Emperor's capital - were 'incapable of civic life',[18] merely members of the emperor's wider household. Said Aelius Aristides of Rome,

> 'If one has beheld the city itself and the boundaries of the city, one can no longer be amazed that the entire civilised world is ruled by one so great.' (*Ad Romam* 9)

---

11 *Satire* 3,126f..

12 Ibid., 3, 188-9.

13 Ibid., 3, 249-50.

14 P. Southern, *Domitian - Tragic Tyrant*. (London and New York, 1997), p. 4.

15 R. Saller, 'Patronage and friendship in early Imperial Rome: drawing the distinction', in A. Wallace-Hadrill (ed.), *Patronage in Ancient Society*. (London and New York, 1989), p. 49.

16 Ibid., 57.

17 Note that Concordia was from the first one of the tutelary deities of the re-founded Carthage and included as such in the formal name of that profoundly Romanised city.

18 Veyne, *Bread and Circuses*, p. 397.

I have chosen four Church Fathers as representatives of a Christian engagement or interaction with the surrounding culture. Clement, despite some doubters, and Hermas were almost certainly Romans by birth and disposition. Minucius Felix was from Cirta in North Africa but had clearly practised as a advocate for some time in the imperial city and was very much Roman in outlook. Hermas, who was possibly a freedman, we know little about but it is clear that he played a leading role in a Christian house-church in Rome. Hippolytus, one or many, was of Greek background but is clearly identified with the fortunes of the Roman church.

1 Clement

1 Clement is traditionally dated[19] to the end of the reign of Domitian (81-96 CE) who assumed the purple on the death of his brother Titus. He succeeded to the throne after a decade of peace and prosperity, but this did not necessarily ensure broad acceptance of his rule in Rome. He did not enjoy a good relationship with the senate, which fact both fed and confirmed his insecurity, but the people of Rome, declares Southern, never had serious cause for complaint while he was alive.[20]

We know virtually nothing concrete about the life of the author of *1 Clement*. Traditionally listed as the third bishop of Rome after the apostle Peter,[21] Clement was credited by Eusebius with the authorship of this letter to the church in Corinth[22] and Hermas speaks of a Clement in the church at Rome who was its official charged with corresponding with other churches abroad.[23] Irenaeus maintains that our Clement was personally associated with the apostles Peter and Paul, while both Origen[24] and Eusebius[25] identify him with Paul's associate at *Philippians* 4,3. Whether or not one accepts the advice that he was a monarchical bishop in Rome - and this is most unlikely - depends largely on whether one believes either that Rome enjoyed a monoepiscopate before the end of the first century or that the Christian community was, at that time and for some time afterwards, governed by a college of presbyters drawn from the leadership of the house churches forming the Roman congregation and of which number Clement was probably a senior and widely respected member.

---

19 See L.W. Barnard, 'Clement of Rome and the Persecution of Domitian', *New Testament Studies* 10 (1964): 251-60, for a discussion of the arguments. J. Fuellenbach, *Ecclesiastical Office and the Primacy of Rome* (Washington, 1980), p. 3, suggests between 93 and 96, while T.J.Herron, 'The Most Probable Date of the First Epistle of Clement to the Corinthians', *Studia Patristica* 21 (1989): 106-21, argues for an earlier date, c. 70 CE. O.M.Bakke, *Concord and Peace* (Tübingen, 2001), pp. 3, 8-11, suggests a date between 95 and 110 CE given the difficulty of precisely identifying historical events, such as official persecution, in its background.

20 Southern, *Domitian*, 59.

21 Eusebius, *Ecclesiastical History* 3.4.9; 21.1. See also Irenaeus, *Adv. Haer*. 3.3.3.

22 *Ecclesiastical History* 3,16,1.

23 *The Shepherd, Vis.* 2.3.4.

24 *Comm. In Joan.* 6.36.

25 *EH* 3.15.34.

The author of this letter is clearly influenced by the society about him. If not Roman by birth he was certainly Roman in attitude and disposition. He may well have been a freedman, even a member of the imperial house. [26] Bakke supports Jeffer's contention that the letter demonstrates above-average literary skills for a 'Greek-speaking resident in Rome'. [27] The letter and its use of the Septuagint also shows a familiarity with a Hellenistic-Jewish tradition[28] but this would be no more than would be expected of the place and time.

The precise historical context of the letter - whether it reflects persecution of the Roman church by Roman authorities or internal strife within the community itself (which would provide an appropriate setting for the primary concerns of the letter itself) - is not clear. What is clear is that the church at Rome, under the pen of a senior figure within that church (whom we shall call Clement), addressed particular concerns to its sister church at Corinth over what appears to have been the virtual overthrow of the established leadership of that church and their replacement by those who engineered their fall. Whether this was a case of 'new' Christians, or outsiders, or one particular house-church or group claiming primacy of oversight of the entire Christian community in Corinth is not clear but the outcome of this 'regime change' was unacceptable to our author – and also, one presumes, to the leadership of the Roman church - as contrary to good order. Our author offers no judgement as to the relative merits of the leadership qualities or style of either the new or the old regime; it is simply that such change, without due process, is contrary to natural order and the divine will for the ordering of the church.

At 1.1 there is a reference to 'sudden and repeated misfortunes and calamities which have befallen us', that is, troubles or problems of some kind afflicting the Christian community at Rome. It is widely, though by no means universally agreed that this must refer to a persecution of Christians (and of Jews?) towards the end of Domitian's reign. Eusebius speaks of Nero and Domitian 'slandering' Christian teaching,[29] of Domitian putting to death many distinguished persons in Rome and being the second emperor (after Nero) to promote persecution against Christians,[30] and banishing from Rome Flavia Domitilla, the niece of the consul Flavius Clemens, for being a Christian.[31] Dio describes Flavia Domitilla as both the wife of Flavius Clemens and a cousin of the emperor, and says that she was accused of atheism, a common complaint against those who practised Jewish customs. [32] It is possible here that Dio has indiscriminately included Christians with Jews; that is, by 'Jewish' here he actually means 'Christian'. There is, however, no non-Christian evidence that

---

26 See both J.S. Jeffers, *Conflict at Rome: Social Order and Hierarchy in Early Christianity*. (Minneapolis, 1991), and Bakke, *Concord and Peace*, p. 7, who finds the former's arguments on this 'reasonable and plausible'.

27 See Bakke, *Concord and Peace*, p. 7 and Jeffers, *Conflict at Rome*, p. 32.

28 Bakke, *Concord and Peace*, p. 4.

29 *EH* 4.26.9.

30 Ibid., 3.17.1.

31 Ibid., 3.18.4.

32 *History* 67.14.1.

Domitian actually persecuted Christians. Some Christians may have been, but not *qua* Christians, among the victims of Domitian's brutal purges. Our author says at 7.1 that 'we [i.e. the Roman Christians] are in the same arena [sc. as them] and the same contest is before us'. This is possibly (though probably not) a reference to a present or at the very least a recent persecution. At 7.2 he urges the Corinthians to put aside non-essential matters and to focus on the rule of the tradition, what is acceptable to God and - with a clear linkage to talk of persecution and martyrdom - the saving blood of Christ. Bakke provides a useful, though brief summary of the traditional view which posits an external persecution as the background for 1.1 and contrasts this with that which suggests that the 'misfortunes and calamities' refer to internal strife within the church at Rome.[33] For our purposes, however, this particular dispute is of little account except insofar as it may shed light on events in Corinth.

What cultural and/or intellectual influences are at play in this letter? To what extent and how do these influences affect not only the presentation of Clement's ideas but even the content of those ideas themselves? Bowe sees overall in the letter a rhetorical style aiming at persuasion, not command.[34] The primary focus of the author's concern is communal discord and not essentially ecclesiastical office. He employs a rhetorical commonplace against strife and division, common not only to Roman thought but to all antiquity. Bowe indeed properly observes a particular rhetorical type in this letter. Of the three basic forms of rhetoric identified by Aristotle and others, the first, the deliberative or symbouleutic, is the most suited to Christian paraenetic purposes; *1 Clement* is such a letter. It is self-described as an entreaty (*enteuxis*) (63.2) and a *symboulē* (58.2), a form of counsel for peace traditionally given to cities in the Greek world. The very structure of the work is clearly shaped by contemporary rhetorical convention.[35] Chapters 1 and 2 comprise an *exordium* in which the author praises his readers and speaks of their deserved fame from of old thereby seeking to secure their goodwill. He speaks of their many great qualities, consistent with the rhetorical model, of their humility, their piety, their charity, their kindness, their virtue, their honour, their nobility of spirit, and their fear of God. Chapter 3 comprises an appropriately brief *narratio* in which he speaks of the jealousy, envy, strife, sedition, disorder and conflict now present in the Corinthian church, reflecting both the rhetorical subject of 'war and peace'[36] and, by contrast, the 'goods' of nobility, fame, honour and virtue.[37] Chapters 4 - 61 comprise a lengthy probatio: 4.1-39.9 the *thesis* and 40.1-61.3 the *hypothesis*. This includes the extensive use of examples (of jealousy, envy, and strife, of repentance, obedience, humility, peaceableness, order, reconciliation, honour, and so on), artistic proofs like

---

33 Bakke, *Concord and Peace*, pp. 8f.

34 I acknowledge here my extensive use of B.E.Bowe's fine monograph, *A Church in Crisis: Ecclesiology and Paraenesis in Clement of Rome*. (Minneapolis, 1988).

35 See O.M.Bakke, 'The Rhetorical Composition of the First Letter of Clement', *SP* 36 (2001): 155-162.

36 See Aristotle's *Rhetoric* 1.4 (1359a).

37 Ibid., 1.5 (1360b).

emotional appeals (such as that against *hubris*[38] at chapter 21 - see below on this) and non-artistic proofs[39] like the law (the scriptures) and reference to witnesses both ancient (such as key figures from the Old Testament) and more recent. At 7.5 he suggests that '[we] review all the generations [of witnesses]'. He employs scriptural maxims (see chapters 13-15 on humility, order, and peaceableness). [40] 'War and captivity',[41] mentioned as symbolic attributes of the troubles at Corinth at 3,2, are one of the traditional 'topics' of the symbouleutic genre, the discussion of 'strife and faction' likewise part of the traditional fare. The letter also shares with Chrysostom, Aristides and Quintilian an abundant use of examples - example and analogy being common rhetorical devices - of both *upodeigmata* (examples) and *upogrammoi* (models). A preference for the general over a particularity of detail - evident in both Chrysostom and Aristides - is likewise evident in *1 Clement* whose author has often irritated scholars who simply want to know more of what actually happened in Corinth itself.

At chapters 59-61, as our author moves towards his *peroratio* (chapters 62 (recapitulation) and 63 (emotional appeal)), he turns his pen to prayer. He appeals to God as the true audience for his exhortation to aid the Corinthians in their strife, for mercy, for peace, for concord. He reminds all that all human authority on earth derives from the gift of God alone. 'O you who alone is able to do these things and far better things than we' (61.3). Here is traditional rhetoric turned, transformed indeed, into a powerful evangelical tool.

The level of the engagement of and interaction with the surrounding Roman society on the part of the author of *1 Clement* is considerable. His concern and that of the Roman congregation which he represents at those events in Corinth which he describes, though of course somewhat dramatically at 3,2 as 'jealousy, envy, strife, sedition, persecution and disorder, war and captivity', is driven by a very Roman desire for order and stability. Though symbolic, these do stand in his mind over against the Christian virtue of love, the discussion of which quality at 49,5 implicitly demonstrates remarkable convergence with the Roman virtues of Order and Concord promoted by Augustus, by permitting neither schism nor sedition but rather doing all things in harmony (*homonoia*). Talk of *stasis* owes a particular debt to Hellenistic political rhetoric (cf. Aristotle, *Pol.* 5.6.1; 5.7.5;[42] *Eth. Nic.* 9.1167a 34[43]). Our author, in the manner of Hellenistic political commentators, contrasts

38 Ibid. 2.2 (1377c).

39 Ibid. 1.15 (1375a).

40 Ibid. 2.21 (1394a).

41 Ibid. 1.4 (1359b).

42 Aristotle speaks of 'factional conflict' as involving several varieties, including the overthrow of oligarchy by the prosperous who have no share in the spoils of office (5.6.1) and of such conflict even being instigated by one sharing power who yet desires sole power (5.7.5).

43 Aristotle speaks here of faction caused by the rivalry of two claimants to power. True civic concord is not only about agreement on ideals but about unanimity on purposes and direction.

eustatheia (political stability) (61,1: with *peace* and *concord*; 65,1: with *peace* and *concord*) with *stasis* (faction, sedition) (cf. Philo, *Leg. ad Gaium* 113[44]). 'Peace and concord' are, of course, a recurring theme in the letter - perhaps *the* theme - and this mirrors a standard classically rhetorical position. Dio Chrysostom's *Four Orations*, in this respect at least, share a common rhetorical milieu with *1 Clement*. Maier observes that 'Clement drew from pagan political rhetorical *topoi* when depicting the divisions in the Corinthian church and when exhorting his audience to pursue ideals of harmony and concord' and reflects particularly on the alleged *hubris* of the usurpers there.[45] He points to Aristotle's *Rhetoric* 1378b as providing the *locus classicus* of the 'hybrist'. Aristotle argues there that 'the young and the wealthy are the hybrists (*hubristai*)'.

Thus when Clement at 3.3 speaks of the 'dishonourable' rising against the 'honourable' and the 'young against the old' he probably had Aristotle in mind with the latter pairing. Maier points to three authors roughly contemporary to Clement who identify *hubris* as a defining feature of those who foment communal discord: Dionysius of Harlicarnassus (*Roman Antiquities*); Plutarch (*Precepts on Statecraft*); and Dio Chrysostom (*Discourses*) whose attraction for Clement is well documented (see above). In the causes of the discord in Corinth Maier declares that Clement 'was adopting an association of vices believed throughout pagan antiquity to be typical of the hybrist'.[46] He also suggests, however, the influence of the Maccabean literature which pictures Antiochus Epiphanes and his supporters as hybrists and says that 'In *1 Clement* we most probably have an instance of mixture of a pagan rhetorical *topos* with a biblical profile of the boastful enemy of the Lord'.[47]

Scholars argue over whether or not chapter 20 of the letter on the ordered nature of the universe is primarily Stoic or Jewish in background -

(1) 'The heavens moving at [sc. God's] appointment are subject to him in peace ... (11) All these things did the great Creator and Master of the universe ordain to be in peace and concord, and to all things does he do good,...'.[48]

This section is certainly influenced by Stoic thought. There are echoes of Cleanthes' *Hymn to Zeus*, elements of both a determinism and a providence consistent with Stoic thought, and Epictetus' caring, protecting and providential God is suggested. Shaw comments that 'with the Stoics the ultimate frame of reference for individual men was not the *polis* ... but rather the universe - Nature itself'.[49] And

---

44 'Ares who ends war and creates peace ... [and] Gaius the enemy of peace, the comrade of war, who transformed the settled order (*eustatheian*) into uproar and faction (*staseis*).'

45 H.O.Maier, '*1 Clement* and the Rhetoric of υβρις', *SP* 31 (1997): 136.

46 Ibid., 140.

47 Ibid., 141.

48 W.C. van Unnik, 'Is I Clement 20 purely Stoic?', *VC* 4 (1950): 185, argues against the traditional view of a Stoic background for this key chapter declaring that a Jewish one is the more likely, while W. Ullmann, 'The cosmic theme of the *Prima Clementis* and its significance for the concept of Roman Rulership', *SP* 11 (1972): 87, argues that the background is not Jewish but oriental (and thereby Stoic).

49 B.D.Shaw, 'The Divine Economy: Stoicism as Ideology', *Latomus* 44 (1985): 35.

in this cosmic order 'each person had a definite place…and a role to play, whether as slave, father, husband, king, or councillor, and also had specific duties attached to that role' (see Epictetus, *Encheiridion* 4,6,26; 15,17,24). Bakke identifies chapters 19 to 21 as employing 'a common *topos* of deliberative rhetoric that urges concord'. [50] He observes, as do others, that in both Palestinian and Hellenistic Judaism we can find similar notions regarding the ordering of the universe. [51] Yet no Jewish texts use the phrase 'peace and concord' with respect to elements in the universe so this must come from a Greek source. [52] Given that in his view 'Clement's basic purpose with the chapter is to present the harmony and peace of nature as a model for the Church to imitate'[53] – and in my view he is correct here - he then suggests both Dio Chrysostom (*Or.* 40.35-37) and Aelius Aristides (*Or.* 23.77) as possible sources for the notion of the universe acting as a model for civic concord. [54]

The providentially ordered universe, for Clement, is prescriptive for the ordering of society and of the church. This is the key to understanding this work and is consistent with the Augustan virtues of peace, concord and stability. The call at 54,2 for the usurpers to relieve pressure in the Corinthian church by going into voluntary exile also reflects very clearly the traditional Roman solution to civic discord through exile, voluntary or otherwise. Such a call, says Bakke, is consistent with the honour-shame culture which characterised Mediterranean society then and now. Thus 'honour played a fundamental role in the cultural environment of Clement' and 'holding a public office was in [this] cultural milieu associated with great honour'. [55] Bakke also points to the witness of Dio Chrysostom, Plutarch and Aristotle that the love and pursuit of honour is a prime cause of *stasis*. [56] Clement's concern is that the Corinthian church is losing its well-deserved good reputation and that there is a clear connection between sedition and a damaged reputation; the present sedition in Corinth is dishonourable and brings shame upon the community. [57]

These dissident Corinthians in Clement's mind challenge thereby not only Christian but also Roman virtues. Indeed the two in the mind of our author may be one. The author speaks of the Corinthians' previous history as marked by a 'virtuous and honourable citizenship (*politeia*)' (2,8). The *Ante-Nicene Christian Library* translates the phrase as 'a virtuous and religious life'. Indeed, at 54,4 our author speaks of 'those who live without regret as citizens in the city (*politeia*) of God'. Clement uses *politeia* again at 3,4 in the same sense of a membership of Christ's body when he speaks of those who are driven by jealousy, envy, strife, sedition and so on, who abandon righteousness and peace, who leave behind the fear of God, and whose faith is weak, as those who walk neither in the customs of God's

---

50 Bakke, *Concord and Peace*, p. 160.
51 Ibid., p. 162.
52 Ibid..
53 Ibid., p. 163.
54 Ibid., pp. 165f..
55 Ibid., p. 310.
56 Ibid., p. 311.
57 Ibid., p. 312.

commandments nor live out their 'citizenship' worthily to Christ. Not dissimilar language was employed at 21,1, where our author warns of the potential judgement of God on the community if they do not act as citizens worthy of him, 'if they do not perform good deeds well-pleasing before him in concord'. Again we observe the Augustan-like ideals of good citizenship and concord. The Roman ideal for the state is that of Clement's for the church. Chapter 20 - with its profound distaste for anything which could be termed *stasis* or factionalism - and our author's use of the image of the community as a body at 37,5 - all members working together and united in a common subjection to preserve the whole body, the 'decent, ordered, tidy society'[58] of Augustus - also reflect this. No Roman could have said it better. Thus again do Clement's conception of the church as an ordered community and the Augustan conception of the Roman world converge.

This concern for order and concord in the body - in this case, the Christian community - is most evident in the author's reflections on the ordering of its ministry and in particular the ministry of leadership. At 21,6 he urges the Corinthians to both reverence the Lord Jesus Christ and, among things, to respect those who rule them. Likewise, the author's exhortation in the same passage for the community to honour the aged is a quite deliberate allusion to the deposed leaders in the Corinthian community, the elders or presbyters. Our author then speaks at 40.5, in the context of order within the religious life, of the proper services of the High Priest, the ordinary priests, the Levites, and laypersons (ecclesial plebeians) themselves bound to the ordinances of the laity. Each of the brethren must be pleasing to God 'in his [or her] own rank' (41.1).

Jeffers' claim that our author's exhortations to the rich to help the poor, and to the poor to give thanks to God for such benefactors at 38,2 - going beyond the biblical injunctions in this regard with respect to the grateful response required of the poor (the weak) - is based on Roman notions of patronage is probably correct.[59] It is probably also reasonable to suggest that the author's concern for demonstrations of hospitality - at a level more evident than within the New Testament itself - is the result of the influence of Roman aristocratic notions of friendship, even though our author actually makes no explicit mention of the latter. The claim that 'Clement and his congregation came to accept social distinctions among themselves as a basis for ordering their relationships, that is, through the influence of Roman ideology, they came to accept hierarchy as natural to Christianity',[60] may well be true. The Christians represented by this epistle may have accepted distinctions within the ordering of their community - indeed they almost certainly did - but this does not require that such distinctions within the community, such as they were, had necessarily to be based on existing secular ones.

A very significant engagement by the author with the surrounding culture occurs in his employment of military images. At 37,1 he urges his fellow Christians to 'serve

58 R. Goodman, *The Roman World: 44BC – AD180*. (London and New York), p. 166.

59 Jeffers, *Conflict at Rome*, p. 132

60 Ibid., p. 131.

as soldiers' and in so doing to follow earnestly the faultless commands of Christ. He employs similar language at 3,4 of the commands of God. He then employs as illustration those serving in the Roman army. His reference to 'our generals' and to other ranks is possibly one to Roman officers and enlisted personnel and not here to church leaders and other members of the community. Each carries out orders appropriate to his own rank (*en to idio tagmati*) - for not all soldiers are prefects or tribunes or centurions or have charge of fifty men[61] or the like [sc. but most are common soldiers, privates] - orders which come from the emperor and the generals. Later our author uses the same expression - 'each in his own rank' - of Christians within their community (41,1), with respect to the diversity of Christian service. Again the sense that each person has their own defined place in the Roman world and in the universe is carried through by Clement to the life of the church. Jeffers is correct when he declares that 'Clement believes that, just as Rome remains in peace because all obey the emperor, the Christian community will remain in peace when all obey God, the Master, by remaining in submission to the community's leaders'.[62]

Our author is evidently one who has a deep appreciation and admiration for the achievements of the *Pax Romana*. It is difficult perhaps for many today entirely to appreciate the profound sense of peace and security felt by those within the Roman world of the late first century CE, when little over a century earlier that world had been convulsed by civil war and strife, a reminder of which had been experienced only a generation earlier (in the memory of many of those still alive) during the upheavals of the late 60's. At 60,4 Clement urges obedience to rulers and governors on earth, again, of course, within a framework of concord and peace. At 61,1, however, he makes clear that their power is that granted them by God, and any subjection to them must accord with the divine will. Christian prayers for such rule must always be mindful of this fact. Such prayers must be for the health, peace, concord (again) and firmness in exercising the authority given them by God without offence. This last reminds one of Tertullian's injunction that the emperors may be obeyed by Christians but only 'within the limits of godly discipline', that is, excluding idolatry.[63] Yet within those constraints our author appears to accept the reality of Roman order and its modelling of the divine requirements for the church's ordering of its own life. It is for their transgression of these fundamental principles of *peace*, *concord* and *stability of governance* that he requires the removal of those who have wrongly presumed the places of leadership at Corinth contrary to divine/natural order and the reinstatement of those whose authority has been so wrongly usurped.

61 Although Bowes, *A Church in Crisis*, p. 127, notes that there was actually no office for leading 50 men in the Roman army whereas there was such in the desert army of Israel.

62 Jeffers, *Conflict at Rome*, p. 137.

63 *de Idololatria* 15,4.

Hermas: *The Shepherd*[64]

The Shepherd was probably written in stages during the reigns of Trajan (98-117), Hadrian (117-138) and Antoninus Pius (138-161), Gibbon's 'golden age'. When Trajan became emperor at the conclusion of the short and largely insignificant reign of Nerva, he did so with considerable popular and senatorial support. A conscientious, competent ruler, Trajan reformed the administration of the state, particularly in Rome,[65] and reportedly demonstrated a marked respect for the Senate[66] which was by all accounts reciprocated. [67] When Hadrian became ruler he was complicit in the execution of potential rivals. [68] The Senate was apparently coerced into silence by these actions and his ongoing poor relationship with that body, which these executions in part fostered, led to an initial refusal on its part to deify him after his death. [69] His constant travel abroad meant that he spent very little time in Rome itself. He saw himself not as an innovator but as one whose task it was to preserve and, where necessary, to restore the best in the Roman way of life. It was during his reign that the term '*urbs sacra*' began to be applied informally to Rome - it was made official only under Septimius Severus - and in this way reinforced the increasing identification and connection between the person of the emperor and Rome. Antoninus Pius stayed in Rome for much of his reign and managed to both obtain and enjoy the almost unparallelled affection of his senatorial peers. He was deified by the Senate after his much widely mourned death. [70]

The dating of Hermas' *Shepherd* is problematic. Traditionally it was placed towards the middle of the second century CE, given that the Muratorian Canon[71] says that its author was the brother of Pius, bishop of Rome at that time. This dating is now almost universally challenged and modern opinion tends towards a late first century date, at least for the earlier sections of the work. Jeffers suggests that most of the work would have been completed by the end of the first century and the remainder by 135 CE at the latest,[72] Bauckham that *Visions* 1 to 4 were certainly written immediately prior to the Domitian persecution at Rome, and Hahneman that 'the internal evidence of the Shepherd supports an early date for all its parts'.[73]

---

64 See G.M.Hahneman, *The Muratorian Fragment and the Development of the Canon* (Oxford, 1992), pp. 61-71, for a useful summary of the history of the reception of *The Shepherd* within the church.

65 Dio, *History* 68, 5,4; 6,2-3.

66 Ibid. 68, 5,2; 7,3.

67 See Pliny's *Panegyricus* as an example of this.

68 Dio, 69,8,2.

69 Dio, 69,23,3.

70 Dio, 13,3.

71 Lines 73-77.

72 Jeffers, *Conflict at Rome*, 106f.

73 R. J. Bauckham, 'The Great Tribulation in the Shepherd of Hermas', *JTS* 25 (1964): 28 and Hahneman, *The Muratorian Fragment*, p. 41. C. Osiek, 'The Genre and Function of the *Shepherd of Hermas*', *Semeia* 36 (1986): 114, suggests that Visions 1-4 were written

Assuming that the work was compiled in stages during a time when, apart from some rather celebrated martyrdoms - notably those of Justin and Polycarp in the East - the church benefited from a period of relative peace and prosperity, it would seem that the church in Rome had settled into a somewhat comfortable existence in which it began to accommodate itself to various aspects of Roman life. It is in this context that Hermas issues his challenge to the church, warning it of the dangers of such accommodation and the alleged compromise of Christian ethics in the face of the attractions of the surrounding culture. Prophets normally call for repentance when times are relatively unchallenging for the people of God and this would seem to reflect the setting for this particular work.

Osiek declares that the author of the *Visions* at least must have been a freedman[74] and that his own concern about wealth and social-climbing was addressed predominantly to a large and influential freedman group within his own faith community.[75] While Giet has suggested that the work may been authored by three different writers - *Visions* 1-4 by a contemporary of Clement of Rome, *Similitude* 9 by the brother of Pope Pius in the mid-second century, and *Vision* 5 - *Similitude* 8 and *Similitude* 10 by someone else[76] - this is now widely disputed. Earlier even than Giet many scholars supported the multiple author approach - Coleborne later even suggested six different authors![77] - but most scholars believe that the work reflects a unitary approach and could well have been authored by a single person writing over a significant period. [78] Henne suggests the somewhat unusual view, not widely supported, that there was actually no 'Hermas' at all. [79] He maintains that the name itself has only a symbolic significance, that it is a Doric form of the name Hermes and as such is meant to evoke the notion of a divine messenger charged with transmitting a story of transformation. Another issue which arises again and

---

towards the end of the first century, *Sim.* 9 near the middle of the second and the rest of the work by the end of the third quarter of that century. C. Osiek, *Rich and Poor in the Shepherd of Hermas* (Washington, 1983), p. 6 offers a good summary of the various arguments, as does P. Henne, *L'Unité du Pasteur d'Hermas* (Paris, 1992), pp. 7f. Stewart-Sykes, 'Hermas the Prophet and Hippolytus the Preacher: The Roman Homily and its Social Context', in M.B.Cunningham and P.Allen (eds), *Preacher and Audience: Studies in Early Christian and Byzantine Homiletics* (Leiden, 1998), p. 36, note 6, comments that Hahneman's chapter on the dating of Hermas (34-72) has 'transformed' the discussion and that 'there is little point in repeating his extensive arguments here'. I would agree.

74 Osiek, *Rich and Poor*, p. 130.

75 Ibid., p. 132.

76 S. Giet, *Hermas et les pasteurs: les trois auteurs du Pasteur d'Hermas*. (Paris, 1963).

77 W. Coleborne, 'The *Shepherd* of Hermas: A case for Multiple Authorship and Some Implications', *Studia Patristica* 10 (1970): 65-70.

78 See J.Reiling, *Hermas and Christian Prophecy: a Study of the Eleventh Mandate*. (Leiden, 1973), p. 23 and especially Hahneman, *The Muratorian Fragment*, pp. 46-61 whose detailed arguments on the identity of this single author - he opts for a contemporary of Clement of Rome - like those on the question of the dating, need not be repeated here.

79 P. Henne, 'Hermas, un pseudonyme', *SP* 24 (1993): 136-9.

again in Hermas scholarship is that of Hermas' status within the Roman church. It is generally agreed he was not a presbyter - though the argument is more from silence than otherwise - but that he was probably a recognised prophet. Yet the whole thrust of the document does suggest some form of leadership role within at least his own immediate church 'family'.

At *Vis.* 2,2.7, 4,2.4 and 5 our author speaks of a 'great tribulation' which is coming. O'Hagan suggests that the first passage certainly implies that a trial of faith is somehow involved - a great eschatological trial[80] - but that the unqualified term *thlipsis* elsewhere in the treatise can simply mean 'persecution'.[81] Bauckham does not deal with the reference at 2,2.7 but confines his treatment of the question to *Vision* 4.[82] He argues that these references do not simply refer to a period of persecution - either anticipated or already experienced - though they will imply such a one as imminent.[83] All that can be said with any certainty here is that Hermas makes brief and tantalisingly obscure references both to past persecutions of Christians - which could be to events during the reigns of either Nero or Domitian - and to future trials of faith for Christians - which could refer either to specific persecutions or to the last, great eschatological trial. To pin any of Hermas' 'tribulation' references to a specific time (or place for that matter) is impossible. He refers also at other points to the martyrdom of Christians, at *Vis.* 3,1.9 to those who have suffered for the name, and at 3,2.1 to the methods of torment inflicted on the persecuted - crucifixion and being thrown to the beasts among them - but again in such a way as cannot be dated with any precision. In the absence of specific evidence pointing to actual persecution in the text one must assume that the 'tribulation' referred to by Hermas is not a specific bout of persecution but an eschatological crisis faced by the church at Rome as it settles into an easy accommodating relationship with the world around it. The 'crisis' is then one which is both immediate and future in that it is met at every point where the allegiance of the Christian to the Gospel is to be tested.

Osiek declares that the *Shepherd* meets the qualifications of apocalyptic literature, employing the definition given by Collins.[84] Yet the function of the *Shepherd* as *paraenesis*[85] (a usual but not unknown component of apocalyptic literature) does

---

80 A. P. O'Hagan, 'The Great Tribulation to Come in the Pastor of Hermas', *SP* 4 (1961): 306.

81 See, for example, *Vis.* 2,3.4 and *Sim.* 9,21.3.

82 He says that he is in this paper concerned 'solely with [sc. Hermas'] use of apocalyptic material in Vision IV', *Hermas et les pasteurs*, p. 27.

83 Bauckham, 'The Great Tribulation in the Shepherd of Hermas', 31f. Osiek, 'Genre and Function', 117 also sees reference here to coming eschatological conflict.

84 Osiek, 'Genre and Function', 118. John J. Collins, 'Introduction: Towards the Morphology of a Genre', *Semeia* 14 (1979), 9, speaks of 'a genre of revelatory literature with a narrative framework, in which a revelation is mediated by an otherworldly being to a human recipient, disclosing a transcendent reality which is both temporal, insofar as it envisages eschatological salvation, and spatial insofar as it involves another, supernatural world'.

85 See Stewart-Sykes, 'Hermas the Prophet and Hippolytus the Preacher', where the author calls Hermas 'a parainetic prophet' (p. 38) and at p.42, where he poses the 'hypothesis

set it apart from much of that genre. [86] Its underlying theme of *repentance* is an unfamiliar element in apocalypticism, and the historical and political concerns normally associated with Jewish apocalypticism are, for example, lacking in the *Shepherd*; yet its immediate intellectual context is Jewish thought developed in a Hellenistic milieu. [87] The *Shepherd*, in terms of its function and form, concerns the translation of an eschatological vision into realistic terms. The work concerns a series of revelations to Hermas, transmitted in the first instance by an ancient lady who through the time of the revelations is transformed into a younger woman and who is to be identified with the Church itself, and in the second by the eponymous shepherd of the treatise, whose particular revelations form the bulk of those delivered to Hermas. The work comprises five Visions - although the fifth actually introduces the twelve Mandates which follow (the ancient/young woman reveals the first four visions, the Shepherd the fifth) - and then the ten Parables which follow them. The Mandates and the Parables are revealed to Hermas through the Shepherd. The principal theme of the work is that of a repentance to which Hermas is called both individually but also, and more importantly perhaps, as a member if not leading figure of the Roman church. The overwhelming context of the work is of a church which is perceived as essentially faithless in its engagement with the surrounding culture, particularly in a time of relative peace, stability and prosperity when the church has grown soft and flabby. As we will see below, the immediate crisis faced by the church here is not one of external persecution but an internal one of eschatological proportions. As Osiek says in her fine commentary on the work: 'Hermas is more afraid of his listeners losing their faith than losing their lives'. [88]

The work clearly reflects more than a nodding acquaintanceship with Greco-Roman literature and thought. [89] The figure of the Sybil, of whom there were a number of prominent statues in Rome itself, may provide for Hermas a model for the woman-church (the revealer of *Visions* 1-4). The personification of the seven Virtues at *Vision* 3.8.2f. through the seven young women is traditional in Greco-Roman mythology and may even, for Hermas, suggest the traditional Hellenistic form of the caryatids at the base of a tower. The discernment of angels - both good and evil - at *Mandate* 6, 21f. may reflect a two-way paraenetic theology with roots in both Greek and Jewish moral traditions. The call in *Mandate* 8 to restraint (*enkrateia*) is common to both Jewish and to Greco-Roman moral teaching. The contrast between the heavenly and the earthly spirits at *Mandate* 9.11-12 is also a Greco-Roman commonplace. On *Mandate* 11.2 - concerned with discerning prophecy - Osiek comments that 'the accusation that the false prophet says what his clients want him

---

that the *Shepherd* is constructed from only slightly redacted homilies' (p. 42).

86 Note there the comment of Stewart-Sykes, ibid., 62 that 'Hermas shows no sign of a rhetorical education'. Even a brief reading of the work can only support this claim.

87 See Reiling, *Hermas and Christian Prophecy*, pp. 25f..

88 C.Osiek, *Shepherd of Hermas: a commentary*. (Minneapolis, 1999), p. 20.

89 I am here, as elsewhere, very much in debt to Osiek's work.

to say is a common critique of Greco-Roman oracular prophecy'.[90] The metaphor of filiation - for example, evil desire as the daughter of the devil - employed by Hermas at *Mandate* 12.2.2 was known in both Jewish and Greco-Roman literature and the notion of the slave of desire (*Mandate* 12,2.4-5) was a familiar rhetorical *topos*. The parable of the elm and the vine - *Similitude* 2 - was a well-known literary motif for human relationships in the Greco-Roman world.[91] The image of protective female heavenly figures - such as those which surround Hermas at *Similitude* 9.11.1f. - are likewise Greco-Roman commonplaces. The notion that Christians lived in the world as if in a foreign land - see *Similitude* 1[92] - was 'already a traditional eschatological motif, inherited from the Platonic and Stoic philosophical traditions, and possibly also from the Jewish diaspora experience'.[93] The reference at *Vision* 1.3.4 to the 'god of the powers' shows both Jewish and Stoic traces. The concern expressed over an unhealthy indulgence of the body at *Vision* 3.9.3 is primarily Stoic although this was also a commonplace in the second century. The virtue of *autarkeia* (self-reliance) - exhorted at *Similitude* 1.6 - is possibly adapted from Stoic thought though it may just have easily come from a Epicurean source.[94] Cicero in his *Tusculan Disputations* points to a Stoic notion of self-sufficiency as a desirable virtue (5.40-1, 81-2[95]). None of this, of course, proves that our author drew his inspiration for this from sources other than from within the Christian community but it does suggest most strongly that he is influenced in the presentation of his thought at the very least by non-Christian notions.

Two social institutions in the Roman world and of particular importance in Rome itself were those of patronage and the *paterfamilias*. There are reflections of the Roman practice of patronage in the *Shepherd* at *Vision* 3.2.4 - where Hermas is probably the client to the lady's patron - at *Mandate* 4.2.1 - where Hermas is client and the Shepherd now patron - at *Similitude* 2 - where the author speaks of the intercessions which the poor can make on behalf of the prosperous who support them materially - and at *Similitude* 8.4.1, where the Shepherd is again imaged as a patron who demands that Hermas serve him. These passages suggest not only the use of a familiar relationship image but also that such relationships existed within the Christian community at Rome. Osiek here sees a spiritualisation of the institution of patronage whereby the *obsequium* and *operae* normally owed by the client are, in the ecclesial context, intercessory prayer. At *Vision* 1.3.1 the old woman condemns

---

90 Osiek, *Shepherd of Hermas: a commentary*, p. 142.

91 See Ovid, *Metamorphoses* 14. 661-68: 'The vine is supported by the elm to which it has been united.'

92 Cf. *Hebrews* 13.14.

93 Osiek, *Shepherd of Hermas: a commentary*, p. 158.

94 See Epicurus, *Letter to Menoeceus* 127-32 (L&S 21B) and *Vatican sayings* 45 (L&S 25E): 'Natural philosophy does not make people boastful and loud-mouthed, not flaunters of culture, the thing so hotly competed for among the multitude, but modest and self-sufficient, and proud at their own goods, not at those of their circumstances'.

95 'It necessarily follows that the happy life [sc. for the Stoics] is in the power of the man who has the final good in his power.'

the corruption of Hermas' 'family' by their attention to the demands of daily life and holds Hermas directly responsible both for this state of affairs and for its remedy. It is also clear that the reference to 'family' is not merely to Hermas' immediate family but to the Christian community to which he belongs and in which he would seem to exercise some responsibility. Here again is the issue of Hermas' particular status within that community. Here is undoubtedly at work the image of the Roman *paterfamilias* who was always held responsible in law for his family's behaviour. Likewise, at *Mandate* 12.3.6, Hermas' primary, even exclusive, responsibility for his *oikos* suggests the image of the *paterfamilias*. At *Similitude* 7.2 Hermas' direct responsibility for the sins of his household - what Osiek identifies as 'the social embeddedness of family members in the head of the household'[96] - again suggests the role of *paterfamilias*. Steve Young also suggests, in his treatment of the call to Hermas to 'be a man' (*andrizou*), the role of *paterfamilias* for Hermas.[97] He speaks of the tensions over his leadership role as *patronus-paterfamilias*, that his failure to care for his household provides the context for understanding his failure 'to be a man'. Under old Roman law the *paterfamilias* was responsible for damages resulting from the actions of his children or slaves. This suggestion of Hermas as *paterfamilias* is important for our understanding of the early Roman church and for its own self-understanding. For if the references to Hermas' family are merely to his immediate relatives then it is merely a Roman commonplace that he is responsible for their actions. If, however, his *oikos* here is the Christian (house) church to which he belongs, then the implications for the relationship between leaders of the Christian community and the regular members of the congregations - where the former are responsible for the actions of the latter before God - are immense and the pastoral and liturgical consequences significant. For the notion of the Christian clergy as 'fathers' to their flock is wide-ranging and immense in terms of the pastoral relationship in particular and reflects a movement, evident already in Clement's depiction of the non-leaders of the church as the *laos*, which is fostered here and indeed further developed.

It is probably correct to suggest that a primary concern of Hermas in writing this treatise was to make clear that the preoccupation of many Christians with commerce and wealth-production and the acquisition of a comfortable, not to say luxurious, lifestyle - and a concomitant solid standing in the surrounding society - was incompatible with the living of the Christian life. Osiek suggests that Hermas addresses his remarks to those Christians in Rome who 'are economically comfortable, upwardly mobile, and inclined to find vigorous fidelity to the demands of religious visionaries uninteresting if not downright threatening'.[98] We can accept that these were probably for the most part freedmen, given that both the *ordines* of Rome were rarely concerned with business dealings - that is, normal commercial transactions

96 Osiek, *Shepherd of Hermas: a commentary*, p. 192.

97 S.Young, '*Being a Man: The Pursuit of manliness* in the Shepherd of Hermas', *Journal of Early Christian Studies* 2 (1994): 237-255.

98 Osiek, *Shepherd of Hermas: a commentary*, p. 192.

- and that much of their wealth was both inherited and largely in land, and that much of ancient literature certainly points to the freedman class of Rome as that principally concerned with the acquisition of personal wealth through commercial enterprise.

Our author's references to 'wealthy' Christians are legion, recognising as we must that the notion of 'wealth' here is an entirely relative matter. These were probably not Christians fabulously wealthy by conventional Roman standards - one is reminded of Pliny's claim that one needed a fortune of 20,000,000 sesterces to be accounted rich in Rome - but those who had accumulated large enough fortunes either to enable one to pursue a comfortable lifestyle or to put oneself within reach of it. At *Vis*. 3,6.5 the lady speaks of those Christians whose preoccupation with wealth production and business interests has forced them, in time of persecution, to deny their Lord. Only when their wealth is taken away, she says, are they of real use to God (3,6.6). This is not speculation about theoretical possibilities but presumes both that Christians are actually diverted from piety by material preoccupations - Hermas himself in his former life is given by the lady as a classic example of this tendency - and that some Christians have in the past actually apostasised on account of a desire to preserve their wealth and social standing. At *Vis*. 3,9.2f. the lady condemns those wealthy members of the community who refuse to adequately support the poor of the community. While these categories of 'rich' and 'poor' are often elsewhere purely theological ones, here they are not exclusively so. Yet this does not mean that Hermas is particularly interested in issues of economic justice or the actual plight of the poor.[99] Hermas' real concern with the rich and poor here, I would suggest, is the likely deflection of the self-driven rich from their proper service of God. His major concern is actually with the rich. The poor, for Hermas, are of interest only in so far as their circumstances provide opportunities for the rich to demonstrate charity and compassion. At *Mand*. 3.5 the shepherd argues for honesty and truthfulness in business dealings, implying that these cannot be taken for granted either among pagans or Christians so engaged. At *Mand*. 10,1.4 he criticises well-off Christians not only for their commercial dealings but also for their seeking after approval from and friendship with pagans. At *Sim*. 1.10 he urges Christians not to pursue the wealth of the heathen but rather that wealth which they have, presumably, from God. He declares that the wealthy servant of God is too busy for the things of God, for the service of God. The rich must, he says, assist the poor who can intercede for them with God. The poor man is indeed obliged, as he is in *1 Clement*, to intercede with God for his benefactor. Again, the image suggested is that of a patron-client relationship. For only working together as do the fruitful vine and the sterile elm may rich and poor eventually work together for God. And, in any event, all wealth comes first from God. The shepherd does not entirely rule out a career in commerce for the Christian, however, for he declares at *Sim*. 4,7 that one business and, by implication, only one enterprise, can be served

99 Osiek in 'The early second century through the eyes of Hermas: continuity and change', *Biblical Theology Bulletin* 20 (1990): 118, observes that here 'Hermas sees a prophetic task: to recall [sc. the rich] to the attentiveness to the less fortunate and indifference to wealth and power that are part of the traditional ethos he has received'.

alongside the service of God. There is a certain pragmatism here. But the shepherd nowhere claims that wealth and business dealings *per se* are evil or ungodly. It is only their tendency to distract the believer from the things of God which concerns him. What is repudiated is an extravagance and luxury which turn the believer away from the faithful and unhindered service of God (*Sim.* 6,2.1f.). He declares also that Christians, if they must pursue earthly wealth, should not seek it among the heathen (*Sim.* 8,9,1). Nowhere does Hermas demonstrate any interest in the matter of wealth and poverty within the broader Roman society. His only concern is with how those Christians who seek to emulate their heathen counterparts at business and leisure imperil their very souls and effectively thereby deny the Gospel.

At *Mand.* 8,10 and at *Sim.* 9,27,2 the shepherd stresses the importance of hospitality, though only within the Christian community itself; he nowhere, however, suggests the establishment of a wide-ranging 'community service' programme by the church authorities, even for the benefit of Christians. Jeffers suggests that the parable of the Master and his Counsellor/Friends at *Sim.* 5,2.6 and in comments about friendship made by him at *Mand.* 5,2.2 and 10,1.4 - the second mentioned concerning fellowship between Christians and pagans - is influenced by the notions of friendship to be found among the Roman elite. [100] The engagement and interaction of Hermas in this treatise with the society and culture of late first/early second century Rome is largely, though not exclusively, concerned with the matter of Christian wealth and commercial dealings in this world, and their impact perhaps on qualifications for entry into the next.

At *Sim.* 1,1 the shepherd urges Christians to remember that they, as servants of God, are living in a strange or foreign country. Your (heavenly) city, he says, is far from this city (ibid.). By this later reference he almost certainly means the city of Rome. He speaks at 1,3 of the Lord of this city and at 1,4 of the Lord of this country. By these he almost certainly means the Emperor. The Christian must choose, he declares at 1,5, between the law of the (heavenly) city and that of this present, earthly one. He adds that the Christian must keep in mind that possession of land by the Christian will serve no good purpose when the Master of the city expels him for resisting the earthly law (1,5). The Christian should seek the purchase of souls in distress instead of land (1,8) for the wealth of his own city is to be preferred to that of the heathen (1,10). These few remarks cannot be read as displaying on Hermas' part either an anti-imperial or an anti-Roman prejudice. He recognises clearly the reality of the rule of the emperor and the prominence of the city in that rule. But, as with his attitude to business enterprise and personal wealth production on the part of believers, neither the glories of the city nor an obedience to the rule of the emperor can be allowed to take precedence over or compromise in any way a prior allegiance to the rule of God and his law for the Christian.

He also demonstrates an almost Clement-like desire for Roman-style order and harmony in society, though not perhaps to the same extent as the author of *1 Clement*. He, like Clement, condemns schisms and dissensions (*Sim.* 8,7.2 and 5,9.4)

100 Jeffers, *Conflict at Rome*, p. 130.

and schismatics (8,7.6), mentioning the last in the same breath as 'law-breakers'. At *Sim.* 9,32.2 he refers to the Lord's preference for peace. Clearly the issues of social harmony and communal peace are ones which had some importance for Hermas in the life of the faith community. And, to the extent that this is so for him, he cannot but have been influenced by Augustan notions of order and concord which shaped the contemporary attitudes of the citizens of Rome and the empire.

It is clear, then, that the *Shepherd* is shaped both in the presentation of its ideas and in those ideas themselves by contemporary Greco-Roman thought. Hermas does not so much reject Roman notions of wealth production as he does the tendency for the accumulation of riches to get in the way of discipleship. He positively embraces Roman notions of order and class, of patronal and patrifamilial status, and happily translates these into the life and ordering of the church.

Minucius Felix, the *Octavius*

It is generally accepted that the *Octavius* was written in Rome sometime in the opening years of the third century (see below). The city was, as elsewhere in the Empire, greatly affected by the civil wars of 193-197. While the actual battles raged elsewhere - across Asia Minor, Syria and Gaul, for example - political battles for imperial supremacy took place with no less ferocity in Rome itself. Powerful figures in the capital, and the general populace with them it would seem, first chose support for Didius Julianus, then Pescennius Niger, and finally Clodius Albinus. When Septimius Severus (ruled 193-212) returned to Rome in 197, he forced the cowed Senate to declare Commodus a god[101] and displayed great brutality against opponents both actual and perceived.[102] He is reported as having put to death nearly 30 senators.[103] The rule of his son (M. Aurelius Antoninus) (212-217) was marked by warfare on the frontiers and by violence at Rome. Many people, including relatives, political opponents and those who simply failed to support particular actions of his (e.g. the jurist Papinian), were executed and this caused great apprehension in the city. His introduction of Roman citizenship to all inhabitants in the empire in 212,[104] while probably reflecting its already debased value, would not have been well received in the city, whose inhabitants still valued their own citizenship.

Whether the events depicted in the *Octavius* represent an authentic debate cannot be determined but Clarke does make the point that the placement of a debate on a leisurely holiday was a 'well-established literary convention'.[105] Rendall places the present writing - an account of a supposed debate between Octavius Januarius, a

101 *Scriptores Historiae Augustae*, 12,8.

102 Ibid., 13 & 14, passim.

103 Ibid., 13,1.

104 Dio, 78,9,5.

105 G.W.Clarke, 'The Historical Setting of the *Octavius* of Minucius Felix', *JRH* 4 (1967): 267-86. See also J. Beaujeu, *Minucius Felix: Octavius*. (Paris, 1964), p. xxii. Cicero, at *de Oratore* 1.vii.24, for example, speaks of Lucius Crassus, Marcus Antonius and others

convert Christian, and Q. Caecilius Natalis (some person by this name is known as a magistrate at Cirta c. 210 CE), a pagan, and moderated by Minucius Felix himself - somewhere in the early third century after the publication of Tertullian's *Apologeticum.* [106] 'The tone of the *Octavius*, Clarke says, 'with its heavy stress on the philosophical pedigree of Christian tenets and its noticeable lack of nervous urgency, readily fits into the philosophically-inclined atmosphere and the largely tolerant context of Severan Rome.' [107] The dialogue was not written in the heat of turmoil and persecution but at a time of relative security for Christians - although there were localised though imperially sponsored persecutions of the church in both Alexandria and Carthage in the early years of the first decade of the third century. Septimius Severus and his house were, however, quite secure in the capital and it seems that this young Christian advocate felt safe enough himself to produce a protreptic writing designed to exhort pagans to conversion. He was also confident enough, as we shall observe later, to offer significant critiques of both imperial practices and the imperial office itself.

Lactantius[108] and Jerome[109] both maintain that Minucius Felix had been a prominent advocate practising at Rome and it is generally accepted that Minucius Felix came originally from North Africa, such are the very particular references to the African town of Cirta in the text. Minucius Felix's own comment at 14,3-4,

> 'as a rule, truth of the clearest kind is affected by the talents of the disputants and the power of eloquence. An audience, as everyone knows, is easily swayed',

demonstrates his first-hand acquaintance with the reality of justice and the law in which he mirrors Plato's *Phaedo* 88d[110] to address an underlying theme, common among Christian writers of the time, of the potential duplicity and the deceptiveness of rhetoric. This was of course also the concern of Plato; that eloquence alone, with no regard for issues of truth, might allow the weaker argument to triumph over the stronger and more righteous. This concern, however, did not prevent Plato in the *Phaedrus* from utilising the conventions of rhetoric in his argument. Minucius Felix likewise expresses a concern that Caecilius' eloquence and not his lack of argument might win the day (14) but this does not prevent him from the employment of rhetorical conventions (see below).

Real event or not, says Rendall, Minucius Felix 'represents the cultured and professional classes of the metropolis'. [111] The scenery and atmosphere and colour

---

retiring from Rome to Tusculum to engage in a debate on political issues emerging in the Senate.

106 G.H. Rendall, *Minucius Felix: the Octavius*. (Cambridge, Mass.), 1977, p. 307.

107 Ibid., p. 280.

108 *Div. Inst.* V.1.21.

109 *De Vir. Illustr*. 58.

110 In this passage, where the immortality of the soul is being discussed, it is observed how the eloquence of those who participate in the debate sway one this way and then another.

111 Rendall, *Minucius Felix: the Octavius*, p. 305.

of the work are taken from cosmopolitan Rome and the author draws his style and vocabulary from the tradition of Cicero and Seneca, particularly from the former. The *Octavius* is a piece of protreptic discourse. Its form is shaped by the common dialogue model, again drawn principally from Cicero. [112] While its intention is primarily protreptic it is also apologetic and didactic in that it provides a teaching model for Christians addressing pagan objections. It is primarily protreptic, however, in that it is intended to convert, not merely to explain. Beaujeu declares that the dialogic form employed by Minucius Felix conforms to the spirit of the Sceptics of the New Academy. Apart from the very obvious influence of Cicero and of Seneca, the *Octavius* also shows traces of the *Attic Nights* (18.1) of Aulus Gellius which also has three players in its dialogue and is also set at Ostia. The influence of both Cicero and Seneca on the *Octavius* is, however, not only in the presentation of ideas but also on those very ideas themselves. The passage at 5,6 -

> '[Caecilius:] But seeing that with mad and fruitless toil we overstep the limits of our humble intelligence, and from our earth-bound level seek, with audacious eagerness, to scale heaven itself and the stars of heaven, let us at least not aggravate our error by vain and terrifying imaginations'-

is a prime example of the Sceptic approach[113] and the *Octavius* provides a setting in which such scepticism is overcome by an essentially Stoic argument. Clarke identifies the influence of Cicero, most 'notably' of the *De natura deorum*, the *De divinatione* and perhaps the now lost *Hortensius* (as a model protreptic), on Minucius Felix. Such influence can be seen at 17.5f. with its description of the cosmic order brought into being by a supreme Creator - direct, almost word-for-word copies of Cicero's *De natura deorum* 2.115[114] and 2.37.95[115] - at 18.4 with the image of the universe as an ordered house as evidence of the existence of a lord and author - reflecting

---

112 See particularly the *De natura deorum* which features a three-way dialogue between representatives of three schools of philosophy – Epicurean, Stoic and Academic – on their respective theologies (dealing with divine existence, nature and providence).

113 G.W. Clarke, *The Octavius of Marcus Minucius Felix*. Translated and annotated. Ancient Christian Writers. 39 (New York, 1974), p. 184, note 42, sees echoes of Horace, *Od.* 1.3.38, Virgil, 6.135, and Aul. Gellius, *Attic Nights* 9.12.

114 (Stoic) Balbus : 'Not merely did the creation [of the stars and the heavens] postulate intelligence, but it is impossible to understand their nature without intelligence of a high order (*sine summa ratione*).' Minucius Felix: 'Not merely did the creation [of the stars], their production and co-ordination require a supreme maker and perfected intelligence, but further they cannot be felt, perceived and understood without a supreme order of skilled reasoning (*sine summa ratione*).'

115 Balbus here quotes Aristotle from the latter's lost dialogue *de Philosophia* where he marvels at the wonderfully ordered state of the universe and declares that if persons previously restricted to dwellings below the earth were to be released above they could not but acknowledge that this state was the handiwork of gods.

Cicero's notion of the universe as the gods' 'home' at *Republic* 3.9.14[116] - and in the same passage with the qualifier 'moderator' for the sun, reflecting *Tusculans* I.28.68. [117] Here Octavius challenges Caecilius' depiction earlier, against the idea of the Christian God, of a fortuitous creation, of a spontaneous, chance and random happening with no single Mind behind it (here there is the suggestion of atomism influencing Caecilius' thought), with the Christian/Stoic notion of a providential Mind behind all creation. Caecilius' ideas themselves were drawn by Minucius from Cicero's presentation of Epicurean thought by the dialogue partner Velleius at *De natura deorum* 1.8.18f. (demolished according to Cicero by fellow dialoguer, the Academic Cotta (1.21.57f.)) and from *The Nature of the Universe* of Lucretius.

The *Octavius*, at a number of points then, reflects the same sort of Stoic thinking which is found in *1 Clement*. As we have seen, at 17,5f. Octavius speaks of order in the universe, and of the creation, production and co-ordination of the stars requiring a supreme Maker and a perfected Mind (17,6). He speaks of the fixedness of the seasons, of the *ordo* held together by *ratio* (17,7). He speaks of the ordered provisioning of the animal world (17,10), of a beauty and a form which declare the work of God (17,11). In this universe order, obvious foresight and law presume a lord and author (18,4). All this, for the author, points to the one God as sovereign over all. The author is not afraid to demonstrate familiarity with the world of learning. At 19,1, as further evidence for the existence of a single creator God, he quotes Homer and at 19,2 Virgil. He is happy to employ a wide variety of philosophers, early Platonists, Aristotle, Stoics, Xenophon the Socratic, even Plato himself (making a direct reference to both *Timaeus* 28c[118] and 41a), to support his argument that God is one (19,4-20.1). At 19.14 he says that, with respect to the unity of God,

> 'Plato speaks more plainly [sc. then the rest], both in substance and expression, concerning God; his language would be quite divine, were it not sometimes debased by an alloy of political bias'.

He quotes *Timaeus* 28c, or rather paraphrases it, and says that this is 'almost exactly what we [Christians] say [about God]'. [119] He will use Epicureans, Stoics, and Plato to argue concerning the place of fire in the universe (34,2-4), and says, praising with faint damns, that the philosophers have borrowed from the prophets the shadow of a garbled truth (34,5). He will ridicule where it suits him, but he will not condemn the

---

116 'Xerxes ordered the Athenian temples to be burned solely because he thought it wicked for gods to be shut in and confined by walls, when their *home is this entire world*.'

117 'The guide and controller (*moderator*) of [the sky, the speed of its revolution, the alternations of day and night, the interchange of seasons] is the sun.'

118 Plato here refers to the Maker and Father of this universe. This latter text is a patristic favourite in both East and West.

119 *Timaeus* 28c is also alluded to at 26.12 when Octavius wonders why, when Plato found it hard to discover and to speak of God, it was not so when it came to him speaking about angels and demons (at *Symposium* 202d f.).

wisdom of the world outright, employing it, where appropriate, to expound the truth and final wisdom of God.

Clarke also sees evidence of the use of a copybook *controversia* in the *Octavius*. Minucius Felix has turned his Ciceronian material partly into a copybook exercise, such as was employed in the schools of rhetoric. He has a *pro* and a *contra*, an *actio* and a *responsio*, and an arbiter. He employs the traditional thesis topic of *an providentia mundus regatur* (whether the world is governed by providence) and sums up the achievement of his rhetorical aims in a self-congratulatory manner in chapter 39. Minucius Felix has clearly made extensive and deliberate use of a formal rhetorical style in this work. Both the first four chapters of the dialogue and the first of Caecilius' own speech (chapter 5) provide an *exordium* in which first Minucius Felix lays the ground for an outcome favourable to his cause and Caecilius demonstrates unwittingly that his own cause is lost from the outset. Octavius' speech possesses an *exordium* of sorts - he goes on the attack immediately in attacking Caecilius' whole presentation and offers a type of *partitio* in which he identifies that single truth which he is to establish (16) - but did not actually need to given that Minucius Felix has already provided one in his opening remarks. Likewise, Octavius does not offer a formal *narration*, although this has been effectively provided by the entire speech of Caecilius (5-13) in which the latter sets up (aided no doubt by the judge's intervention at the end of Caecilius' delivery) the coming triumph of the Christians. [120] Minucius Felix questions, even before Octavius has spoken, whether in his eloquence Caecilius has even offered or established any proofs (*probatio*) (14). Octavius' proofs lie in his systematic and devastating refutation of Caecilius' assertions. His single truth - or series of truths - that divine providence exists, that God is one, and that Christians are virtuous, provides the framework in which his argument is set. He argues for the interconnectedness of all life (17), for the existence of a controlling mind (cleverly using the illustration of the orderly house as evidence for a master) (18), employs the witness of the poets and the philosophers - Caecilius' own witnesses - as proof for his own cause (19), savages Greco-Roman religious belief and practices (20-24), demolishes the argument that Rome's own piety has brought her empire (25-26), refutes Caecilius' allegations of Christian immorality (28, 30-32) and that Christ was a malefactor deserving of death (29), argues for divine care for the world (32-33), brings philosophers on his side to argue for the coming conflagration (34), opposes the notion of fate (36), and argues that Christian poverty is a virtue and not a vice (ibid.). God is present, and not at all disinterested in Christian suffering and endurance which themselves provide a discipline and not punishment (37). At 39 Minucius Felix admires Octavius' use of argument, illustrations, and use of authorities and at 40 Caecilius admits defeat and the force of his opponent's arguments for providence, God, and the virtue of Christians. Minucius Felix, then, has employed the conventions of rhetoric to argue the case for conversion to Christianity but acknowledges at the end that such eloquence as was put to such good use can only be seen itself as a gift from God.

---

120 Note that a piece of deliberative rhetoric does not necessarily require a *narratio*.

The conscious engagement and interaction of Minucius Felix with the city of Rome is very apparent. While he does reflect something of his African origins and while the work itself does demonstrate an awareness of the world beyond Rome, its particularly Roman flavour is unmistakeable. His knowledge of Roman history and religion may owe much to the use of the traditional *exempla* and also to the influence, even the actual texts, of Cicero and Tertullian, but Minucius Felix undoubtedly appreciates and engages quite intentionally with the society and culture in which he lives and works and worships and employs that understanding and engagement with at times telling effect. One of the most significant elements of any society or culture is its perception of its own history; this becomes how, in part at least, it sees itself. In the *Octavius* Minucius Felix identifies his own understanding of such a self-perception on the part of the Romans and challenges it. Octavius, in challenging Caecilius' defence of Roman religion in chapter 6, and in offering by way of response a critique of the claimed nobility of Rome's origins, was actually imitating a common rhetorical *topos* found in Tacitus, Sallust and Cicero among others. His understanding and presentation of aspects of the history of Rome - though brief and utterly polemical in intent - is, however, compelling. Against the argument that Rome owes its greatness and its empire primarily to religious fidelity and piety and to its sense of justice (6.2.3; 12.5) - Tertullian deals with this matter also in his *Apologeticum*[121] - Octavius asks how this can be when the Romans were in origin a collection of criminals, that Rome was in its beginning a city of refuge for such criminals, and that Romulus had indeed killed his brother Remus mainly to establish his credentials within this markedly criminal environment (25, 2). The history of the city and its growth, he says, is more associated with rape, pillage and the despoliation of the conquered than with piety (25, 3). All that the Romans hold, occupy and possess is the spoil of outrage (23, 5). Every Roman triumph meant a new impiety (23,6). The Romans, says Octavius, have grown great not by religion but by sacrilege (23,7). Thus does he answer Caecilius' proud jibe that the Romans possess their empire and rule without the aid of the Christian God (12,5).

At 18, 6 Octavius asks rhetorically, 'when has monarchy (*regni societas*) ever started in good faith or ended without bloodshed?', offering examples from the past, of Persia and Thebes, of Romulus and Remus, of Pompey and Julius Caesar. This sentiment he draws almost literally from the *Pharsalia* of Lucan who declared that '*nulla fides regni sociis*'[122] and '*populique potentis quae mare, quae terras, quae totum possidet orbem non cepit fortuna duos*',[123] the last four words echoed by Octavius himself when he says that with Pompey and Caesar 'the fortunes of a world empire could not find room for two (*et tam magni imperii duos fortuna non cepit*)'. Nature, he goes on, provides the model of one only leader or monarch and therefore

121 See Tertullian's *Apologeticum* 25,2 where he challenges the widely held notion of the Romans that they enjoy their pre-eminence in the world as reward for their religious observance.

122 I.92.

123 I.110.

there is properly but one God having supreme power.[124] At 33,1[125] he implicitly and unfavourably compares the majesty of the emperor to that of God when he declares with little subtlety that God, for whom the whole world is as a single household[126] - the evidence of Cicero's *Republic* 3.9.14 demonstrates that this is an adaptation of a Stoic notion - has no need of ministers formally reporting to him, for he more than adequately knows his own realm. He implies that the emperor is only as powerful or effective as his weakest official. Not so the God of the Christians! At 37,7 Octavius declares that some may be 'deceived by the fact that people who do not know God abound in wealth, are full with honours and occupy the seats of power'. There are certain persons, he says, so lifted up by sovereignty and dominion, that their natural temperament is traded freely for a degraded mind, licence and a lust for power. Does he mean here to allude to the emperors, including Rome's present ruler/s? But it is all an illusion, he suggests, for such wealth and power can be taken away in an instant - as it was for Commodus and other like emperors before him - by death and other acts of violence. Those who are raised high, he says, have only further to fall. Even with a large retinue, in danger you are on your own. We are all equal, he declares. Virtue alone gives mark (*Omnes tamen pari sorte nascimur, sola virtute distinguimur*) (37,10).[127] There are clear echoes of Seneca's *De beneficiis* 3.18[128] and 3.28.1[129] in this passage. Many Romans would have heartily agreed. The Republican spirit, even in late second century Rome, was not entirely dead. The knowledge of God alone provides the basis for genuine happiness, he says. But here Minucius does not so much condemn the imperial system as to make clear that it is subordinate to the power of God; that it cannot replace that power. That God alone, in the end, can provide what is truly needful for life. The imperial system - and this would echo Tertullian's view - must know its place, its *limits*.

At 24,2 Octavius declares that emperors do not wish for deification, even fearing it, for they clearly prefer to stay alive! At 32,1 he would appear to condemn cult paid to images of the emperor. At 29,5 - a reference at 29,4 to the Egyptians choosing a human for their worship may or may not be to the emperor - he again condemns the practice of the deification of kings and princes, declaring that such persons may be worthy of honour but not of worship as gods. Supplication made to their images and prayers to their Genius, their *daemon* - Octavius probably has in mind here the cult of the *Genius Augusti* which in Rome stood in for the cult of *Roma et Augustus* - are simply forms of treating even the living emperors as gods (ibid.). He ridicules pagans, as did Tertullian, for thinking it safer to swear falsely by the genius of Jupiter than by

---

124 As we saw above he then, in chapter 19, provides support from poets and philosophers for the unity of God.

125 See also 18,4, Seneca, *Ben.* 7.1.7, and Tertullian, *De Pudicitia* 7.11.

126 He obviously compares this with the imperial *domus* which received great emphasis under the Severans.

127 See also 16,5 and 31,8 for similar sentiments.

128 'Virtue embraces all, freedmen, slaves and kings.'

129 'There are the same things for all, all have the same origin, no-one is more noble than the next person.'

that of their emperor. Minucius Felix may accept the legitimacy of the government of the emperor under God but will not compromise on the practice of the imperial cult. At 23,9f. Octavius condemns the practice of deifying human beings generally and declares that this is the origin of the Roman pantheon. He draws to his side the witness of the historians Nepos, Dio Cassius and Diodorus to testify that this is so (ibid.). With respect to the traditional apotheosis of the emperors *post mortem* we have seen how he declares that these do not seek to be gods, but rather wish to remain men - and presumably thereby alive; in fact they fear to become gods (24,2). Octavius points also to the logical absurdity of the notion; gods cannot die, he says, therefore the dead cannot become gods (24,3).

At 5,4 Caecilius refers to Christians as 'untrained in study, uninitiated in letters and ignorant even of the lesser arts' and yet still pronouncing views on the majesty of the universe; at 12,7 accuses them of being 'ignorant and uncultured, rude and boorish'. At 31,6 Octavius replies that Christians do not take their place 'among them meanest of the people' and reject 'your official titles (*honores*) and purples'. This does not mean that Christians cannot hold formal office at all but rather that Christians do not put as much store by them as do the pagans; that Christians, for their part, raise their eyes to a higher prize. At 4,6 Minucius himself, when describing how he and his two companions sat down together to engage in their debate, says that he sat between the two protagonists as arbiter, but not as a mark of rank or distinction, for friendship always assumes or creates equality (*nec hoc obsequi fuit aut ordinis aut honoris, quippe cum amicitia pares semper aut accipiat aut faciat*). Clarke recognises in the final phrase - *amicitia pares semper aut accipiat aut faciat* - a proverb commonly employed at the time. Now it is, of course, possible that Minucius is merely making an innocent observation in the spirit of the occasion. I would suggest, however, that this remark compares an alleged Roman obsession with rank and distinction - seen in the humiliating practices of patronage, for example - with the ideal Christian view of a world governed by a God who is no respecter of persons. The *Octavius* reflects both a Roman conservatism and suspicion of things new in its desire for order but also unfavourably compares the former's obsession with class and status with the egalitarianism of the Christian God.

At 16,5 Octavius declares that the rich are so engrossed in business activities that they look more to their gold than to heaven, while the poor – 'our poor' he calls them - more readily ponder wisdom and pass on its teaching. At this point Octavius would seem to mean by the 'rich' non-Christians and by the 'poor' Christians. Here he does not so much attack wealth *per se* as merely recognise, as did Hermas and Clement, that it can easily prove a distraction to the service of God. At 36,7 he again does not so much condemn wealth *per se* but rather declares that Christians would properly rather be good by innocence and patience than prodigal by hoarding wealth. Is this a reference solely to the pagan world, or is it, as more explicitly in *The Shepherd*, a recognition of an increasing problem in the church of upwardly mobile Christians seeking the glory and ambition normally associated with a secular existence? Earlier, at 36,3 he had said that most Christians are reputed poor, which may be literally true or may just be a pious reflection. The poor can be rich, Octavius says, towards God.

The *Octavius* is a protreptic piece intended to urge the conversion of the educated of Rome, represented here by the Epicurean/Sceptic Caecilius, to the embrace of the Christian God. Minucius employs arguments directly from contemporary philosophy to do so, particularly from Cicero (and principally from his *De natura deorum*) and the Stoics. He argues that the very order of the universe requires the existence of a single supreme creative Mind, that is, one God. The primary thrust of the argument is monotheistic and in the contrived but reasonable context of a debate between existing Greco-Roman philosophical schools, the Epicurean, with his view of a universe inhabitated perhaps by gods but certainly ones uninvolved in its creation and essentially indifferent to human affairs, is converted to a Stoic (Christian) view of divine creation and providence. He also challenges Rome's perception of itself as founded on its piety, accepts the reality and legitimacy of imperial rule (under God) while yet condemning the imperial cult and the apotheosis of dead emperors, challenges Roman class and status consciousness, and while not condeming wealth production *per se* senses that it probably obstructs a sense of ultimate fidelity to the Gospel. All of these are intended to underscore his argument for the existence of single Creator God and to make clear the implications of that existence for those who would acknowledge it.

'Hippolytus of Rome'

The general consensus among Hippolytus scholars is that two and possibly three or more writers were responsible for the treatises traditionally ascribed to Hippolytus of Rome. [130] Much of the debate centres around the identity of the figure on the so-called Statue of Hippolytus discovered and reconstructed by Pirro Ligorio in Rome in the sixteenth century and the treatises listed thereon.[131] While many scholars have argued that the statue is of the Roman anti-pope Hippolytus and that the treatises listed are from his pen alone, Brent, among others, persuasively argues that the statue is not meant to identify a particular person but rather to stand for the collective personality of a particular ecclesial community - what Brent calls one of a number of 'house-schools' within the largely fractionalised Christian community in Rome at the end of the second and beginning of the third centuries - which community contained the two or three authors whose writings are represented both on the chair

130 A. Brent, *Hippolytus and the Roman Church in the Third Century* (Leiden, 1995), pp. 338f. suggests that there were three. Note, however, C. Bammel's useful discussion of the arguments put forward by J.Frickel, *Das Dunkel um Hippolyt von Rom. Ein Lösungsversuch: Die Schriften Elenchos und Contra Noetum* (Graz, 1988) in 'The state of play with regard to Hippolytus and the *Contra Noetum*', *Heythrop Journal* 31 (1990): 195-9, for one author only.

131 For the history of this see Brent, *Hippolytus and the Roman Church in the Third Century*, pp. 3-50.

of the Statue and in the tradition of 'Hippolytus'. For example, the *Contra Noetum* and the *Refutatio*, probably the two best known of the Hippolytan writings and neither of which appears in the list, almost certainly came from different hands, yet from within the same community, and probably represent different stages in that community's history. The issues involved are simply too complex for adequate treatment or coverage here and the reader is directed to Brent for a comprehensive and most scholarly discussion.

For our purposes it will be sufficient to refer to the author or authors of these various writings as 'Hippolytus', recognising that it is most probable that the author of the *Refutatio* (or *Elenchos*) was an earlier figure writing at a time when the 'Hippolytan' community stood very much in opposition to the bishop Callistus, while the author of the *Contra Noetum*, the *de Antichristo* and the *Commentary on Daniel* was the Roman presbyter martyred with bishop Pontianus in 235 soon after the death of the emperor Severus Alexander and associated with the apparent reconciliation of that community with the dominant church faction at Rome. It will need to be acknowledged that this confusion as to the identity of these 'Hippolyti' makes it difficult to draw any conclusions as to his/their engagement with the surrounding culture except in the most general terms and explains, I trust, the relative brevity of the treatment of this Father.

Notwithstanding this, of course, the fact is that 'Hippolytus' has actually little to say about the immediate society in which he lived and wrote. The extent of his engagement and interaction with its culture, except perhaps on a particular intellectual and philosophical level, and as compared with his near contemporary Tertullian in Carthage and his fellow 'Romans' (see above), is, notwithstanding the abundance of 'his' writings, sparse. According to Butterworth[132] the style and method of argument in the *Contra Noetum* is derived from that of a Cynic diatribe, with attempts to identify personally with the audience (3,2; 4,8; 9,1 *et al.* where he consistently addresses his readers as 'brethren'), the use of the first person plural (7,3; 9,1; 12,5; *et al.*), and the portrayal of the Noetians as *anoetoi* (8,3). The author of the *Elenchos*, on the other hand, says Brent, employs both Stoic and Platonic concepts in his presentation of the *logos*. [133] In the *Elenchos* our author provides lengthy description of various of the ancient schools of philosophical thought, among them the Platonic (for which he shows that different interpretations can make Plato both the promoter of the notion of one, ingenerable and incorruptible God and of that of the existence of multiple gods), the Aristotelian, the Stoic (where God is the one originating principle of all things whose providential care pervades everything), and the Epicurean (whose gods have a providential care for nothing in creation which was in any case the product of chance). But nowhere, except perhaps for a possible preference for the Stoic view, does he indicate or demonstrate anything of his own reliance on these

132 R. Butterworth, *Hippolytus of Rome, Contra Noetum: Text introduced, edited, translated, in Heythrop Monographs*, (1977), pp. 122-131, cited in Brent, *Hippolytus and the Roman Church in the Third Century*, p. 123.

133 Brent, *Hippolytus and the Roman Church in the Third Century*, pp. 355f..

for the development of his own theology. But this, of course, is not his purpose. That rather is to demonstrate how the various Christian heresies are derived in some way or other from the Greek philosophical schools. At 6,21,1f. the author claims that the Valentinians stand in clear succession to Pythagoras (astronomic system) and Plato (aeonic emanation), while at 7,14,1 Basileides is said to derive his system from Aristotle.[134] This is particularly so in the matter of Aristotle's notion of deity as 'conception of conception' which renders God, for Hippolytus, a non-existent entity.[135] This is a fairly standard approach for the time, seeing in philosophical systems the foundations of heresy, but it does not reflect of necessity an anti-philosophical approach on the part of the author. It is interesting to note that our author apparently did not include Stoicism - his philosophical school of choice - explicitly as a source of Christian heresy.

This is also some evidence in the writings of Hippolytus of the use of rhetorical conventions. While the *Refutatio* does not lend itself readily to the conventions of rhetoric it yet offers clear evidence of such a framework. It begins with an *exordium*, a brief *narratio*, and a *partitio* of sorts in which the author outlines his approach to the issue. The major part of the writings comprise proofs (*probatio*) for Hippolytus' refutation of heretical theologies and their sources in philosophical thought and they end with a *recapitulatio* as part of a *peroratio*. The *Contra Noetum* has no obvious *exordium*, but does have a *narratio* which runs for the first three chapters. Chapters 4 to 16 comprise the *probatio* and 17 and 18 the *peroratio* with a recapitulation of Hippolytus' arguments. Stewart-Sykes, in a discussion of a homily taken from the *catanae* on the Psalms,[136] sees a clear rhetorical framework in the compilation of this homily: *premium*, *narration*, brief *egression*, *narration*, and then longer and shorter *probatio*. 'This preacher', he says, 'is rhetorically trained' and his use of the term *oikonomia* 'to mean plan, or plot, of salvation reflects the use of the term in the rhetorical schools to mean the arrangement of a plot'.[137]

Bobertz identifies in the *Apostolic Tradition* the exercise of the role of the Roman *patronus* in the *Cena Dominica*.[138] In this study Bobertz deals with what he recognises as 'the maze of social relations surrounding the description of privately sponsored Lord's Suppers (chs. 27-29), and especially the role and status of the sponsors of those suppers, local patrons of the Roman Christian community'. These *cenae dominicae* were evidently dinners provided for the local Christian community and paid for by wealthier members of the Christian community. This demonstrates the hierarchical structure of the social environment in which the church found itself and the influence of that environment on personal relationships within the community

134 The question which emerges here, of course, is whether Hippolytus' Aristotle is the authentic one or his own creation.

135 See Aristotle, *Metaphysics* 12 and *Refutatio* 7.7 and 9. For Aristotle the prime mover as such is pure activity, and this activity is the conception of conception.

136 Stewart-Sykes, *Preacher and Audience*, pp. 47f..

137 Ibid., p. 56.

138 C.A. Bobertz, 'The Role of Patron in the *Cena Dominica* of Hippolytus' *Apostolic Tradition*', *JTS* 44 (1993): 170-84.

itself. The 'clients', the *vocati*, must act in such way, presumably with appropriate deference, as will enhance the honour and prestige of the 'patron'. The relationship between the *patronus* and the chief officials of the community - bishop, presbyters and deacons - is not, however, clear. What we do have here, however, is evidence of 'a growing point of tension within the Christian community. Namely, the relationship between the still emerging authority of the Christian priesthood, in the orthodox Roman community concentrated in a single bishop since the middle of the second century, and the social authority of patrons in a genuinely hierarchical society'. [139]

Select Bibliography

Rome:

M.Goodman, *The Roman World: 44BC - AD180*. (London and New York, 1997).

F.Millar, *The Emperor in the Roman* World. (London, 1977).

R.Saller, 'Patronage and friendship in early Imperial Rome: drawing the distinction', in A. Wallace-Hadrill (ed.), *Patronage in Ancient Society*. (London and New York, 1989), pp. 49-62.

C.Wells, *The Roman Empire*. (London, 1984).

***1 Clement*:**

O.M.Bakke, *Concord and Peace*. (Tübingen, 2001).

B.E. Bowes, *A Church in Crisis: Ecclesiology and Paraenesis in Clement of Rome*. (Minneapolis, 1988).

J.S Jeffers, *Conflict at Rome: Social Order and Hierarchy in Early Christianity*. (Minneapolis, 1991).

***The Shepherd*:**

G.M.Hahneman, *The Muratorian Fragment and the Development of the Canon.* (Oxford, 1992).

C.Osiek, *Rich and Poor in the Shepherd of Hermas*. (Washington, 1983).

C.Osiek, 'The Genre and Function of the *Shepherd of Hermas*', *Semeia* 36 (1986): 113-121.

C.Osiek, *Shepherd of Hermas: a commentary*. (Minneapolis, 1999).

The *Octavius:*

G.W.Clarke, *The Octavius of Marcus Minucius Felix*. Translated and annotated. Ancient Christian Writers 39. (New York, 1974).

Hippolytus of Rome:

C.A.Bobertz, 'The Role of Patron in the *Cena Dominica* of Hippolytus' *Apostolic Tradition*', *JTS* ns 44 (1993): 170-84.

139 Ibid., 182.

A.Brent, *Hippolytus and the Roman Church in the Third Century*. (Leiden, 1995).
J.Mansfeld, *Heresiography in context: Hippolytus' Elenchos as a source for Greek Philosophy*. (Leiden, 1992).

Chapter 3

Carthage and the Fathers

North Africa and Carthage in the imperial period

Rome ruled North Africa effectively from 146 BCE following the end of the Third Punic War and the destruction of Carthage. Roman Africa was (re)created as a province under a proconsul as early as 40/39 BCE. By 36 BCE Octavian had become undisputed master of Africa and a process of Romanisation proper had begun. Roman expansion in Africa was slow but there is no evidence that African opposition to Rome was stronger or more passionate than elsewhere. Africa was not strategically important to Rome and there was little serious military resistance to the Roman presence in the region. Carthage was probably first settled in the ninth century BCE, traditionally by Phoenician refugees from Tyre. After the fall of Tyre in 574 BCE, it became the Phoenician western capital. Prior to her disastrous wars with Rome there is evidence of Greek influence in Carthage and this may explain the facility which many upper-class Carthaginians had with the Greek language.146 BCE saw the destruction of the city and in 122 BCE there was a failed attempt by the Gracchi brothers to establish a new colony, Junonia, on the old site. While this never eventuated, many of the settlers brought over from Italy remained in the region. In 44 BCE Julius Caesar planned to establish a new Carthage but his death intervened. In 35 BCE Statilius Taurus raised ramparts on the site and in 29 BCE the official re-founding of Carthage was proclaimed. Carthage was granted the status of a colony and some 30,000 settlers were sent out from Italy. In 16 BCE the formal inauguration of the city was proclaimed by Sentius Saturninus. We know very little of the history of Roman Carthage from that time until towards the close of the second century CE, part from reports of riots, possibly over grain shortages, in the late 180s during the proconsulate of P. Helvius Pertinax, the future emperor. Carthage had, by the second century CE, become one of the largest and wealthiest cities in the Roman world, second only in the West to Rome itself. Its population is estimated to have been in the high six-figures. It enjoyed success not only in the law, the arts and commerce, but was a major centre for a diverse array of religious practices. Apuleius spoke of Carthage as that place

> 'where every citizen is a cultivated person and where all devote themselves to all fields of knowledge, children by learning them, young men by showing them off, and old men by teaching them … Carthage, venerable mistress of our province, Carthage, divine muse of Africa, Carthage, prophetess of the nation which wears the toga.'[1]

1 Apuleius, *Florida* 20 10.

Jews only appeared in Carthage in the Roman period but by the late second century they were a significant community within the city. There are traces of a Jewish cemetery with some 200 tombs and evidence for at least one synagogue. Since the Jewish presence in Carthage began only at this time, there developed in Carthage a Rabbinic form of Judaism. Frend argues, against Barnes,[2] that Tertullian's reference to the Jews as persecutors of the Christians is one to a contemporary situation and not merely to an historical one and provides evidence for an ongoing hostility between the Jewish and Christian communities in Carthage in the time of both Tertullian and a half century later in that of Cyprian.[3]

The elite Romano-Africans had by the second century CE reclaimed their heritage as Africans - see, for example, the worship of both Caelestis and Saturn, the one very public, the other markedly private - but had also established themselves as clearly Roman. The Carthaginian *ordo* were no mere agents of Rome, but proud Africans whose actions were blessed by Rome. But Carthage was not a sovereign and independent entity and the citizens of the city were thoroughly (or rather saw themselves as) Roman. The political significance of the local public cults, apart from the imperial cult, was negligible. Religion in Carthage was a wide and freewheeling affair, where magic and astrology were rife. Vespasian had established the imperial cult in North Africa between 70 and 72 CE as part of a wider plan to legitimise the rule of the Flavians.

Formal educational instruction in Roman North Africa was normally in Latin, sometimes in Greek, but never in Punic.[4] In the urban centres Punic was replaced over time by Latin, though in the areas beyond the cities and towns many people continued to speak mainly Libyan (Berber). Africa was described by Juvenal as the 'nurse of pleaders [that is, advocates]',[5] as a place, unlike Rome, where one could still make a living through oratory. Recitations apparently still drew large audiences in Africa in the second century of the Common Era, though these were more oratorical than poetical in nature. A prominent teacher of rhetoric and philosophy at Rome, the African Cornutus produced in the time of Nero oratorical handbooks in both Latin and Greek. Roman Africa produced some significant figures in literature:[6] the historian Suetonius, the rhetoricians Cornelius Fronto and Cornutus (see above), the writer Apuleius, and the grammarian Sulpicius Apollinaris. It also produced some key political figures: the senator-consul Pactumeius Fronto (cos. 80 CE), the jurisconsult P. Pactumeius Clemens (cos. 138 CE), the lawyer Salvius Julianus, urban prefects Q. Lollius Urbicus, from Cirta, and Laetus, and any number of emperors.[7] Worthy

2 T.D.Barnes, 'Tertullian's Scorpiace', *JTS* ns 20 (1969): 132.

3 W.H.C.Frend, 'A Note on Jews and Christians in Third-century North Africa', *JTS* 21 (1970): 291-6.

4 See Apuleius, *Apology* 98.

5 Juvenal, *Satires* VII, 148.

6 See the introduction to the chapter on Rome (Chapter 2) for comments on Latin culture and the *quadriga* of Latin intellectual thought.

7 See the conflicting views of T.D.Barnes, 'The Family and Career of Septimius Severus', *Historia* (16 (1967): 87, note 1 and A.R.Birley, 'The Coups d'Etat of the Year 193',

of note also is the fact that one third of the 29 senators executed by Severus in 197 were closely connected by birth or property ownership to Proconsular Africa; yet many Africans were also appointed by Severus to major provincial and gubernatorial positions. Birley, basing his figures on Alföldy's extensive investigations, reckons that of the 31 provincial governors appointed between 197 and 211 whose origin may be known, 19 were either certainly, probably or possibly from Africa (and 10 of these were appointed to 18 one-legion praetorian provinces). This, he says, is not so much a case of regional chauvinism but rather a understandable wish on the part of the emperor to work with men known to him.

Tertullian

Tertullian wrote most of his extant corpus between 193 and 220 CE during the reigns of Septimius Severus and his son Caracalla. He wrote in both Latin and Greek - though no Greek treatises survive - and he clearly came from an affluent and educated background. He was not himself a member of the clergy and probably trained as an orator though not as a specialist jurist. [8] He clearly identified himself with the self-styled New Prophets of Carthage in the latter half of his life but there is no reason to class him as a schismatic. [9] No-one could seriously suggest that Tertullian's engagement and interaction with the society and culture of North Africa, and most particularly with that of Carthage itself - its history, religion, social life, politics, economy, physical environment and so on - forms the dominant feature of his thought. Nevertheless, it is a significant feature; for in any number of his writings he sometimes condemns that culture in the most strident terms, sometimes (though not as often) he clearly demonstrates an appreciation of it, often he praises it with faint damns, or damns it with faint praises. He often employs the surrounding culture as background to the images he employs. Sometimes particular aspects of that culture itself are his immediate concern, and not merely useful as analogies or as illustrations for something else. In a number of his extant treatises - *de Baptismo*, *de Carne Christi*, *de Oratione*, *adversus Praxean*, and *de Pudicitia* among them - he hardly (if at all) makes reference to the physical and social world he inhabits, beyond that of the church and its thought; that is, in these particular works his theological and biblical reflections are not conditioned at all explicitly by the society around him; some, like the *adversus Hermogenem* and the *de Patientia*, display no outward signs of engagement with any aspect of the surrounding culture, but in fact implicitly do so (for example, the work against Hermogenes is explicitly directed at this person but is actually directed against Plato's view that matter is eternal and uncreated, and that on patience is influenced throughout by Stoic thought); but in the greater number of treatises - including the *Apologeticum*, *de Corona*, *de Fuga*, *de*

Bonner Jahrbuch 169 (1969): 265, on this.

8 D.Rankin, 'Was Tertullian a Jurist?', *Studia Patristica* 31 (1997): 335-42.

9 D.Rankin, 'Was Tertullian a schismatic?', *Prudentia* 18 (1986): 73-80; D.Rankin, 'Tertullian's Consistency of thought on ministry', *Studia Patristica* 21 (1989): 271-6.

Idololatria, *de Ieiunio*, *de Pallio*, *de Praescriptione Haereticorum*, *de Resurrectione Carnis*, *Scorpiace*, *de Spectaculis*, and *ad Uxorem* I and II - such references, by way of background, illustration, analogy or imme̅diate and direct concern (that is, as topics in themselves), are legion and often central to his theme.

Given the voluminous nature of Tertullian's writings, it is surprising that there are not more references in them to particular events in Carthaginian history. What there are of them, however, are employed by him with telling effect. At *de Pallio* 1,1, in apparent but mocking echo of Apuleius,[10] Tertullian addresses the citizens of Carthage thus:

> 'Men of Carthage, ever princes of Africa, ennobled by ancient memories, blessed with modern felicities, I rejoice that times are so prosperous with you that you have leisure to spend and pleasure to find in criticising dress.'

Tertullian makes only one clear reference to the time of the original founding of Punic Carthage. At *de Monogamia* 17,2 he argues somewhat ironically that chaste pagans from the past will eventually act as judges against those Christians who repudiate the ideal of monogamy. Among others, he says, there will arise a queen of Carthage (being Dido whom Tertullian describes as the 'chaste and excellent ')[11] who will condemn those Christians who deny monogamy, such a queen coming as she did as a refugee from Tyre, living on alien soil, the foundress of so great a city (sc. Carthage), and one who, as example, spurned a second marriage with Aeneas, preferring, in a marvellous reversal (but not contradiction) of the Pauline adage, to 'burn rather than to (re-)marry'.[12] At *ad Nationes* II.18,3 Dido is again held up as an example to the wife of the Carthaginian general Hasdrubal who preferred death for herself and her children rather than join her husband in submitting to Scipio. Thus, Tertullian employs this particular aspect of the history of Carthage to both embarrass and perhaps to shame his co-religionists to take issues of personal morality more seriously. Here, as he does in *de Pallio* more explicitly, he implies an alliance of traditional Carthaginian virtues and Christian values.

At *Apologeticum* 25,8 Tertullian alludes to Carthage as the city loved by Juno (= Caelestis?)[13] and suggests that she surely would not have wished it to be destroyed (as it was in 146 BCE) by the race of Aeneas (i.e., the Romans), with whom the chaste and virtuous and role-model Dido had spurned marriage. This forms part of Tertullian's argument against the notion that Roman piety and religiosity led to the grant by the gods of their empire and in favour of one which suggests that the gods are often simply powerless to actually protect their own. He then observes that the Romans have actually not paid much honour (in terms of worship) to the fates which

---

10 See pages 57-8.

11 *De Anima* 33,9.

12 See also *ad Martyras* 4,5 and *de Exhortatione castitatis* 13,3 where similar sentiments are expressed.

13 Virgil, *The Aeneid* i.16-18. 'Now Juno is said to have loved Carthage best of all the cities in the world'.

gave them Carthage against the manifest desire and prayers of Juno.[14] At 26, 1ff., Tertullian argues rather that it is in any case the Christian God - and not the pagan ones - who dispenses empires and charts their various courses. At *ad Nationes* I,18,3, in response to charges that Christians display only contemptible obstinacy in the face of persecution and peril, Tertullian argues that such fortitude was also demonstrated (and praised and not despised) among the ancestors of the accusers.

Tertullian also makes some reference to the re-founding of Carthage in Roman times. At *de Pallio* 1,2 he refers to the official pronouncement of the inauguration of Carthage under Octavian (in 16 BCE) by Sentius Saturninus as one of the crucially defining moments in the (to Tertullian) regrettable, even shameful, Romanisation of Carthage. This process is symbolised for him by the adoption by Carthaginians of the *toga* in place of the *pallium*. [15] Yet the apparent patriotic and anti-Roman diatribe of the *de Pallio* are less significant (and real) than might seem to be the case at first glance. [16] The contrast Tertullian offers, though couched in seemingly patriotic terms, is actually not between Rome and Carthage but rather between education and learning, on the one hand, and an acquisitive materialism on the other. The pallium, unlike the Roman toga, can be justified in terms of either a Cynic or a Epicurean indifference, or of a Stoic seeking after an alignment with the natural order. There is a call here to neither a form of Punic nationalism nor a Punic cultural revival. Despite the claims of a Cynic-like agenda and diatribe-style Tertullian does not issue a call for a renunciation of empire. He offers, in Barnes' terms, a resolution of the Athens-Jerusalem antithesis[17], that of Christianity and classical culture. The pallium, says Tertullian in chapter 5, owes no duty to the political process. Its only

---

14 See likewise *ad Nationes* II.17.7.

15 D.E.Groh, 'Tertullian's polemic against social co-optation', *Church History* 40 (1971), 13, describes *de Pallio* as 'a particular instance of Tertullian's general concern to bring appearance and inner reality into correlation'. He maintains that for Tertullian 'the *pallium* represents [sc. in this treatise] a divine dress donned to express values opposed to those of societal man in his craving for public dignity and glory, symbolised by the *toga* (14).
The *pallium*, on the other hand, proclaims a 'renunciation of the pursuit of public office and social rank' (ibid.).

16 It is interesting to note Tacitus' observations on the British scene where a similar assumption of the toga by the natives reflected that process of Romanisation so despised in North Africa by Tertullian:

> 'In the same way, our national dress came into favour and the toga was everywhere to be seen. And so the Britons were gradually led on to the amenities that make vice agreeable - arcades, baths and sumptuous banquets. They spoke of such novelties as "civilisation", when really they were only a feature of enslavement' (*Agricola* 21).

Champlin speaks of the African bourgeois aristocracy's 'concern for Latin and things Roman at the expense of things African' (E.Champlin, *Fronto and Antonine Rome*. (Cambridge, Mass. 1908), p. 17). Indeed, says Champlin, this was more evident in Africa than in other Latin-speaking provinces.

17 Champlin, *Fronto and Antonine Rome*, p. 231.

care is not to care. At 5,4 he claims that the pallium (and thereby the city whose true heritage it somehow, in Tertullian's eyes at least, represents) owes no duty to the forum, the election-ground, the curia, will not hover about the governor's residence[18] - all Roman innovations - will not plead, will not act as magistrate, will not act as soldier, or as king. But in its very symbolic withdrawal from public life it accords its own invaluable benefit to public life. It prescribes medicines to morals. It does more for the community than do all political works. It stands over against vice, lethargy, ambition, inhumanity, gluttony, gambling, impurity, and intemperance which characterise all those who wear the toga. The palliated word (*sermo palliatus*) alone will rid society of these things! In this the pallium, which for the sake of argument Tertullian identifies with all past Carthaginian virtues, offers real learning in its alliance with the Gospel. It is the vesture of the better philosophy. At 6,1 he identifies the wearing of the pallium with moral probity and integrity and also at 6,2 with particular scientific arts and achievements of public utility. He identifies the Roman toga with all that is dishonourable. At the end of the treatise (6,2) Tertullian confers on the pallium

> 'likewise a fellowship with a divine sect and discipline. Rejoice, Mantle, and exult! A better philosophy has now deigned to honour you ever since you have begun to be a Christian's vesture!'

Tertullian's embrace of classical culture, in all its claimed purity, could not be more emphatic.

Tertullian demonstrates a variety of attitudes towards the imperial office and its incumbents. These range from the conditionally positive to the downright hostile. At *ad Scapulam* 4.5f. Tertullian employs the good emperor-bad emperor motif when he makes the improbable claim that Septimius Severus himself was attentive to Christians. At *de Pallio* 4,5 he continues the use of the above motif with the observation that some past Caesars were lost to shame - the positive edge is the implication that some were not - and refers specifically to a 'second Nero', by which he almost certainly means Domitian.[19] His conditional acceptance of imperial authority is underscored at 15,8 where Tertullian speaks of the limits to the honours owed to an emperor being '*intra limites disciplinae*', the limits of Christian discipline on idolatry and the obedience owed to God (see also *Scorpiace* 14,3). At *Apologeticum* 2,16 Tertullian refers in passing to the allegation that Christians are the enemies of the emperors, a charge he later strenuously refutes. At 21,24 he declares that, on the contrary, the emperors also would have believed in Christ - as did Pontius Pilate[20] - if they were 'not necessary to the age'. This appears to suggest

---

18 Do we have here a description of the morning parade of clients so much a part of the Roman custom of patronage?

19 Juvenal, *Satire* 4,38, speaks of late Flavian Rome as enslaved to a bald-headed Nero (*calvo Neroni*), a clear reference in the context to Domitian.

20 See *Apologeticum* 5,2 and Eusebius, *EH* II,2 for the improbable story of Pilate reporting favourably on the Christian faith to the emperor Tiberius.

that imperial opposition to the Christian faith was all part of the divine purpose, given Tertullian's next comment which suggests that Christians were not able, in their turn, to become emperor, presumably again as part of such a plan, as themselves needing to stand over against the God-denying age. Evans points out that in Tertullian's view the emperors, for their part, were necessary for the *saeculum*, which is itself subject to demons and will be brought to an end by judgement on the final day, and therefore cannot be themselves Christian. [21] At *Apologeticum* 32,1 Tertullian speaks of the need for Christians to pray for the emperors, for the empire and for the very interests of Rome. For like many of his contemporaries, Christian and non-Christians, and Cyprian later, he had a sense of the impending end of the age and of the horrors which would probably attend this.[22] Thus Christians were bound at the very least to pray for the endurance of the empire for it was that alone which caused the delay of that inevitable end. Christians in praying for the emperor and the empire prayed for the *mora finis* (39,2). At *de Idololatria* 15, passim, however, Tertullian refers to feast days celebrated in the emperor's honour. These, he concludes, are acts of idolatry, being worship given to a human being (15,1). At *Scorpiace* 9,7 he refers negatively to the governors and kings (emperors) as slayers of the body and declares that only the one God can rule the soul. There is no particular single position running through these references to the imperial office. Yet there is evident an underlying respect for the office itself (see *Apologeticum* 21,24; *de Pallio* 4,5; and *ad Scapulam* 4,5), if not for all its occupants (see *Scorpiace* 9,7 and *de Pallio* 2,7). This remains, of course, only for so long as such respect does not compromise that sovereign allegiance owed to God (see *de Idololatria* 15, passim, *Scorpiace* 14,3, and *adversus Marcionem* IV, 34, 17).

Tertullian's account of the imperial cult largely accords with what else we know about its practice in his own time. Worshippers, certainly in the period before Decius, swore by the *genius* of the emperors and offered and vowed sacrifices for their safety (*pro salute*) (*ad Scapulam* 2,5). At times, however, Tertullian can point to an incompatibility between actual practice and underlying theory. At *Apologeticum* 13,8, for example, he declares that 'with perfect propriety you give divine honours to dead emperors, much as you do while they are alive'. While this was not strictly true in theory (according to contemporary evidence), Tertullian goes on at 28,3 to demonstrate that it was often effectively true in practice. For the average Roman was naturally more likely to fear and respect the present power of the living emperor than that of a more remote divinity. 'You do homage with a greater dread and a more intense reverence to Caesar', he declares, 'than to Olympian Jove himself' (ibid.). Yet, at 17,2 Tertullian can also declare that the pagans rank worship of the majesty of

---

21 R.F. Evans, 'On the Problem of Church and Empire in Tertullian's *Apologeticum*', *SP* 14 (1976): 27 and 35.

22 The so-called 'crisis of the third century' which many believe began with the death of Commodus but intensified towards the middle of the third century.

the Caesars immediately after the worship (*religio*)[23] they regard as due to the gods. The Christians, he says, will, however, neither propitiate the images of the emperors nor swear by their *genii*. At *Apologeticum* 33,1 Tertullian maintains that Christians both owe and actually render *religio* and *pietas* to the emperor.

For Tertullian, the emperor is appointed by God (*ad Scapulam* 2,6; *Romans* 13,1). The emperors receive their *imperium* from God (*Apologeticum* 30,1). Christians therefore have a scripturally-founded obligation to pray for the emperors as for all lawful rulers (31 and 32). In the imperial office Christians see and respect the ordinance of God (32,2). 'On valid grounds', says Tertullian, 'I might [actually] say Caesar is more ours than yours, for our God has appointed him' (33,1). Though Christians decline to swear by the *genii* of the emperors (Caesars), they swear by their safety, as being more august than any imperial *genius*. And believing that emperor to be appointed by the Christian God, Christians thereby desire the emperor's well-being (*ad Scapulam* 2,6). We Christians, he declares, pray for the well-being of the emperor to that god, the only God, who can actually bestow it (2,9). Christian prayers do more for the emperor's well-being than do pagan ones (*Apologeticum* 33,2), for the emperor is appointed by God and, in any case, the Christian God is real! And not only do Christians pray for the emperor, but also for their ministers and for all in lawful authority (39,2). Apart from the Christian attitude to lawful authority established by God and attested to in Scripture (*Romans* 13, *1 Peter* 2, 13-14; *Titus* 3,1)[24], the theological basis of Tertullian's attitude towards the imperial cult is clear. 'We are', he declares, 'worshippers of one God' (*ad Scapulam* 2,1). We have no master but God alone; those whom you regard as masters (the emperors?) are only humans, and one day they themselves must die (5,4). 'What we worship is the one God' (*Apologeticum* 17,1). 'Give all reverence to God, if you wish Him to be propitious to the emperor. Give up all worship of, and belief in, any other being as divine. Cease also to give the sacred name [sc. god] to him [sc. the emperor] who has need of God himself' (34,3). 'One soul,' says Tertullian, 'cannot be owed to two [lords] - God and Caesar' (*de Idololatria* 19,2). According to *1 Peter* 2,13, he declares, 'the ruler indeed must be honoured, yet so that he be honoured [only] when he keeps to his own sphere, when he is far from assuming divine honours; because

23 *Religio*, as employed by Tertullian, normally means either a religious 'system', or 'piety'/'reverence'. We find the first rather neutral use of the term at *Apologeticum* 16,8; 24,1; 25,12; 26,3; 35,3 and at 39,1 (where, interestingly, he specifically employs it to denote the common confession of Christians), at *ad Nationes* I,10,36 and 17,2, and at *ad Scapulam* 2,2. He employs it in the second sense, as piety, at *Apologeticum* 35,5 of the 'homage' due Caesar as a lesser majesty (than God), at *ad Nationes* II,17,13 of the simple 'piety' of the ancient Romans, and at *de Pudicitia* 5,1 of the 'religious regard' owed to parents as second only in worthiness to God.

24 Tertullian actually makes very few references to these key texts, at *ad Scapulam* 2,6; *Scorpiace* 14,1f.; and *de Idololatria* 15,8. He makes none explicitly in the *Apologeticum*, which is strange, unless one counts the possible allusion at 33,1 where he says 'for our God has appointed (*elegit*) him [sc. the emperor]'. There may also be an allusion to such texts at *ad Nationes* I,17,4.

both father and mother will be loved along with God, but not put on an equality with him' (*Scorpiace* 14,3).

Tertullian's pagan opponents, according to the former, allege that the Christians 'do not worship the gods and do not offer sacrifices for the emperor', making them guilty therefore of both 'sacrilege and treason' (*Apologeticum* 10,1). Tertullian would happily concede the first allegation but not its claimed implications. For him, the Christians are the truly civic-minded who alone can actually do something beneficial for the emperor. At *ad Scapulam* 2,5 Tertullian also claims that treason is laid falsely to their charge, even though no Christian, he maintains, supported either Albinus or Pescennius Niger in 193-7. At *Apologeticum* 24,1 he declares that the Christian confession of the one and only God acquits them of the '*crimen laesae publicae*' - that chiefly against the Roman religion - and at 28,3 he speaks of a second ground of accusation (the first is clearly their failure to worship the Roman gods, which so offends the Romans and renders the Christians un-Roman in Roman eyes (24,9)), that of treason against a majesty more august. Yet the allegations of *sacrilegium* and *maiestas* - particularly the second named - do not accord with the evidence of contemporary accounts of trials of Christians. In the nine reliable pre-Decian *acta martyrum* the motif of loyalty to the emperor, or more particularly to the Imperial cult, is brought up by an accuser or a local official other than a Roman official on only one occasion (the *Acta Polycarpi* 8,2). The overwhelming weight of evidence is that local concerns[25] involved the threatened abandonment of local cults rather than any possible non-observance of the Imperial cult. To the emperor, says Tertullian, we render such reverential homage as is lawful for us and good for him. Christians, of course, remain unutterably opposed to physical sacrifices, whatever the circumstances (*ad Scapulam* 2,8). We Christians, he declares, regard the emperor as the human being next to God and as less than God alone. He is greater indeed than the gods themselves who are actually subject to him (*ad Scapulam* 2,7). We sacrifice for the emperor's safety (*pro salute*) but only to our God and his (2,8). This we do 'according to the emperor's own desires' (2,7).[26] Christians pray for the emperors, for the empire, and for the protection of the imperial house (*Apologeticum* 30,4), which latter began to receive increasing focus under the Severans. The Christian may call the emperor Lord - for Septimius claimed the title of 'Lord' - but not in God's place (34); under no circumstances, however, will he call him 'god'. 'Never will I call the emperor God ... not even himself will desire that high name applied to him' (33,3). Christians will pay no vain, nor false nor foolish honours to the emperor (35,1), for it is homage to a lesser majesty [than that of God] (35,5). It is indeed a curse to give the name of god to Caesar (34,4).[27] Tertullian even scorns the deification of dead emperors. 'I see so many rulers, whose reception into the heavens was publicly announced, groaning now in the lowest darkness with great Jove himself' (*de Spectaculis* 30,3). The Christian will properly pay honours due

25 See Pliny, Ep.10, 96f.

26 See also *Apologeticum* 30,4.

27 For to do so was the anticipate his death, a capital offence.

to the emperor - for which they have a sufficient prescript from scripture - but only within the limits of discipline, so long as they keep ourselves separate from idolatry (*de Idololatria* 15,8).[28] Tertullian is adamant that his overarching concern is the protection of the emperor as the chosen of God. He wishes thereby to prove his care for the emperor and his house. The problem is that this, for many like Pliny and other Roman officials, was not the point; it was for them a matter of *religio* and not of *imperium*, a religious and not political matter.

Tertullian makes a few, but nevertheless significant references to Roman administration and the law, apart from those to the emperor himself (see below). Some relate directly to the treatment of Christians at the hands of the Roman authorities and to the place which Christians may and do occupy in Roman society. Tertullian's attitude towards Rome and things Roman is at best ambivalent and often multi-layered. He is both highly critical, and at times savagely so, and yet also profoundly supportive of different aspects of what is called *Romanitas*. At *Apologeticum* 35, for example, he tries to refute the accusation that Christians are enemies of the state. He asks sarcastically whether there is never a whiff of hostility to the emperor from the Senate, knights, army or from within the imperial palace itself (8).[29] Yet at *de Corona* 13,3 he refers to Rome as the 'Babylon' of John's *Revelation*.[30] At *de Resurrectione Mortuorum* 24,18 he speaks of the coming fall of Rome, bringing in the ten kingdoms and introducing the Antichrist (*2 Thessalonians* 2,1-10), as the only obstacle standing in the way of the End and Judgement. At *de Spectaculis* 7,3 the city is described as that in which the demons' assembly has its headquarters. These references to Rome - negative and even hostile as they are - are conventional and not necessarily or exclusively anti-Roman. The city simply becomes a convenient symbol for all in the empire that was opposed to God.

Elsewhere I have argued that the level of Tertullian's knowledge of the law and legal process suggests that he was court-room orator or advocate - with only such knowledge of the law and judicial process as was needed by him to ply that trade - rather than a specialist or professional jurist.[31] He clearly employs what limited knowledge he does have of particular laws and legal processes quite effectively. His use of the legal concept of the *praescriptio* in *de Praescriptionibus* to deprive his heretical opponents of scriptural support is perhaps the most obvious example. At *de Corona* 4,5 Tertullian confronts the claim that there is no explicit scriptural injunction against the wearing of crowns. He readily acknowledges this but argues instead that both tradition and custom stand against the practice and brings into the debate the standard Roman legal procedure or rule whereby custom counts where there is no

---

28 In the passage above Tertullian uses the stories of the Three Brothers and Nebuchadnezzar (*Daniel* 3,19f.) and of Daniel himself and Darius (*Daniel* 6) as examples of acts of resistance to giving rulers beyond their proper due.

29 Tertullian at *ad Scapulam* 2,5 challenges accusations of *maiestas* against Christians by, in part, declaring that no Christians supported Albinus, Niger or Cassius.

30 See also *de Cultu Feminarum* II.12,2; *adversus Marcionem* III.13,10; *de Resurrectione Mortuorum* 22,10 and 25,1; *Scorpiace* 12,11.

31 Rankin, 'Was Tertullian a Jurist?'.

formal legal precedent. At both *adversus Marcionem* IV. 21,2 - 'no-one bears witness except in a case decided by judicial process', referring to the dominical injunction to shake off the dust from one's feet as a witness against those who refuse the claims of the Gospel - and V.1.3 - that profession concerning oneself is only rendered valid by the authority of a second person, 'one signs, another counter-signs, one seals, the other registers the document in the public records', referring to the question of who will confirm Marcion's exclusive choice of Paul's testimony for his version of the canon - Tertullian makes use of particular and well-defined legal procedures to illustrate the lines of a particular biblical or theological argument. At *de Monogamia* 16,4 he refers to the Julian laws on child-rearing - with their penalties for those who do not produce offspring (see also *ad Uxorem* I.5,2) - and declares that Christians appearing before the judgement bar of Christ are not subject to such regulations. Before Christ, he declares, and he is here arguing for celibacy as a legitimate option (even preference) for the Christian, both the childless (that is, those engaged in a 'spiritual' marriage) and the unmarried (the virgin) shall receive their full portion. At *Apologeticum* 4,8, on the other hand but for precisely the same purpose, Tertullian refers favourably to the repeal by Septimius Severus of the Papian Laws against celibacy[32] which set down penalties for those not having children at an early age. He sees this as a sign of a willingness on the part of the Romans, notwithstanding their veneration of antiquity and of long-established custom, to amend or put aside laws which are no longer considered appropriate. The laws, he implies, are not set in stone. Thus, the alleged failure of Christians to honour tradition - understood by the Romans as the *mos maiorum* - ought not necessarily to be condemned.

In the *Apologeticum* Tertullian is particularly critical of the Roman judicial process with particular respect to its treatment of Christians. He is as much saddened by what he sees as an abuse of the system for which he clearly has much respect - it is after all probably his natural habitat - as he is by its patently unfair dealing with his co-religionists. At *Apologeticum* 2,14 he argues that the treatment of Christians in court is perverse and contrary to normal judicial process; that while Christians are happy to confess their 'crime', magistrates invariably want them to deny it and, if necessary, to lie in order to secure an acquittal. What of the rule of law? Tertullian asks; what of the requirement for the law properly applied to bring evil to light, and to bring confessing persons to the establishment of their guilt and to the application of an appropriate punishment? This is what after all, he says, the Senate has decreed and emperors have mandated. This empire, he declares, is surely run by the rule of law, and not by tyranny. He is offended by all this as much as an advocate committed to due process as he is as an sectarian apologist.

He is concerned also not only with proper judicial process but also with the question of the Christian community's involvement in the surrounding society and any suggestion of their contributing in any way to a breakdown of law and order. At

32 The *Lex Papia Poppaea* of 9 CE was designed to supplement the Julian law of 18 BCE to tighten sanctions against celibacy and an unwillingness to bear children (Tacitus, *Annales* iii,25). It was ineffective in overcoming the attraction to many Romans of childlessness.

Apologeticum 38,2 he acknowledges that various public associations (*factiones*) are prohibited, and properly so, for reasons of public order. But this school (*secta*) (that is, Christianity), he says, should properly be placed among the *licitae factiones*, for it does nothing which the clearly *illicitae factiones*[33] do, and for which they pose no threat to public order (38,1) for it has no political interest in this State (38,3). This, however, does not mean that Tertullian is suggesting that the Christian community, through this indifference to political matters (which he implicitly suggests should be seen by the Romans as a veritable virtue), poses a threat to social stability.

At *de Corona* 13,1 Tertullian describes how the various orders in public and civil life wear crowns appropriate to their status. He reports that magistrates in both Athens and Rome and in all the provinces wear crowns to indicate their particular office. But Christians, he says, have their own orders, magistrates and places of meeting; they belong to Christ alone and therefore require no identifying civic crowns. Christians are foreigners in this world and therefore the crowns of this world have no place on their heads. At *de Idololatria* 17 and 18 Tertullian canvasses the question of Christians holding civic office or serving under those who hold such office. At 17,1 he recognises that it is possible in theory for a Christian to hold civil office, or to serve those in office, and to avoid any taint or connection with idolatry - and thereby implicitly recognises the place of the empire and its structures in the divine purpose - but not likely in practice. At 18,8 he declares, somewhat uncompromisingly, that the powers and dignities of this world are not only alien but hostile to God. At *adversus Marcionem* IV.27.5 Tertullian interprets the criticism by Christ of all those who seek the best places and public salutations (*Luke* 11,43) as referring to those who seek high public office. At *de Paenitentia* 11,4f. he questions whether the seeking after public office - with all its difficulties, annoyances, humiliations and so on - is worth the fleeting joy of a single year of occupying the same! He follows this up with a question for his co-religionists, asking whether they are prepared, for the sake of eternity, to put up with at least as much bother for God and his divine offices (such as martyrdom) as these competitors and candidates endure for the sake of attaining public office? At *ad Scapulam* 4,1 he argues that magistrates can perform their public duties effectively, but yet still do so with compassion. Tertullian would appear here again, at least implicitly (cf. *de Corona* 13,1), to accept the actual institutions of government as notionally valid within the divine plan. Yet his attitude to civic institutions could only be described here as at best ambiguous and hardly likely to inspire official confidence. What Tertullian saw as indifference could well have been seen by the authorities from time to time as hostility. Tertullian demonstrates a general respect for Roman governmental institutions and for the concept and rule of law and for Roman law (*Apologeticum* 38,2), but believes that the latter's reputation is sullied by perverse applications of it (*Apologeticum* 2,14 and *de Fuga* 12). Christians, he says, are respecters of the law, but unlike the Romans, respecters also of its spirit, of its intention (*Apologeticum* 30,4). But such respect shall not

33 Neither the expression *religio licita* (or *illicita*) nor *factio licita* (nor *illicita*) had any legal standing in Roman times. Both are apparently Tertullian's own inventions.

compromise the Christian's prior allegiance to the law of God; for the divine law is superior to the secular (*de Idololatria* 17,1).

Tertullian's use of rhetorical forms in the construction of many of his treatises has been too well established by Sider[34] and others[35] to require much more comment here. Sider points to Tertullian's use of the *exordium*, the *narratio* (with a *propositio* or *partitio* or both), the proof, comprising both *confirmatio* and *reprehensio* (though more 'interwoven and inseparable'), and a *peroratio*. He also makes use of a *praemunitio* and an *amplificatio* to bookend the proof. Sider also argues, however, and persuasively so, that 'it is becomingly increasingly clear that in the disposition of his material Tertullian moves well beyond the imitation of rhetorical rules to an imaginative correlation of form and content'.[36] This demonstrates Tertullian's utter immersion in his rhetorical training for only such immersion would allow such flexible employment of the rules. This would, of course, be explained by Tertullian's profession as an orator rather than as a jurist.

Tertullian was certainly a well-read person, though whether he drew from complete works of the authors referred to or from *exempla* is not clear. He makes use of some of the great figures of ancient literature and philosophy - Aristotle, Epicurus, Herodotus, Homer, Lucretius, Plato, Plutarch, Varro, and the Stoics Zeno, Chrysippus and Cleanthes among them - and some of the lesser lights - including Cornelius Nepos and Claudius Saturninus from whose writing '*de coronis*', for example, he gained much background information for his own *de Corona* (7.6 and 10,9). While at *Apologeticum* 46.18 and *de Praescriptione* 7.9 Tertullian would appear to condemn philosophy unreservedly - note his famous 'What has Athens to do with Jerusalem?' from the latter - he yet at *Apologeticum* 14.7 would also appear to afford it some value at least with respect to the figure of Socrates. Indeed at *adv. Marcionem* II.27.6 - 'The Father, who is invisible and unapproachable, and placid, and (so to speak) the God of the philosophers' - where Tertullian's suggests that Marcion's good and utterly transcendent God has more in common with the philosophical view of the Supreme Principle than with the orthodox Christian one, and at *de Testimonia animae* 4.1-8 and 5.9-11 - though in these passages the Christian view, for example, of the soul is more noble than the Pythagorean', 'more complete than the Platonic' and 'more worthy of honour than the Epicurean' - Tertullian speaks of the study of philosophy as a preparation of sorts for the Gospel.[37] At *de Pallio* 6,2 he is even prepared to speak of Christianity as a 'philosophy', albeit a superior

---

34 R.D.Sider, *Ancient Rhetoric and the Art of Tertullian*. (Oxford, 1971).

35 As early as 1924 F.H.Colson, 'Two examples of literary and rhetorical criticism in the Fathers', *JTS* 25 (1964): 364-77, recognised the influence of rhetorical conventions on Tertullian's style. See also G.D.Dunn's 'Rhetorical Structure in Tertullian's *Ad Scapulam*', *VC* 56 (2002): 47-55 for a fine recent example of the study of this influence on Tertullian, and M.S.LeTourneau, 'General and Special Topics in the *De Baptismo* of Tertullian', *Rhetorica* 5 (1987): 103, who reports that Tertullian 'consciously, frequently, and skilfully exploited the topics of classical invention'.

36 Sider, *Ancient Rhetoric and the Art of Tertullian*, p. 21.

37 See Justin Martyr and Clement of Alexandria later.

one. Christianity is itself a philosophical 'school'. Tertullian regularly employs both *schola* and *secta,* commonly used terms for philosophical schools, of the church.

One major concern, however, remains; for Tertullian philosophy or more properly philosophical speculation is the fount of heresy. This, for example, he makes clear at *de Anima* 3,1 where he speaks of the philosophers as the 'patriarchs of heretics'. This is perhaps the greatest source of his disenchantment with philosophy. Tertullian is certainly no Platonist not withstanding his high regard for the latter and his evident desire in many of his writings to take him seriously. His expressed regret, at a number of places, at having to challenge Plato, is not ironical but heartfelt. *Adversus Hermogenem*, for example, is directed against a Platonist dualism though it does not mention Plato by name. *De Anima* is in many ways anti-Platonist. For here Tertullian speaks, against Plato, of the soul as 'sprung from the breath of God, immortal, corporeal, having form, simple in substance, intelligent' and so on. He opposed Platonist notions about the origin of the human soul, believing with the Stoics that it is corporeal and created and originates at birth (*de Anima* 4.1). At *de Carne Christi* 11 Tertullian declares that everything which exists must have something through which it exists and that that something must be a body. The soul exists; it must therefore be a body. In this he reflects a Stoic materialism demonstrated by Nemesis in his *de Natura Hominis* where the latter quotes Cleanthes in declaring that the soul is corporeal (78,7f.). At *de Anima* 25 Tertullian cites Cleanthes as witnessing to the birth of the soul. [38] For Plato, however, the soul was unborn and unmade (see his *Phaedrus*), for the Christian the soul knows birth and creation. Yet it is also true that in Tertullian's belief that human free choice provided the cause of sin - against notions of fatalism - he was influenced as much by Plato as by the Stoics. In Tertullian's reflections on this subject at *adv. Marcionem* II.5-9 we see echoes of *Republic* 380b,[39] 613a[40] and 617e,[41] *Laws* 728e,[42] and *Theaetetus* 177.[43]

Tertullian's famous paradox at *de Carne Christi* 5 - that the crucifixion and the resurrection are credible because there are '*ineptum*' - supposedly comes from an Aristotelian notion and is not evidence of Tertullian's raw fideism or lack of reason.[44] Tertullian quotes the Presocratics at *de Anima* 14,5 - where he cites Strato,

---

38 The anti-Stoic Plutarch in *On Stoic self-contradictions* also speaks of Chrysippus arguing that the soul is engendered and is so after the body (1053d).

39 'To say that God, who is good, becomes the cause of evil to anyone…no-one should assert.'

40 'All things that come from the gods work together for the best for him that is dear to the gods.'

41 'The blame is his who chooses: God is blameless.'

42 'Nothing that nature gives a man is better adapted than his soul to enable him to avoid evil.'

43 'The evildoer fails to see that the effect of his unjust practices is to make him grow more and more like [a pattern of deepest unhappiness] and less and less like [God].'

44 E.F.Osborn, 'The Subtlety of Tertullian', *VC* 52 (1998): 361, says that 'Subtlety and surprise are part of [Tertullian's] offering to the careful reader. *Ratio* is his favourite word and his paradoxes are rhetorical, always capable of rational resolution'.

Anesidemus and Heraclitus to argue for the unity of the soul as diffused over the whole body and yet as in every part the same - Pythagoras at 28,2 - while critical of Pythagoras Tertullian yet calls him 'excellent in some respects' - and Lucretius, *The Nature of the Universe* 1,305[45], at 5,6 - 'The soul must have a body; if it were not corporeal it could not desert the body [at death]'. In this last Tertullian, arguing, as we saw above, alongside the Stoics, for the corporeality of the soul, contests the Platonic and Aristotelian views and at 28,2 challenges Plato and the Middle Platonist Albinus on the transmigration of souls.

The most significant philosophical influence on Tertullian was undoubtedly Stoicism. His *de Patientia* is clearly so influenced. We find it also in his constant employment of military images, a traditional Stoic *topos*. At *Apologeticum* 39, 1 his reference to the church as a 'body' with common knowledge of piety, a shared discipline and a common bond of hope probably owes as much to Stoic thought as it does to the well-known Pauline ecclesial image. The notion of an ordered world (as for the Stoics) is evident at *Apologeticum* 17, *de Anima* 27, and *adversus Hermogenem* 26 and 29 (especially the latter). His emphasis on human free will as the source of sin is not only Platonist but also Stoic. At *adversus Praxean* 5 and at *de Spectaculis* 2f. his notion on the relationship between nature and reason and the ideal of living according to nature is clearly Stoic-influenced. In his christological thought - particularly in the *adversus Praxean* and the *Apologeticum* - his notion of the mutual interpenetration of the natures by way of *perichoresis* or *krasis di'holon* is Stoic.[46] We also saw above the Stoic background for Tertullian's notion of the corporeality of the soul. His famous description of the soul at *Apologeticum* 17,6 as 'naturally Christian' in the spontaneous human references to deity echoes Seneca's suggestion at *Epistulae morales* 117.6[47] that the notion of deity is implanted in every person.

Tertullian gained much of his rhetorical knowledge from Cicero. He cites him, for example, at *de Anima* 24,3 on memory, at 46,11 on prophecy, at *Apologeticum* 11,6 on eloquence, at 50,14 on pain and death; and at *de Pallio* 5,5. Tertullian refers to the letter of the younger Pliny to Trajan (*Ep.* X, 96-97) at *Apologeticum* 2,6f. and to other writings of his, though without actually naming him, at 8,5, 33,4 and 40,3-4. He alludes to but nowhere names the satirist Juvenal at both *Apologeticum* 33,3 (an allusion to *Satire* 3.41 perhaps: 'I know not to lie') and at *de Pudicitia* 1,1 (*Satire* 6,1 on the subject of chastity). Tertullian has an undoubted soft spot for the Stoic philosopher Seneca. [48] At *de Anima* 20,1 he refers to him as '*Seneca saepe noster*'

---

45 'For nothing but a body is capable of touching or being touched.'

46 See my 'Tertullian's Vocabulary of the Divine "Individuals" in *adversus Praxean*', *Sacris Erudiri* 40 (2001): 5-46. Diogenes Laertius speaks of Chrysippus' notion of the *krasis di'holou* (7.151) as does Alexander of Aphrodisias which he describes as a 'mutual coextension' of substances which preserve their peculiar natures in this 'blending' (*de Mixtione* 216,14f.).

47 'For example, we infer that the gods exist by the fact (among other evidence) that all have an innate conviction of their existence.'

48 R.Braun, 'Tertullien et les poètes latins', in R.Braun, *Approches de Tertullien: vingt-six études sur l'auteur et sur l'oeuvre (1955-1990)* (Paris, 1992), p. 26, declares that 'l'influence

and employs him for support of the notion that the natural properties of the soul are inherent within it. He also employs him as an authority at 42,2, in a discussion about sleep as the mirror of death, at *Apologeticum* 12,6 on Roman superstition, and at 50,14 on pain and suffering. Tertullian feels no such warmth for the historian Tacitus. Him, at *Apologeticum* 16,2 (see also *ad Nationes* I.11,1), he blames for the insulting belief that Christians worship the head of an ass. At 16,3 he calls him 'that chatterbox' and at *ad Nationes* II.12.26 reports that the story of the origins of Saturn may be found in his writings. Tertullian cites the historian Sallust - the first governor of Africa Nova (Numidia) in 46 BCE - at both *de Anima* 20,3 and *Apologeticum* 9,9. He mentions the historian Tranquillus Seutonius at *de Anima* 44,2, alludes to his *Nero* at *Apologeticum* 22,12, and cites him as a mine of information on games and the gods associated with them at *de Spectaculis* 5,8. Tertullian also refers to the work of Cornelius Nepos, a contemporary of Cicero and writer on antiquities, employing him for support at *Apologeticum* 10,7 for his own view that Saturn was nothing but a deified human being. Tertullian, as one might expect, makes considerable use of the epic poet Virgil[49], quoting him at length to support or to illustrate his argument. He does so at *Apologeticum* 7,8; 14,2, 25,8 (Juno), and 25,16; at *ad Nationes* I.7,2; II.13,14.26; 17,6; at *de Pallio* 1,31 and at *de Spectaculis* 9,3. He alludes to him clearly at *adversus Marcionem* I.5,1 and II.13,20; at *ad Nationes* II.12,20 and at *de Praescriptionibus* 39,4. Tertullian thus makes significant use of at least three of the 'quadriga' of Arusianus Messius - Virgil, Sallust and Cicero - three of the alleged Big Four of Latin literature.

Tertullian evidences not only a knowledge of Jewish practices from the past but also something of the Jewish presence in Carthage itself. Many of his references, of course, do not actually always require the presence of a significant Jewish community in the Carthage of his day and may simply reflect a grasp on his part of the scriptures and of Jewish-Christian relations historically. A number of Tertullian's references to the Jews, however, clearly have to do with the Carthage of his own time. At *de Pudicitia* 8,7, referring to the parable of the Prodigal Son and what he terms the squandering of God's substance by the Jews, he declares that the Jew of the present day is a beggar in alien territory, serving the princes of the age; that is, the Jews belong to another higher realm but have accommodated themselves to this one. At *Apologeticum* 21,25 he refers to Christians suffering from Jewish persecution, and his comment, at *Scorpiace* 10,10, that the Jewish synagogues are the founts of persecution suggests that this may apply to the contemporary scene. At *adversus Marcionem* V.5,1, he displays some familiarity with the customs of the Jews of Carthage and even, let it be said here, some sympathy with them (notwithstanding *Scorpiace* 10, 10 above), reporting how the Jews of Carthage, as did their forebears, great each other with the 'peace' formula employed by Paul.

At *Apologeticum* 42, 2 Tertullian argues that whatever differences in belief and lifestyle may exist between Christian and non-Christian Carthaginians, there is still

---

de Sénèque sur Tertullien est indéniable'.

49 See ibid., 22f., for a lengthy discussion of Tertullian's use of Virgil.

much that they have in common as fellow citizens of the city. We, he declares, share the forum with you, the meat-markets, the baths; we may not share the bath with you at the Saturnalia, but we do bathe (42,2). We sail ships as you do, we go to war as you do (!)(42,3). We do not eat at the Liberalia with you, but we do eat, and the same things from the same shops! Yet at *de Ieiunio* 12,3 Tertullian can speak of the need for Christians to prepare themselves for the 'last times', for persecution and for torture, and to put aside self-indulgent living as represented, for example, by the baths, which are not to be preferred to that other washing, the sacrament of baptism. He gives the counter-example of the pseudo-martyr Pristinus who apparently preferred the luxury of the baths to Christian baptism and who, inebriated by drink provided by his co-religionists to ease the pain of torture, became incapable under questioning of bearing appropriate Christian witness. By way of analogy, at *adversus Marcionem* III.3,2, Tertullian employs the image of the first arrivals at the public baths taking the best places to illustrate how Christ vigorously lays first claim to a person's faith. At *de Virginibus velandis* 11,4 he employs the example of heathens veiling brides as they are led to their husbands as argument for the veiling of Christian women, and demonstrates also knowledge of other local customs such as the accepted ages for marriage observed within the predominantly pagan society of Carthage.

Though Tertullian clearly comes from an affluent Carthaginian family - his education and general manner would indicate this - it is not clear whether he literally imports into his understanding of the Christian community the social divisions of the secular world. It is clear, however, that he at least uses the language of that world to articulate the nature of clerical-lay relationships. He does not explicitly employ the language of *honestiores* and *humiliores* but he does so implicitly. He refers at *de Baptismo* 17,2 and *de Fuga* 11,1 to the distinction of clergy and laity as *maior* and *minor locus* much as Cyprian did later. He employs the notion of the Roman *ordines* when he refers explicitly to the laity as the *plebs* at *de Monogamia* 12,2, *de Ieiunio* 13,3, *de Anima* 9,4 and *de Exhortatione castitatis* 7,3. He refers to the laity, somewhat disparagingly, as both *grex* (herd) at *de Fuga* 11,3 and as *pecus* (cattle) at 11,1f.. His commitment to social and communal harmony and peace as cornerstones of the Christian life is evident in his delegation of the right to baptise in *de Baptismo* 17. Notwithstanding this reflection of Roman (and thereby Romanised Carthaginian) patterns of social relationships in his understanding of status in the church he does not seem to suggest that the concept of patronage played much part in this.

In chapters 11 and 12 of *de Idololatria* Tertullian deals with the question of how, if at all, a Christian might engage in public trade and whether commercial dealings are an appropriate activity for a Christian. This was an important issue in a city which existed principally by trade, a veritable city of merchants. Tertullian does not exclude all trades from Christian involvement but only those where there is the possibility of either direct or indirect contact with idolatry or the materials of idolatry(11,3). Here perhaps is an early example of ethical investment! But how then are we to live?, some Christians seem to have asked. Faith, says Tertullian, fears not famine, that is, unemployment and destitution (12,4). At *de Pudicitia* 19,24 Tertullian again speaks of the dangers implicit in living and working (earning a living) in a city devoted to pleasure and to business when he speaks of the daily temptations to be faced by Christians in business, official duties and trade. It is of course unlikely that Tertullian would have bothered to involve himself in expressing these warnings were considerable numbers of Christians not so involved.

Tertullian's employment of references to the society and culture around him is of considerable interest to the student of both the history of the early church and the ancient world. He uses these for a variety of purposes, illustrative, polemical or even apologetic. He employs some polemically to attack aspects of that culture and this is particularly so in the matters of religion and social behaviour. He employs others apologetically when seeking either to explain Christianity to a pagan audience or even when he wishes to shame a Christian one into adherence to particular practices of discipline or lifestyle where he believes that a given pagan practice has something of value, no matter how marginal, to teach his co-religionists. His use of both philosophical writings and major figures from Latin literature is by no means negligible.

Cyprian

The Severan period ended with the death of Severus Alexander in 235. In his place Maximinus the Thracian became emperor. Almost immediately a rebellion broke out in Africa led by the three Gordians, father, son and grandson. Although Maximinus eventually lost his throne the revolt itself was short-lived and was crushed with brutal reprisals. The equestrian and allegedly pro-Christian Philip the Arab became emperor in 244 - having been acclaimed by soldiers of the Army of the East - with his son Philip the Younger (who became Caesar before August 247), and was eventually himself overthrown by his own general Decius sometime shortly after July 6th 249. Alarmed by what he saw as a decline in the fortunes of the empire Decius determined upon a test of loyalty for its citizens (and others?) by the requirement that each declare their allegiance publicly by offering sacrifices under the watchful eye of commissioners appointed for the task. The imperial cult was not involved in the process nor was it an action specifically targeted against Christians. Yet the latter were perhaps the most obvious members of the empire to resist the requirement, and action against them - though only very few were actually killed - was swift and brutal. In 251 Decius was killed in action against the Goths and was succeeded by Gallus. At the same time the great plague then racing around the known world - Rome saw some 5000 deaths daily and in Alexandria some 50 per cent of the population either died or fled - reached Carthage.[50] Partly in response to this new crisis for the empire the emperor allegedly ordered a new round of empire-wide sacrifices and, with it, a renewed bout of persecution. Yet it lacked the utter violence of the previous episode and the church weathered it reasonably well. In the following year Aemilianus (briefly) and then Valerian, a former rigorous censor

50 Cyprian himself speaks of the terrible social consequences of this plague at *de Mortalitate* 16.

under Decius, succeeded Gallus who (Valerian, that is), it is said, was not, initially at least, particularly ill-disposed towards Christians. They were even apparently a large number of well-placed Christians in the imperial household. Yet in 257 this emperor also ordered a fresh round of loyalty-testing sacrifices, more specifically targeting Christians. Indeed, according to Millar, the imperial *epistulae* issued in relation to this action specifically referred to the church and provided for the confiscation of Christian property, both individual and episcopal[51] and a prohibition, under pain of death, against Christians gathering at their cemeteries. The persecution, in comparison with those under Decius and Gallus, was relatively mild but was specifically directed against the leadership of the church, particularly against the bishops.

Although little is known for sure about the life of Caecilius Cyprianus Thascius - the accounts of both Dio and Herodian stop before the time of his conversion to Christianity, the unreliable *Historia Augusta* is in any case largely silent for the period 244 to 259, and Cyprian's deacon Pontius' *Vita Cypriani* is too hagiographical to be relied upon - we do know that he was the highly articulate, well-educated, propertied son of a well-to-do Carthaginian family, a man with his own innate sense of his social position as a *persona insignis*. Trained as a rhetor he was, by all accounts, himself a highly regarded teacher of the art in Carthage. At *ad Donatum* 2 he attacks his former profession - though his own writing as a Christian was yet characterised by an exuberant, even exaggerated rhetorical style - when he writes,

> 'In courts of justice, in the public assembly, in political debate, a copious eloquence may be the glory of a voluble ambition; but in speaking of the Lord God, a chaste simplicity of expression strives for the conviction of faith rather with the substance, than with the powers, of eloquence'.

He became a Christian in the mid-240s under the influence of the presbyter Caecilius. In late 248 or early 249, following the death of the bishop of Carthage, Donatus, and against the significant opposition of a number of influential clergy in the city, he was elected and consecrated as bishop himself. When the emperor Decius put forth the decree in 250 that all citizens perform ritual sacrifices as tokens of their loyalty to the state and to the imperial house, Cyprian urged his flock to be steadfast, non-confrontational and non-provocative, but unlike his episcopal colleague in Rome, the martyr Fabius, he fled the city and sought to govern the church in Carthage by edict from his place of hiding. Many questioned both the wisdom and the morality of his decision - and his personal courage - and some who had opposed his election saw a chance to destabilise his position. This manifested itself particularly in their support for the granting of absolution to those who had lapsed and sacrificed by confessors awaiting their fate in prison. Cyprian from his self-imposed exile challenged this practice and its implicit threat to his own authority. In 251, after he had returned from hiding, a council of African bishops meeting in Carthage confirmed his stance but his struggle with dissidents in his own see continued for much of his episcopate until his death under Valerian in 258. Despite the fact that Cyprian apparently came

51 F. Millar, *The Emperor in the Roman World*. (London, 1977), pp. 569f..

from the highly Romanised elite of Carthaginian society neither his treatises nor his letters betray much conscious engagement, save his rhetorical background (see below), with the surrounding culture. Cyprian virtually never quotes from non-Christian literature. It is one thing that differentiates him from his '*magister*' Tertullian. At *ad Donatum* 3 he speaks at one point of the old life which he has now left behind him. He speaks of previously - that is, prior to his conversion - 'knowing nothing of my real life, a stranger to truth and light'. He speaks of his former life as characterised by feasting, sumptuous clothing, civic honours and magisterial office, and the patronage of many clients. His life now, on the other hand, is marked by thrift, simple dress, privacy and lack of glory, and alone-ness.

Given Cyprian's previous role as a professional teacher of rhetoric it is hardly surprising that his treatises should show the influence of the conventions of contemporary rhetorical theory and practice. Two of his best known works, by way of example, demonstrate this clearly. The *De unitate ecclesiae catholicae* begins with a classic *exordium* at chapter 1 where Cyprian seeks the goodwill of his readers. Chapters 2 and 3 comprise a *narratio* which provides a background to the coming discussion. Chapter 4, in the style of Tertullian, comprises a *praemunitio* whereby Cyprian prepares the way for his argument proofs. Chapters 5 to 20 provide the *probatio* where the primary witness is that of scripture. The *peroratio* begins at chapter 21 (through to 24) in which Cyprian makes a series of emotional pleas to the 'virgins' to hold fast to the unity of the church. The *de lapsis* also provides clear evidence of the use of rhetorical conventions. The first three chapters comprise the *exordium*, chapter 4 a brief *narratio* in which Cyprian lays on the emotional appeal of 'I grieve, brethren, I grieve with you', 'I wail with the wailing, I weep with the weeping'. Chapters 5 to 31 provide the *probatio*, again mainly by way of the witness of the scriptures, and chapters 32 to 36 the *peroratio* with a recapitulation of his argument and appeals to the emotions of his readers.

The so-called 'crisis of the third century', as understood by contemporaries, probably dates from the end of the reign of Marcus Aurelius but was perhaps most obvious and critical, in terms of a combination of wars, frontier threats, famines, plagues, manpower shortages, a sense of moral decline, around the middle of the third century and up until the turn of the century. An atmosphere of general pessimism certainly becomes evident following the military setbacks under Marcus Aurelius and the civil wars following the death of Commodus and the collapse of the Antonine dynasty. Following the demise of the Antonines the theme of restoration was foremost in the public pronouncements of contenders for the throne. Official imperial propaganda of the time spoke of the need for a *saeculum novum* and for emperors to be *restitutores orbis*. All claimants to the imperial throne in 193 put forward programmes of restitution and this set in train a constant refrain in future imperial propaganda. Though the title had appeared in the time of Hadrian, Severus Alexander was the first emperor to be celebrated epigraphically as *restitutor orbis* and from the time of Gordian III in the 250s it became a normal title for Roman emperors. Both Ulpian and Philostratus stressed the manpower shortage in the empire[52] and Cassius Dio spoke of the period after the golden age of Marcus Aurelius as one of iron and dust.[53] An unknown orator in the reign of Philip spoke of tyrants, destruction, depopulation through civil war, poor management of justice, finances, the military and the frontiers, of a confused and decaying empire.[54] This language is reminiscent of Cyprian at *ad Demetrianum* 3f. where he speaks of the divinely-ordained aging of the world and of those things, like poor harvests, scarce natural resources, manpower shortages, maladministration of justice, moral decline, civil war, disease (plague), and so on, which evidence this.[55] He speaks, in a manner which was not uncommon for early Christian writers, and which imitated Stoic thought, of the 'growing old' of the present age.[56] Diogenes Laertius speaks of the Stoic view of the world as perishable[57] and Stobaeus reports that Cleanthes spoke of the cyclical growth and decline of the world and the universe as a living organism.[58] Demetrianus, proconsul of Africa, had apparently blamed the present wars, famines and pestilence then afflicting the province on the impiety of the Christians. Thus, the treatise is usually dated to the year 252, the time of the great plague then spreading throughout the empire and reaching Carthage itself. Cyprian's response was that the decay and decline of the world's failing estate - diminishing natural resources, a dropping off in agricultural produce, a lessening of justice, reductions in civic concord, a lowering of moral discipline - is quite natural and expected. The world, like all things which according to God's law must have both a beginning and an end, is no longer robust and is, in fact, dying. Minucius Felix, following Sallust, spoke likewise of the decay of the world, as did Lactantius later following Seneca. The latter had spoken of Rome's biological development from *infantia* through to the inevitable *interitus* (ruin).[59] At *de Mortalitate* 25, written in the same period, Cyprian speaks of the world 'collapsing', of the world as a house worn out and wearied. Here we see the very Roman notion - present very clearly in Seneca and in much Stoic thought - of history as a process of 'biological senescence' but tempered in the present period by the suggestion or belief that the crisis could be turned about and health, represented by the stability of traditional order, restored. Cyprian clearly felt that the emperors of his time had failed to exercise their authority appropriately and that this was evidenced by the general breakdown in law and order and general security. In the Christian life he saw an escape not only from sin but from these ravages wrought by a sinful world.[60] Yet at *ad Demetrianum* 9 he acknowledges that divine punishment for the sins of humankind may provide no such escape at all. And

52 Ulpian, *Digest* 50.6.3; Philostratus, *Gymn.* 1f. and 14.

53 71.36.4.

54 *Eis basilea*, 7ff.

55 3 and 5.

56 *Ad Demetrianum* 3. Note also that Parisinus and CSEL II read 'saeculum' for 'mundum'.

57 7.141.

58 1.17.3.

59 *Divine Institutes* 7.15.14ff.

60 Ibid., 2ff.

these scourges happen, says Cyprian, and this is his point, not because we Christians do not worship the pagan gods, as Demetrianus alleges (though that is true), but because Demetrianus and his fellows do not worship the one, true God.[61] Thus, far from the old Roman adage that *Pax Romana* derives from *Pax Deorum*, Cyprian asserts here that *Pax Romana* derives rather from *Pax Dei*! Christians pray for the safety of the empire but only, unlike the pagans, that it might have time to repent.

Cyprian speaks, too, of kingdoms - and it is almost certain that he has the Empire in mind here - that do not rise to supremacy through merit, but by chance.[62] He speaks, like Minucius Felix, of the criminal origins of Rome, probably against the claims of apologists for Roman piety:

> 'A people is collected together from profligates and criminals, and by founding an asylum, impunity for crimes makes the number great; and that their king himself may have a superiority in crime, Romulus becomes a fratricide; and in order to promote marriage, he makes a beginning of that affair of concord by discords. ... The Roman kingdom, therefore, did not grow from the sanctities of religion, nor from auspices and auguries, but keeps its appointed time within a definite limit.'

The Roman empire will not last forever. It has a beginning and an end. Cyprian looks at history and asks when an alliance in royalty ever began either with good faith or without bloodshed.[63] He includes as examples - he is arguing for a belief in only one God (and for this purpose cites both Plato and Hermes Trismegistus in support)[64] - the Roman founding twins, and Pompey and Julius Caesar, and points to nature, to the bees with one ruler, and to other types of flocks and herds, for proof of his argument. In *ad Fortunatum*, where he exhorts his readers to martyrdom, he attacks the practice of idol worship, arguing that one God alone is to be worshipped, and portrays Antiochus Epiphanes, as frequent a target of the early Christians as were the Maccabees frequent models of virtuous and heroic resistance against tyranny, as the Antichrist.[65] Some indeed even of Cyprian's correspondents are ready to style the persecuting emperor Decius as the Antichrist[66] but Cyprian himself does not appear to be of such a mind. Whatever demonic forces he might see at work in the persecutions of both Decius and Valerian his generally positive attitude towards the empire will not allow him to cast it in such terms. Yet at *ep.* 55.9.1 he refers to Decius as 'that savage tyrant' and clearly lays the blame on him, rather than on his advisers or ministers, for the persecution of Christians.

---

61 *Ad Demetrianum* 9.5.

62 *Quod idola dii non sint*, 5.

63 Ibid., 8.

64 Ibid., 6. Cyprian points to Plato's view that there is but the one God and all the rest are angels and demons and to Hermes Trismegistus that there is one God, incomprehensible and beyond our estimation.

65 1;2 and 11.

66 See ep. 22,1.

There are, of course, clear evidences of the influence of the Roman cast of mind in Cyprian. His commitment to Roman (and Stoic?) notions of unity, order and harmony in family, community and church is unquestionable. At *de habitu virginum* 8 he speaks of the tension between spousal obligation and church discipline - though he has no doubt as to where the Christian's ultimate obligations lie - and at *de opere et eleemosymis* 16 of that between familial obligations and those owed to God. He quotes *Matthew* 10,37 - 'He who loves father or mother more than me is not worthy of me' - in this regard, a text as offensive to the Roman sense of *pietas* as to its original Jewish hearers. His *de unitate ecclesiae catholicae* is, of course, replete with calls for the necessary unity of the church as reflecting the unity of Christ but this is no doubt inspired also, at least in part, by Roman notions of order. At *ep*. 11.4.1 he speaks naturally of the traditional authority of the *paterfamilias*, at *ep*. 27.1.1, against a background where Cyprian condemns special favours to the lapsed, of a proper familial *pietas* which led Mappalicus the martyr to instruct that peace be granted to his lapsed mother and sister. At *ep*. 55.13.2 Cyprian regards as extenuating circumstances the case of an apostate who sacrificed on behalf of his whole house and thereby endangered his own soul but protected the lives of the household, thus carrying out the responsibility of a true Roman *paterfamilias*. Under the old Roman law the *paterfamilias* was responsible for the infractions of the members of his household and it may be that Cyprian sees in this particular lapsed Christian an example of the translation of this concept into the Christian arena. In *epp*. 46, 48 and 60.1.1, and elsewhere, Cyprian gives particular attention to the need for communal unity and concord.

Cyprian, says Clarke, saw himself as a *persona insignis* and his clergy, for the most part, as not so. At *ep*. 3.1,1 he implicitly refers to the proper subservience of his deacons when he refers to their '*locus*' as different to that of a bishop.[67] Many scholars have written on Cyprian as *patronus*.[68] Burns observes that 'loyalties were cemented and discipline exercised by the sort of personal patronage which Cyprian used during his exile' and that '[the church's] patronage was exercised through an established bureaucracy'. Bobertz argues for the existence of 'the primary prerequisites of patronage networks' in the larger urban Christian congregations of the second and third centuries and speaks of Cyprian setting about 'establishing new "client" clergy in Carthage'. He speaks of the '*beneficia* of forgiveness, reconciliation and readmission to the church', of Cyprian as 'bishop and patron of the laity', and declares that 'Cyprian's biblical references to the gospel qualities of the "humble and meek, docile, tranquil, and modest", are used to define the proper characteristics of loyal "client" clergy'. Bobertz also characterises *epp*. 38, 39 and

---

67 See also 12.1.1.

68 J. Patout Burns, 'Social Context in the Controversy between Cyprian and Stephen', *SP* 24 (1993): 38-44; C.A. Bobertz, 'Patronage Networks and the Study of Ancient Christianity', *SP* 24 (1993): 20-27; C.A.Bobertz, 'Patronal Letters of Commendation: Cyprian's *Epistulae* 38-40', *SP* 31 (1997): 252-9; J. Patout Burns, 'The Role of Social Structures in Cyprian's Response to the Decian Persecution', *SP* 31 (1997): 260-7.

40 as Christian letters of patronal commendation, such as Cicero and others wrote in great abundance, to 'introduce three confessors to the church at Carthage and also at the same time to 'establish them as clients of bishop Cyprian'. In *ad Donatum* Cyprian makes a number of references to patrons and clients. At *de habitu virginum* 11, in a manner reminiscent of Minucius Felix and Hermas, Cyprian speaks of the value of charity towards the poor being reciprocated by the poor's prayers for their benefactors. Although the bishop never uses the term *patronus* or its relative *cliens* to describe his relationship with either clergy or laity, it is nevertheless clearly the basis for his understanding of his relationship with them. Indeed, the terms were actually rarely used in polite Roman society, given the social inferiority and degradation they usually implied. It is just possible that the notion of the confessors of the 250s as patrons had begun to make its mark in Carthage, in a land where martyrs already enjoyed high status. The relationship of confessor and penitent lapsed was between persons of unequal status - the confessors were guaranteed entry into heaven and the lapsed excommunication - and the exchange envisaged would have been honouring by the lapsed and forgiveness from the confessor. Was the struggle between Cyprian and the confessors over the right to readmit the penitent lapsed fought out within the context, implied of course and never explicit, of a battle between potential patrons for a crowd of clients? At *ep*. 38.1.1 Cyprian even seems prepared to present the image of God as the ultimate *patronus* - though not explicitly - when he speaks, in the context of his own unusual appointment of the twice-confessor Aurelius to the ranks of the Carthaginian clergy, of God having already cast his vote for the appointment.

If it is true, as his biographer Pontius claims, that Cyprian, on becoming bishop, gave away much of his personal wealth for the relief of the poor by selling off a number of his properties,[69] then he personally embodied much of the actual advice he subsequently gave to wealthy Christians. Pontius also speaks of Cyprian's 'excessively affected penury'. Cyprian makes much in his treatises of the proper use of wealth. At *de habitu virginum* 7 he suggests to a wealthy Christian sister that true riches lie with God - 'she is rich who is rich in God; she is wealthy who is wealthy in Christ' - and that delight in earthly wealth means an improper love of this world and at 10 that the wealthy ought not to vaunt their wealth and that Apostle Peter spoke of being 'rich in the grace of Christ'. In chapter 11 of the same treatise he declares to the sister who objects that wealth and possessions must be used that possessions should be used only for the things of salvation, for meeting the divine commandments. A wealthy Christian might 'lend one's estate to God'. This might even be seen to imply that the generosity of the wealthy towards the poor - 'Move [God] by the prayers of many to grant you to carry out the glory of virginity' - will oblige the latter to pray for them, suggesting a form of patron/client relationship. Exchange your earthly possessions for heavenly ones, he implores. Your wealth must minister to good uses and not simply be used as it will. At *de lapsis* 11 Cyprian attacks a blind love of one's own property as deceiving the unwary and of their wealth fettering would-be

69 *De Vita Cypriani* 2.

confessors like a chain to this world. He speaks of believers being held back by the chains of their wealth; such are not so much possessors (of this wealth) but rather possessed by it, slaves to profit and bond-slaves of their money.[70] Cyprian speaks of those who show a preference for a worldly estate to confession of the faith,[71] urges the avoidance of wealth as an enemy,[72] and again suggests the notion of lending one's possessions to God, with the implication that one will be paid back many-fold in divine blessings. At *de dominica oratione* 20 he speaks again of the Apostle's condemnation of wealth and of the perils of riches, and declares that one who has pity on the poor lends to God, a common theme. At *de opere et eleemosymis* 10 he urges that the faithful prefer their own souls to mammon and to personal and family comforts, at 12 he warns of Pharisee-like Christians who ignore warnings about the proper use of wealth, at 13 he speaks of those who are slaves to their money, bound with the chains (again) and the bonds of covetousness (once loosened by Christ but now bound again in chains to their wealth), at 15 of those whose care for their possessions prevents their labour in the church - the widow at *Luke* 21,3f. is 'found rich in good works' - and at 19 he urges that Christians assign to God the wealth being saved up for their children. A true *paterfamilias* will entrust the guardianship and the future of his children and dependants to God alone; a father who does not do so is unfair and traitorous towards them. To care for the earthly needs of one's children alone is to commend them solely to the devil. At *de unitate ecclesiae catholicae* 26, where he may well see his own example in his reference to the sale of personal property for the sake of the community in the early church (*Acts* 2, 44f.), he condemns those who contravene the Lord's bidding to sell and refuse even to tithe, preferring instead solely to increase their own store.

Unlike the Roman theologians of the second and third centuries who see nothing sinful in the possession of wealth *per se*, only in its misuse and abuse, Cyprian, like his predecessor Tertullian and consistent with the rigorous and hard-edged North African ethos, can see no instrinsic virtue in wealth or possessions and believes that the imperfect creature cannot be trusted to use it wisely on his or her own account but must instead surrender it to the Lord. Wealth is a trap for all Christians, wise or not, and must be got rid of so as to preserve one's own soul. It is for Cyprian a simple choice confronting the Christian - eternal life and possessions cannot be mixed. And there is, as we also find among the Roman Christians, a clear sense that the wealthy will not only 'purchase' the blessings of God through the surrender of their wealth but a clientele from among the poor for their patronal generosity.

Cyprian does not demonstrate much explicit evidence of the influence of the surrounding society on his thought. Yet there is significant implicit evidence for the influence on him of Stoic thought, of Roman notions of civic order, and of the system of patronage. Cyprian appears to see himself as very much standing over against the surrounding culture, particularly in the area of wealth production and

70 *De Lapsis* 12.

71 Ibid., 35.

72 Ibid.

material possessions, but is in fact more influenced by that society than he possibly realised.

Select Bibliography

North Africa:

A.R.Birley, *Septimius Severus: the African emperor*. (London, 1971).

S. Raven, *Rome in Africa*. 3rd edition. (London, 1993).

J.B.Rives, *Religion and Authority in Roman Carthage from Augustus to Constantine*. (Oxford, 1995).

Tertullian:

T.D.Barnes, *Tertullian: a historical and literary study*. 2nd edition. (London, 1985).

E.F.Osborn, *Tertullian: First Theologian of the West*. (Cambridge, 1997).

D.I.Rankin, *Tertullian and the Church*. (Cambridge, 1995).

R.D.Sider, *Ancient Rhetoric and the art of Tertullian*. (Oxford, 1971).

Cyprian:

G.W.Clarke, *The Letters of St. Cyprian*. 3 vols. ACW 43, 44 and 46. (New York, 1984-86).

P.Hinchcliffe, *Cyprian of Carthage and the unity of the Christian Church*. (London, 1974).

Chapter 4

Antioch, Asia Minor and the Fathers

Antioch of Syria

> 'A city becomes good-looking, when it gets more air, open space, shade in summer and in winter sunshine beneath the shelter of a roof, and when, in place of cheap, squat wrecks of houses, it gains stately edifices that are worthy of a great city.'
>
> (Dio Chrysostom, *Discourses* 47.15)

> 'The Syrian Orontes has long since poured into the Tiber, bringing with it its lingo and its manners, its flutes and its slanting harp-strings; bringing, too, the timbrels of the breed, and the girls who are bidden ply their trade at the Circus.'
>
> (Juvenal, *Satires* 3,62-65)

Syrian Antioch was established by Seleucus I in May 300 BCE - one of sixteen cities of the same name established by him - a month after he had founded Seleucia Pieria, later Antioch's principal seaport, on the coast. It became in time the dominant city of the Empire east of Alexandria. Antioch was known in antiquity as variously 'Antioch the Great', 'the Queen of the East' and 'the Beautiful'. Roman occupation of the city began under Pompey in 64 BCE. The site of the ancient city stands as the southwestern gateway of the Amuk plain and at the head of navigation of the Orontes river. This waterway, with its surrounding valley, provides the principal highway between the Amuk region and the sea. This, in part, gave Antioch its prominence and its power. Syria itself, because of its strategic importance for the Empire, became an imperial province under the direct oversight of the emperor and the *legatus Augusti*, based in Antioch, the key figure in the province and in the East generally. Antioch, therefore, enjoyed a significant international role in terms of the Empire and provided both a strategic frontier against the perceived threat of the Parthians and the hub of major trade-routes. The population of the city in imperial times was around 500,000. As Syria became so important in the affairs of the Empire - although no Syrian entered the Roman Senate for 60 years from the death of Hadrian - so it began to play a significant role in the choice of new emperors. The Antioch-based governor was particularly influential in this, and ofttimes a governor or ex-governor of the province (e.g. Hadrian in 117CE, C. Avidius Cassius, 166-75, P. Helvius Pertinax, 179-82, and Pescennius Niger, 190-3) was a prime candidate for the assumption of the purple. In 175/6 Antioch served as one of two major centres for the shortlived revolt of Avidius Cassius.

Seleucus I Nikator gave rights of settlement to Jewish veterans[1] and by the first century of the Common Era there were three major Jewish areas in Antioch. The Jewish community at Antioch increased in size almost continuously from the time of Seleucus I and by the Roman period, despite its relatively late beginnings, comprised one of the three largest Jewish communities in the Roman world. In the Talmudic era it was Antioch and not Alexandria which both Palestinian and Babylonian Jews regarded as the 'big city'. Jews became prominent in Antiochene business life. The city also saw periodic additions to the community through the transfer of Jewish captives to Antioch. The Jews comprised one-seventh of the population although this was reduced by not infrequent pogroms. If *4 Maccabees* is a product of Antiochene Judaism - the city was the site of a memorial to the martyrs - then it may also tell us much about the Christian community there. The influence of Judaism upon Christianity in Antioch - there is every evidence that the Jewish community and the bulk of the Christian community in Antioch co-existed quite comfortably - is well documented and was constant until the Jews were driven out of Antioch in the 7th century.

Ignatius of Antioch: *Epistles*

We know little about Ignatius' life. Eusebius tells us only that he was the bishop of Antioch after Evodius,[2] that he was the second after Peter,[3] and that he was in time succeeded by Heros.[4] It is generally agreed that he went to his death during the reign of Trajan, though there is significant dispute about the actual year.[5] John Malalas suggested the date as 115 but it hard to see why, if this were true, Ignatius would be sent to Rome when the emperor was actually in Antioch. Trevett argues for a date around 107. Ignatius gives us no specific or direct information about either Antioch or any of the cities to which he writes. We do not know Ignatius' precise ecclesiastical status. He claims to be the bishop of Antioch and at times styles himself as 'bishop of Syria' (*Romans* ix.1). Whether he was in fact a type of early metropolitan for the region of Syria - as is certainly the case for the bishop of Antioch in later times - or merely bishop of the church of Antioch with pretensions to the former, or only the head of a particular house-church in the city with a vision of himself as senior minister in the somewhat fractious Christian community there, we cannot know. Neither do we know his civic status. His journey to Rome does not make him necessarily a Roman citizen exercising a citizen's right to be tried in the capital before the emperor. He may have been sent to Rome by the governor - probably Julius Quadratus Bassus (110-13) - as a test case. Even the circumstances

---

1 Josephus, *Contra.Apionem* II.39.

2 *Ecclesiastical History* III.xxii.2.

3 Ibid., III.xxxvi.2.

4 Ibid., III.xxxvi.15.

5 See C. Trevett, *A study of Ignatius of Antioch in Syria and Asia* (Lewiston, 1992), pp. 3-9 for the most useful discussion of the arguments.

of his arrest and subsequent trial are unclear. He makes no mention of the former and the latter postdates his extant writings.

Ignatius wrote seven extant letters, each with a paraenetic purpose, while on his way to a martyr's death in Rome. Six were addressed to particular churches - those at Ephesus, Tralles, Magnesia, Philadelphia, Smyrna and Rome - and one to an individual, Polycarp, the young bishop of Smyrna. In the main Ignatius confines himself to matters of christology, whereby he seeks to combat the heresy of docetism and, at times, that of Ebionitism, and of ecclesiology, encouraging both adoption of the threefold ecclesial office and obedience to the bishop as a means to unity.[6] The letters of Ignatius, declares Schoedel, reflect the conventions of the Hellenistic letter more than they do the Pauline style.[7] There is also clear evidence of the influence of conventions of rhetorical theory and practice in the letters.[8] It is important, however, to also be wary of imposing a particular structure on them. One would assume, for example, even if there were no rhetorical conventions, that an author writing to the churches of Asia Minor and Rome in the second century would almost certainly seek the goodwill or at least attention of his readers,[9] make abundant use of scripture, and exhort them in sometimes emotional tones. Yet, the structure - Carruth calls the letters examples of epideictic rhetoric[10] - is reasonably clear. Each of the letters contains an *exordium* in which Ignatius courts the goodwill of the persons addressed by near-extravagant praise of their faithfulness[11] and a brief *narratio* in which he outlines the background to his concerns, often in the form of a *propositio* (see *Smyrnaeans* 2). The letters are comprised for the most part of a lengthy *probatio* which comprises mainly argument by way of constant appeals to scripture. Each letter ends with a *peroratio* in which Ignatius recapitulates his arguments and encourages, often with great emotion, his readers to faithfulness. A clear example of the influence of rhetoric may be found in Ignatius' use of Stoic-like athletic imagery in *Polycarp* 1.3 - 3.1 and elsewhere.[12] At *Ephesians* 3.1 Ignatius speaks of the need for himself to be

---

6 M.W.Patrick, 'Autobiography and Rhetoric: anger in Ignatius of Antioch', in S.E.Porter and D.L.Stamps (eds), *The Rhetorical Interpretation of Scripture* (Sheffield, 1999), pp. 352f. says that 'Epistolary theory and practice encourage Ignatius to write his letter [to the Philadelphians] on a single subject [unity]' and that in fact he 'writes on one topic per letter'.

7 W.R. Schoedel, 'Theological Norms and Social Perspectives in Ignatius of Antioch', in E.P. Sanders (ed.), *Jewish and Christian Self-Definition*. Vol. 1: *The Shaping of Christianity in the Second and Third Centuries*. (London, 1980), p. 47.

8 See Patrick, 'Autobiography and Rhetoric', pp. 348-65, on the rhetorical structure of *To the Philadelphians*.

9 See S.Carruth, 'Praise for the Churches', in E.A.Castelli and H.Taussig (eds), *Reimagining Christian Origins* (Valley Forge, 1996), pp. 295-310, for a discussion of the opening sections of Ignatius' letters as employing the topics of an *encomium* for a Greek city.

10 Ibid., p. 296.

11 Carruth, ibid., p. 295 calls these 'praise sections'.

12 See Epictetus, *Enchiridion* 29 and Philo, *de specialibus legibus* 4.101 for examples.

prepared (lit. anointed) by the congregation in faith, an allusion to the preparation of a gymnast or gladiator by a trainer. At *Philadelphians* 2.2 he speaks of the runners in God's race. At *Polycarp* 1.3 he urges the young bishop to strive in all difficulties to be the perfect athlete. At 2.3 he speaks of God's athlete - like the pilot and the sailor - striving for the prize of immortality and eternal life. 'Where the toil and suffering is greater', he says, 'the gain is great.'

At *Ephesians* 6.2 Ignatius refers to the Ephesians' 'good order in God' with reference to their adherence to truth and orthodox teaching. This may reflect the Roman or even Hellenistic virtue of order and communal harmony. At 4.1, 4.2 and 13.1 Ignatius speaks of the congregation's concord, in the last of their 'concord of faith'. At 5.3 he declares that 'he who does not join in the common assembly is already haughty and has separated himself [from the assembly]'. At 8.1 he praises the Ephesians for their lack of communal strife, a much extolled civic virtue, and at 13.2 declares that there is nothing better than peace. All of *Ephesians* 7 is given over to extolling the virtues of communal peace. At *Magnesians* 6.1 he urges the church to 'do all things in harmony with God' and at 15.1 farewells them in the 'concord of God'. At *Trallians* 12.2 he urges continuance in 'harmony and prayer with one another'. In the preface to *Philadelphians* he speaks of the church there established in the 'harmony of God' and at 11.2 of the congregation hoping on Christ and waiting on him in 'faith, love and harmony'. 'Peace' is also for him a favourite term. It reflects then both a Roman and a Greek civic virtue.[13] His contemporary Dio Chrysostom of Prusa addressed the issue of *homonoia* very directly in four of his famous *Discourses*, those to the Nicomedians and Nicaeans (38), that to the Nicaeans alone (39), to Prusans and Apameians (40), and that to the Apameians alone (41).[14] At *Philadelphians* 8.2 Ignatius warns against factiousness, demonstrating again a concern for order in the community, ecclesiastical or civil.

At *Polycarp* 4.3 Ignatius argues against the practice of manumitting slaves from the common fund of the church. Harrill 'locates the passage within the context of Greco-Roman rhetorical and literary commonplaces alarming audiences to the dangers of slave recruitment'.[15] Ignatius' rhetoric here, he declares, 'was shaped as much by Greco-Roman commonplaces and models as by early Christian tradition'. His concern reflects as much as anything else 'the literary/moral *topos* of the slave attempting to break out of bondage by questionable means, the *tuphos* of (liberated) slaves'. Ignatius clearly does not condemn the principle of the corporate manumission of slaves by churches but only where it is financed from the common fund. Harrill suggests that the *paranomē* obligations which were a regular feature of such manumission agreements would have established a 'hierarchy of patronage independent of any "monarchical" bishop' and thus reflects a 'power struggle between the Ignatian clergy and wealthy house church patrons over the control of

---

13 Dio Chrysostom, *Orationes* 38-41 and Aelius Aristeides, *Orationes* 23-24.

14 See earlier the apparent influence of Dio on Clement of Rome.

15 J.A.Harrill, 'Ignatius, Ad Polycarp 4.3 and the Corporate Manumission of Christian Slaves', *JECS* 1 (1993): 115. See Cicero, *Dom.* 54 and *Mil.* 89 for examples of this.

such manumitted slaves and thus over the common funds themselves. Like Cicero in seeking the order and unity of the city of Rome in the face of political upheaval, or a Roman governor control in his own province, Ignatius as bishop sought to maintain church order in a time of great turbulence and persecution. Yet it was perhaps his own position as chief patron which he wished to preserve against the claims of his rivals for the affections of the Antiochene church.

It is perhaps unusual that a martyr on his way to a glorious death in Rome and guarded by a troop of Roman soldiers should make no explicit mention either of the emperor to whom he is going or to the imperial cult. At *Smyrnaeans* 6.1, however, Ignatius does make mention of 'rulers visible and invisible' and declares that even for them there is a judgement if they do not believe on the blood of Christ. 'Let not even office exalt anyone', he says. While Schoedel is of the view that these are references to ecclesiastical, and not civil, opponents - he suggests heretics and/or would-be rival bishops - I believe it more likely that here we have an implied reference to the emperor and imperial authority in general. At *Romans* 6.1 Ignatius also comments that it would be better for him 'to die in Christ Jesus than to be king over the ends of the earth', a clear reference to the emperor, though hardly one that can be construed as unambiguously critical.

Mellink, in a quite perceptive piece of writing[16] deals with Ignatius' apparent fascination with his own impending suffering and death; he considers, as part of this work, three suggested explanation of this apparent obsession. He considers Tanner's pointing to the alleged similarities between Greco-Roman views on suicide and Ignatius' own reflections on his impending death,[17] Perkins on interpreting Ignatius' desire for death as an example of a widespread fascination with death and suffering in the Greco-Roman culture of the time,[18] and Brent's to situate Ignatius' reflections within the cultural setting of the procession associated with the imperial cult.[19] He dismisses each as untenable and while I have neither the time nor the inclination to pursue the matter here – I would suggest the reader consult Mellink's work and the three articles cited – I would suggest that Brent's argument, while perhaps tenuous in places, is nevertheless impressive.

Finally, Schoedel comments that Ignatius' refusal to locate the major challenge to the church in the surrounding pagan world, placing it rather in the internal divisions within the church itself, 'has a bearing … on the shape of [his] theology'.[20] In Ignatius the issue of communal concord is clearly the one major theme running through much of his work and one which reflects very clearly the influence of the surrounding culture.

---

16 O.Mellink, *Death as eschaton: a study of Ignatius of Antioch's Desire for Death.* (Amsterdam, 2000).

17 R.G.Tanner, 'Martyrdom in Saint Ignatius of Antioch and the Stoic View of Suicide', *SP* 16 (1985): 201-205.

18 J.Perkins, 'The "Self" as Sufferer', *HTR* 85 (1992): 245-72.

19 A. Brent, 'Ignatius of Antioch and the Imperial Cult', *VC* 52 (1998): 30-58.

20 Schoedel, 'Theological Norms', p. 46.

Theophilus of Antioch: *ad Autolycum*

Little is known about Theophilus. Eusebius names him as the sixth bishop (168-?) of Antioch after Cornelius and Eros and as the author of works against both Hermogenes and Marcion.[21] He was born of pagan parents, received an Hellenistic education and became a convert after much study of the Jewish and Christian scriptures. This much he tells us himself. He was well acquainted with rhetorical forms, notwithstanding his own self-effacing style in this regard, and probably wrote the *ad Autolycum*, an apologetic and protreptic piece in three short books, shortly after the death of Marcus Aurelius in 180. The primary focus of the work is to demonstrate the superiority of Christianity over pagan thought through its linkage to the writings of the prophets which predate those of the philosophers and poets. Good states that the apologetic intent of the work is 'to secure the credibility of the Christian religion' and its protreptic an 'exhortation[s] calling the reader to a new way of life'.[22]

There is ample evidence within *ad Autolycum* of Theophilus' grasp and use of the conventions of rhetoric. His early condemnation of eloquence is simply that of Plato in favour of knowledge and judgement. At 2,1 he describes himself, in the Apostle's words as 'unskilled in speaking' (*2 Cor.* 11:6) but omits the important 'yet not in knowledge'. This feigned humility is simply classic rhetorical ruse. The whole first book is a combination *exordium/narratio* in which Theophilus does nothing to earn the goodwill of his reader but simply to attack him head-on. In these 14 chapters Theophilus provides a *partitio* of sorts in which he lays out the claims of Christianity (2-8, 12-14) and challenges those of Greco-Roman culture (9-11). In book 2 he again offers a *exordium/narratio* (1-8) in which he outlines pagan teaching on the origin of the world and then (9-35) provides his *proofs* of the teachings of the Christian faith through a commentary of sorts on the book of *Genesis*. In the last three chapters of the book (36-38) Theophilus employs the very words and witness of Sibyl and the poets to support his arguments. Thus does he use the witnesses for the opposition in his own defence. In book 3 he first lays out his major claim here - the superior antiquity of Christian witness (1) - and then challenges the value of the witness of Greek literature and Greek authors (2-3). In superb forensic style he argues that witnesses must either have seen those things to which they testify or accurately report those who have (as the writers of the Christian scriptures clearly do). In the fourth chapter he lists the charges laid against Christians - promiscuity, incest, cannibalism and innovation - and then proceeds to demolish these. He points first to the support of the Greeks for some of these (5-8) and then provides scriptural proofs of the superior morality of the Christians (9-15). He then provides a lengthy proof of the greater antiquity of the Judaeo-Christian writings (16-29). He concludes the whole work with a *peroratio* which restates the call to conversion.

---

21 *Ecclesiastical History* IV.xx.1 and xxiv.1.

22 D.Good, 'Rhetoric and Wisdom in Theophilus of Antioch', *Anglican Theological Review* 73 (1991): 323 and 324.

At first sight Theophilus displays what would seem to be the end result of a quality education. He writes at length on pagan histories (2.1), comments on and quotes from various philosophers, among them the Stoics (2.4), Plato (ibid. - see below - and 3.7),[23] and tragedians and poets, Aristophanes (2.7), Sophocles, Euripides, Menander, Thestius (2.8), Sibyl (2.9; 31), Aeschylus, Pindar, Archilochus, Dionysius, Simonides and others as confirming the prophets of the Old Testament on questions of righteousness, judgement, punishment and providence (2.37-38), Herodotus, Thucydides, Pythagoras, Epicurus, Socrates and Hesiod (3.2).

At 2.4 Theophilus had spoken of Stoics who clearly deny the existence of God but who declare that if God does exist he is not providential. This cannot be an accurate reflection of majority Stoic opinion. He then points to other Stoics who allegedly regard the coming into existence of all things as spontaneous and nature as eternal (with no need for divine providence), and others again who regard God as the individual conscience or the universal spirit. He then acknowledges that Plato and his followers, on the other hand, portray God properly as uncreated and as both Father and Maker (alluding to but not quoting directly *Timaeus* 28c). They also, however, he goes on to say, speak of uncreated matter as God and as, with God, both coeval and immutable. Therefore this God cannot, he argues, be the Maker of the universe for they have not demonstrated his unique sovereignty. God's power must be that to create out of nothing and whatever and however God chooses. Plato has something of the truth, to be sure, but not enough.

He refers to the founding of Carthage from Tyre (3.22) and offers a long chronology of Roman history from Romulus to Marcus Aurelius. All this he does to demonstrate that Moses is older than Saturn and therefore both more reliable and more authentic. All this seems erudite and sound. Yet, as Grant claims, much of his 'learning' is a litany of commonplaces, much is taken from existing anthologies and handbooks, but much is also in error. Theophilus acknowledges openly his dependence on the theogonic language of Hesiod and others (particularly the Stoics) - rather than on more usual 'Christian' terminology - in the articulation of his own theogony, intended primarily to supply a Christian counterpart to the pagan versions. Such practices were not unusual as Christian apologists sought to explicate the Christian Gospel in language readily comprehensible to pagans.

Theophilus's work reflects several doxographical traditions (2.4 and 3.2-8). There are any number of views on the level of Theophilus' classical education and knowledge. Some, like Grant, question Theophilus' knowledge of philosophy, while others are keen to point out this Father's adroit use of it. McVey, for example, acknowledges the electicism of Theophilus (quite standard in the second century)

---

23 Theophilus cites Plato, *Timaeus* 28c3-4 at 2.4, 'Now to discover the Maker and Father of this Universe were a task indeed' to demonstrate God as uncreated (though he also criticises him for maintaining that matter is also uncreated and therefore implying that God is not the Creator) and *Meno* 99e at 3.7, 'Virtue is obtained by divine dispensation only and not by nature or teaching', to argue that truth is given only by divine revelation.

but argues that his thought is dominated by Stoic notions of reality.[24] Yet he does not slavishly follow the Stoics and is keen to differentiate himself from them, arguing, for example, against Stoic allegorising. But his basic presuppositions and lines of argument are Stoic and he is 'clearly intent on reading many Stoic notions of genesis into the biblical book of Genesis'. At 1.12, in his explanation of the name of Christians, he employs the Stoic image of the athlete being prepared with anointing. At 2.15 he reflects on the ordered arrangement of the heavens which almost certainly reflects the Stoic notion of an ordered life conforming to nature. Yet he also challenges the alleged inadequacies of the Greek philosophers' views on creation and 'is determined to drive a wedge between the Greek mythopoetic tradition and Greek philosophy especially on the question of cosmogony'. For Theophilus, however, in the end there can be no compromise with pagan thought. The antiquity of Christianity at the very least assures this. Christianity and pagan thought stand indisputably opposed.

At 1.11, having in chapters 9 and 10 declared that pagan gods were all once human beings and are all but idols and human creations (as witness the testimony of 'your' poets), Theophilus declares that he would rather honour the king (the emperor) than the pagan gods, not worshipping but praying for him. The king, he says, is made by the living and true God. The king is not to be worshipped but rather to be reverenced with lawful honour. He is not a god but is appointed by God. He is not to be worshipped but to judge justly. Theophilus employs the language of *1 Corinthians* 9.17 when he says that the king is entrusted with a particular stewardship by God. As he recognises no other king but himself - for 'king' is his name alone - so God recognises no other God. Worship must be given to God alone. Honour the king, advises Theophilus, employing the language of *1 Peter* 2.17, be subject to him, pray for him with a loyal mind. For by this will one execute the will of God. Here Theophilus also directly quotes *Proverbs* 24.21 ('Honour both God and king'). At 3.14 Theophilus refers to *Romans* 13.1-3 and *1 Timothy* 2.1-2 which enjoin subordination to principalities and powers and prayer for these that one might lead a quiet and tranquil life. Subordination to authority must happen even where that authority is hostile and persecuting. Theophilus clearly accepts the reality and the legitimacy of imperial government but only as it is placed under the absolute sovereignty of God.

Asia Minor

In 133 BCE the kingdom of Pergamum under Attalus III fell into Roman hands and became the cornerstone of Roman rule in Asia Minor. Romanisation proper, with civic institutions modelled largely on those found at Rome itself, was for the most part confined to colonies established in those regions not much affected to that point by significant contact with the Greco-Roman world. Where such previous

---

24 K.E.McVey, 'The use of Stoic Cosmogony in Theophilus of Antioch's Hexaemeron', in M.S.Burrows and P. Rorem (eds), *Biblical Hermeneutics in Historical Perspective: Studies in Honor of Karlfried Froelich on His Sixtieth Birthday*. (Grand Rapids, 1991), p. 58.

contact was greater and prosperity more evident, however, the development of local autonomy, certainly under Augustus, was also greater. The new power of the provinces brought with it, however, new restrictions. Trajan and Antoninus Pius restricted the formation of societies and a shift in power took place from the Hellenic *demos* to a wealthy few. The rule of both Marcus Aurelius (who was mostly preoccupied with the Danubian provinces) and Commodus little affected Asia Minor but the region's support for Pescennius Niger against Septimius Severus in 191-3 brought war to the area for the first time since the beginning of the Augustan period.

I have determined to treat the Fathers of Asia Minor, particularly those associated with Antioch, Smyrna and Sardis, as a group while recognising that there are some dangers in so doing. Norris comments that 'we should avoid a concept as broad as an "Asia Minor Theology"'.[25]

Polycarp of Smyrna: *To the Philippians*

The city of Smyrna lay on the coast of Asia Minor 35 miles to the north of Ephesus on the border between Aeolis and Ionia. It served as the terminus of a major route leading into the interior through the Hermus Valley beyond Sardis. By the first century BCE Cicero could describe it as one of the most flourishing towns of Asia, and Strabo the first of the Ionian cities, the 'ornament of Asia'. The imperial cult flourished in Smyrna.

Polycarp was bishop of Smyrna in the mid second century. He was executed at the age of 86 in 155 during the proconsulship of Statius Quadratus. Eusebius calls him a 'companion' of the apostles and an 'apostolic man'.[26] Irenaeus says that he was appointed to the see by the apostles themselves and was the author of a number of letters known.[27] He apparently claimed to have conversed with John, either the apostle or the Evangelist, and Irenaeus in turn claimed to have heard Polycarp preach.[28] He is also said to have discussed in Rome the question of the dating of Easter with the local bishop Anicetus.[29] He was an avowed anti-Marcionite, allegedly calling the arch-heretic 'the first-born of Satan' to his face.[30] Though he did not actively seek or provoke conflict with the Roman authorities he was arrested and eventually martyred. He became a model for those opposed to the confrontational style of Ignatius. He refused at his trial to swear by the genius of the emperor - an account of his trial is contained in the *Martyrdom of Polycarp* - and was executed. He was, in his younger days as bishop, the recipient of one of Ignatius' letters.

---

25 F.W.Norris, 'Ignatius, Polycarp, and 1 Clement: Walter Bauer Reconsidered', *Vigiliae Christianae* 30 (1976): 43, note 68.

26 *Ecclesiastical History* III.xxxvi.1 and 10.

27 In Eusebius, *EH* IV.xiv.3.

28 Ibid., IV.xiv.3 and V.xx.4f.

29 Ibid., IV.xiv.1.

30 Ibid. IV.xiv.7.

His brief, paraenetic and admonitory letter to the Philippians - possibly written not long after Ignatius' martyrdom[31] - betrays no explicit engagement with the culture of the famous city of which he was the bishop. Yet the style of the letter is not untouched by contemporary form or style. Schoedel comments that 'the modern study of the Hellenistic letter shows that the expression of joy in *Philippians* 1.1 [sc. 'I rejoice greatly with you in our Lord Jesus Christ that'] represents a standard device for making the transition from the address to the body of the letter'.[32] There is no complete Greek version, the only complete text being one in Latin.[33] Given that chapter 9 would appear to suggest that Ignatius of Antioch was dead at the time of writing and chapter 13 that he was not has led some commentators to the positing of two original letters. Both Harrison and Berding support the existence of two unrelated letters and they are, in my view, quite right. The purpose of the first letter (chapter 13 with the possible addition of 14), to act as a covering letter for a collection of Ignatius' letters, is inconsistent with the express purpose of the second letter (chapters 1-12), some teaching on righteousness at the request of the Philippians (3,1). The reference in chapter 13 to Ignatius can be found only in a Latin version and may of course be the result of translation problems.[34]

The letter also shows clear signs of the influence of the conventions of rhetoric, particularly in its transparent imitation of Paul.[35] Chapters 1 and 2 comprise an *exordium* in which Polycarp seeks the goodwill of his readers by reference to their charity and faithfulness and by his exhortation to a continuation of this underpinned by their hope in the resurrection and the Lord's teaching on mercy. Chapter 3 comprises a brief *narratio* in which Polycarp explains his purpose in writing - 'I write to you about righteousness, not at my own instance, but because you first invited me' (3,1) - and the letter's primary focus on the command on righteousness as ethical living. Chapters 4 to 9 comprise the *probatio* which consists of arguments for righteousness and faithfulness in the face of heresy (docetism, see chapter 7) primarily drawn from scripture and the examples of Christ himself (8) and the martyrs (9). Chapter 10 begins the *peroratio* with an exhortation to perseverance in good works and 11 with the example of unrighteousness in an erring member. Chapter 12 comprises

---

31 P.N.Harrison, *Polycarp's Two Epistles to the Philippians* (Cambridge, 1936), suggests a date c. 135, while K.Berding, *Polycarp and Paul* (Leiden, 2002), pp. 17f., suggests one c. 120.The later date would suit a work directed in part at least against Marcion while I simply do not find the arguments, such as they are, for the earlier convincing. It does not, for our purposes, actually matter.

32 W.R.Schoedel, 'Polycarp's witness to Ignatius of Antioch', *Vigiliae Christianae* 41 (1987): 5.

33 Chapters 10-12 and 14 are only found in a Latin manuscript.

34 It speaks of those who 'are' with Ignatius.

35 See Berding, *Polycarp and Paul*, pp. 127-141, where he considers in detail Polycarp's alleged imitation of the Apostle and quotes Quintilian, *The Institutes* 10.2.1, who declared that 'it is expedient to imitate whatever has been invented with success'. In the ancient world, and particularly in the second century CE, imitation was not only the sincerest form of flattery but a positive virtue in the convention of rhetoric.

for the most part further exhortations to righteousness in dealing with others and a prayer which makes clear that true righteousness is a gift from God. At 12,1 where Polycarp declares

> 'For I am confident that you are well versed in the scriptures, and from you nothing is hid; but to me this is not granted'.

what we see is not simply an example of his genuine humility (nor evidence of any true lack of knowledge of the scriptures) but rather a classic rhetorical device by way of a traditional 'humility statement'. Chapters 13 and 14 provide a conventional ending to the letter and have no rhetorical significance. The concept of two letters (13-14 and 1-12) would suit the notion of a rhetorical framework because chapter 12 provides a natural end for such a piece while 13 at least (the jury must forever be out on just where 14 fits!) sits awkwardly within such.

His references to a love of money as the beginning of all evil (4,1) may well be no more than a biblical commonplace and may betray no necessary socio-political stance although it is perhaps the major theme of the letter. He repeats this condemnation of greed at 2,2; 4,3; 5,2 and 6,1. That of idolatry at 11,2, and its linkage there to greed, may also be no more than a commonplace and more likely merely made in passing. At 11,1 Polycarp urges that Valens remember his 'place'.[36] At 9,2 he speaks of the martyrs, like Paul, being in 'the place which is their due'. This is very much in the tradition of Cyprian and others for whom the social structures of the surrounding culture and society are not to be cast aside easily upon entry into the church and with a Stoic view of each person needing to know and inhabit his place in the way things are. While parallels to these concerns - particularly those to do with greed threatening the very fabric and stability of the community - may be found in pagan literature - Plato, Aristotle, Theophrastus, Isocrates, Polybius and the Stoics, for example - they are also found in Jewish apocalyptic. Polycarp's principal concern is, maintains Maier, 'sectarian purity' and his paraenesis 'presents a means of constituting the self in a way that promotes strong community boundaries'. His use of a number of forms in the letter - heroic examples to underscore a particular community ethos, the recollection of past teachers (like Paul), lists of virtues and vices, and the language of exhortation itself - 'are all characteristic of the typical Greco-Roman letter of advice or exhortation'.

His direction to the Philippians to pray for the emperors at 12,3, for potentates, and for princes - and for persecutors and enemies of the Cross - are again probably commonplaces. They represent no more than a traditional biblical and patristic respect for civil authority as that appointed of God, and is to be expected of someone who did not seek to provoke conflict with the government. It is unusual that this bishop, living and exercising his ministry in a city which was proud of its role as a centre for the imperial cult, makes no mention of this. Yet, while Polycarp does point to the dangers of idolatry, his major concern is to encourage his co-religionists, to put before

---

36 Here '*locus*' as a translation of the Greek *topos*.

them the hope of the Gospel, to encourage virtue, mutual care, and perseverance in the face of possible persecution, and above all, to dissuade the wealthier Christians, from among whom come the community's leaders, from pursuing the regular desires of their pagan counterparts, viz., wealth and status. Polycarp is little concerned with heresy - though chapter 7 may be an attack on Marcion or on docetists in general - and his major fear is the attraction of the world for the faithful.

This paraenetic piece is focused, personally, scripturally-based (though there is little or no detailed exegesis or exposition of particular texts), and christo-centric. It clearly ties theology to ethics and an incarnational theology in particular (which repudiates docetism above all) to the pursuit of righteousness. There is virtually no engagement with Greco-Roman philosophy and the writing itself intended for a largely uneducated Christian audience.

Melito of Sardis: *Apology* and *Peri Pascha*

Sardis, situated 45 miles to the east of Smyrna in the Hermus River valley, was traditionally the capital of Lydia. A Jewish community was evident in the city and Josephus speaks of their privileges.[37] A number of Jews were members of the city council and the city possessed the largest synagogue yet discovered, one which seated at least a thousand persons. The very hellenised Jews of Sardis were powerful and well integrated into Sardian society. Their powerful position throughout Asia Minor and their wealth and influence made it almost certain that there would be constant strife between Jews and Christians in the province.

We know little of Melito, who is to be placed in the second half of the second century CE, save what we read in Eusebius' *Ecclesiastical History*. That he was well regarded, if indeed not revered by his co-religionists in his time and beyond it, is not, however, in question. Eusebius quotes Polycrates of Ephesus to the effect that Melito was a eunuch (that is, unmarried) and that 'he lived as a citizen entirely in the Holy Spirit'.[38] He was a prolific writer - Eusebius names many works now lost to us[39] - and his extant works include the *Apology* (part extant in Eusebius) - which Grant places immediately after the revolt of Avidius Cassius in 175-6 - and the homily *Peri Pascha* listed by Eusebius but also available independently of the Eusebeian reference.

At *Ecclesiastical History* v.xxvi.5 Eusebius quotes at length from the *Apology* by Melito concerning the Roman Empire. Melito declares to Marcus Aurelius that a present wave of persecution raging through Asia by (imperial) decree has not happened previously. He states that if it is the wish of the emperor that such actions take place

37 *Antiquities* 14.295f. and 16.171.

38 *Ecclesiastical History* V.xxiv.5. L.H.Cohick, *The Peri Pascha attributed to Melito of Sardis: setting, purpose and sources* (Providence, 2000), 13f., points out, as part of her questioning of the authorship of our *PP* by the bishop of Sardis, that Polycrates does not name his Melito as a bishop as he does others in his names in the same passage.

39 Ibid., IV.xxvi.1f..

then he can only believe that it is rightly done, given that no righteous emperor would condone an unrighteous action. Zuntz describes Melito as demonstrating here a 'respectful devotion and even adulation' towards the emperor. Melito asks only that Marcus Aurelius see for himself whether those who are condemned are done so rightly. If the emperor has not in fact instigated this action, then Melito petitions that he protect Christians. He continues with the advice to the emperor that Christianity first arose among the 'barbarians' but began to flower during the reign of Augustus. It became, he says, an omen for the good of the Empire for from that time the power of the Romans became great and splendid. He urges the emperor to protect this 'philosophy' and to nourish it as did the emperor's predecessors. In the time of Augustus, which for Melito's argument sets a useful precedent, Christianity met no evil but only good and glorious responses. Only in the times of Nero and Domitian were emperors persuaded to slander Christian teaching and to institute false charges against the faithful. But this ignorance was corrected by the emperor's (Antonine) predecessors, who rebuked those who sought to harm Christians. He adduces as evidence of this Hadrian's letter to the proconsul Fundanus and that of Antoninus Pius - when the present emperor shared 'in the rule of the world' - to the cities of Asia. He urges Marcus to follow suit. His willingness to accept the legitimacy of the emperor's rule is evident even if his account of events is somewhat flawed or tainted. The fragmentary nature of our acquaintance with this work, however, does not permit us to more than speculate as to the influences which were brought to bear upon its formation.

The extant *Peri Pascha* was clearly written in the latter half of the second century. Hall gives a date of between 160 and 170 for the *Peri Pascha* of Melito spoken of by Eusebius but we cannot be sure, he says, that they are in fact the same work. Cohick indeed provides an extensive and persuasive argument which brings into question both the authorship of the non-Eusebian *Peri Pascha* and its provenance in Sardis itself.[40] Yet because in the end Cohick actually denies outright neither the question of an epsicopal authorship nor a Sardian provenance - merely that neither the Eusebian evidence nor that of the extant homily itself confirms either - we will need to leave the questions finally unanswered.[41] The (non-Eusebian?) *Peri Pascha*[42] is a sermon for the Easter celebration and its extravagant rhetorical forms are similar to the style of the 'Second Sophistic' which flourished in second century Asia.[43] While there is no question that it is a piece of Greek-style rhetoric it does not reflect the conventional

---

40 See L. Cohick, *The Peri Pascha attributed to Melito of Sardis: setting, purpose and sources* (Providence, 2000), pp. 12f., for the authorship question and 31f. for that on its provenance.

41 Final decisions on either question do not actually affect greatly the purpose of my present work.

42 That is, the one for which we have a complete manuscript. My comment does not imply, however, that the two reference points, the Eusebian and the non-Eusebian, are not in fact to the one work.

43 W.Kinzig, 'The Greek Christian Writers', in S.E.Porter (ed.), *Handbook of Classical Rhetoric in the Hellenistic Period 330BC – AD 400* (Leiden, 1997), p. 643, maintains that

rhetorical structures of the time. It has, for example, no obvious *exordium*, *narratio*, or *peroratio*. Its form is almost entirely one of *proofs* with the principal witness that of scripture. But its style is rhetorical with its employment of rhetorical questions, anaphora, and antitheses. Its use of antitheses, for example, in chapters 2 to 8 and 49 to 50 conform very much to the first *topos* listed by Aristotle.[44] While the author quotes freely from the Old Testament, he makes only allusions to passages from the New. This would confirm a relatively early date. The work is clearly anti-Marcionite and possibly owes a debt of sorts to Jewish paschal traditions. Its stridently anti-Jewish tone - see chapters 72 to 79, for example (at 72, 505, Israel is held directly responsible for the crucifixion of Christ) - would sit well with tensions experienced between the Christian community at Sardis and the well-established and highly integrated Jewish one. Stewart-Sykes argues that Melito was in fact himself Jewish by birth and that this in part explains his strong polemic. 'That Christianity is a true Judaism is central to Melito's approach to Scripture.'[45] Melito in part 'defines his Christianity over and against a dominant Judaism', the basis for which position he finds in John's Gospel. Cohick, however, suggests that the *Peri Pascha* is not intended as anti-Jewish polemic but is in fact a reflection of an intra-Christian debate over Marcionitism and simply employs the language of 'Jewishness' to make a particular point.[46] This is in part argued on the basis that Melito in this work never actually refers to the 'Jews' as such but only ever to 'Israel', suggesting a non-contemporary or at least non-specific reference.

At *Peri Pascha* 92 Melito interprets Pilate's washing of his hands at the trial of Jesus as his distancing himself from, even repudiating, the actions of the Jews in killing Jesus. This continues a tradition evident first in John's Gospel and while it is concerned more to condemn Israel than to suggest a particularly pro-Roman stance it does reflect a desire on the part of Melito to imply some measure of civic loyalty. The passages from the *Apology* and the *Peri Pascha*, while not suggesting an absolute commitment to the Roman state on the part of their author/s(?), do suggest a desire at the very least to not be seen as hostile. It suggests a broad acceptance of the reality of Roman power and governance - quite common among Roman subjects in the East - with the expectation only that this power and governing will be exercised with justice, particularly towards the Christians.

---

the *Peri Pascha* has 'all the hallmarks of "Asianism" and provides a splendid example of the gradual Christianization of the γενος επιδεικτικον'.

44 *Rhetorica* 2.1397a.

45 A. Stewart-Sykes, 'Melito's Anti-Judaism', *JECS* 5 (1997): 273.

46 L. Cohick, 'Melito of Sardis' PERI PASCHA and its "Israel"', *HTR* 91 (1998): 372. In her later book Cohick describes Stewart-Sykes arguments that Melito was a convert from Judaism simply 'unconvincing' (*The Peri Pascha*, p. 14).

Justin Martyr: the *Apologies* and the *Dialogue with Trypho*

Justin Martyr was born into a pagan family[47] before the end of the first century CE in Flavia Neapolis in Syrian Palestine as he himself tells us (*1 Apology* 1). He was, he also tells us, a gentile and uncircumcised and had no knowledge of Judaism or the Prophets until he had gained adulthood. He was, as a result of this, dependent for his work on a Greek version of the Old Testament, but also demonstrates an acquaintance with Jewish practices, beliefs, exegesis and sects, reflecting perhaps some Jewish-Christian contact notwithstanding the general disengagement of these communities after 135. He tells us in the *Dialogue with Trypho* that he was successively the student of a Stoic teacher, a Peripatetic, a Pythagorean (for whom he retained the highest regard but who thought Justin ill-equipped or at least ill-prepared for advanced philosophical study) and a Platonist. He elsewhere condemns both the Cynics for an indifference incompatible with a seeking after truth (*2 Apology* 3) and the Epicureans presumably for their pursuit of pleasure (*2 Apology* 15). He was, according to his own account, converted to Christianity in Ephesus by a person who first steered him towards the Hebrew prophets. In time he himself became an itinerant teacher, arriving in Rome sometime during the last years of the reign of Antoninus Pius. He there established a school where his pupils included his best-known disciple, Tatian. In 165 CE, by order of the Prefect Junius Rusticus, he was martyred.[48]

Both of his *Apologies*, which most probably formed a single work with the *Second* a later appendix or supplement to the First and itself occasioned by the death by martyrdom of Ptolemaeus and Lucius under the Prefect Urbicus (*2 Apology* 2,9f.*)*, were written in Rome after 150. The *Dialogue*, though set in Ephesus during the Jewish War of 132-5 (*Dialogue* 1,3), was also probably written in Rome between 155 and 160; it was probably addressed primarily to a non-Christian Gentile audience at Rome favourably disposed towards Judaism and Christianity. These three works, the only extant ones universally accepted as written by Justin, contain significant evidence of an engagement with the surrounding society and culture. Keresztes challenges the traditional view of the two Apologies as apologies in either the 'post-classical and ecclesiastical [sense'], or even 'in the classical rhetorical sense'. At *2 Apology* 15 Justin asks that if the present writing be approved by the Senate others will be converted, presumably to the Christian faith. 'For this end alone did we', he says, 'compose this treatise.' Now what we have here is then used to argue that the *Apologies* are probably an example of protreptic rhetoric addressed formally to the emperor and to the senate. Yet the primary purpose of the work/s is to ask the Roman authorities to modify, in accordance with justice, the treatment meted out to Christians in Asia, not to convert those authorities. Thus, notwithstanding Justin's statement about conversion at the end of the *Second Apology*, this is not the primary intention of the work. It remains an apologetic piece, or set of pieces, intended to

47 His father's name, Priscus, is Roman, his grandfather's, Bacchius, Greek.

48 See the *Martyrium S. Justini et Sociorum*.

explicate the Christian faith and thus secure for Christians fair treatment before the law as a genuine philosophy.

The *Dialogue* is the alleged record of a debate, probably influenced in style by the Platonic model, between Justin, the Jew Trypho and some companions of the latter.[49] It is traditionally regarded as a protreptic piece,[50] possibly based on the Platonic dialogue model,[51] comprising an introduction, which includes an account of Justin's own conversion (1-10); a debate on the Mosaic law (11-31); a lengthy discussion on Jesus Christ as the fulfilment of Old Testament prophecies (this makes up the bulk of the work) (32-120); and a discussion on the conversion of gentiles (121-142). Unlike many of the other Apostolic Fathers and Apologists, Justin is perhaps less concerned with the order and harmony of society than with the order and harmony of truth.

There are a number of the classic elements of the rhetorical format present in Justin's work. In the *First Apology* chapters 1 and 2 comprise an *exordium* in which Justin seeks to cultivate the goodwill of the emperors, describing them as pious, philosophers, guardians of justice, and lovers of learning. In chapters 3 and 4 he provides a *narratio* in which he outlines the unjust condemnation of the Christians by the Roman authorities. Chapters 5 to 64 comprise his *probatio*. In chapter 14 he even recognises the common philosophical mistrust of rhetoric when he declares,

> 'But lest we should seem to be reasoning sophistically, we consider it right,before giving you the promised explanation [to persuade readers to the truth of Christian claims], to cite a few precepts given by Christ himself ... he was no sophist, but his Word was the power of God'.

At chapter 19, in his argument for the resurrection of the dead, he employs a rhetorical enthymeme, arguing from the basis not of provable fact but of probability. At chapter 23 he outlines his three major theses, that Christian doctrine as taught by Christ and the prophets is true and more ancient than Greek thought, that Jesus is the only proper Son of God, and that pre-Christian claims by demons to Christian truth derive from fabrications. The first is argued or 'proved' from chapters 24 to 29, the second from 30 to 53, and the third from 54 to 64. Chapters 65 to 68 comprise a *peroratio* in which Justin recapitulates his basic argument and offers an emotional appeal to the emperors to hear his plea. The *Second Apology* is likewise comprised of an *exordium* (chapter1), *narratio* (2), *probatio* (3 - 13) and *peroratio* (14 - 15). The *Dialogue* has

---

49 See the very full discussion of this writing in T.Rajak, 'Talking at Trypho: Christian Apologetic as Anti-Judaism in Justin's *Dialogue with Trypho the Jew*', in *Apologetics in the Roman Empire*, pp. 59-80.

50 Rajak's argument, ibid., 75f., that it is less likely that Justin in *Trypho* was seeking the conversion of pagan Gentiles or Jews, than that it had 'a principally Christian readership' is supported by F. Young, 'Greek Apologists of the Second Century', in *Apologetics in the Roman Empire*, p. 84 .

51 Ibid., 63, where Rajak claims that Justin at the beginning of the dialogue 'signals that his presentation is borrowed from Plato'.

no obvious *exordium* but does possess a lengthy set of *proofs*, and a *peroratio* by way of an exhortation to conversion.

Justin's engagement with the higher learning of his own day was significant. For Justin, who apparently wore the philosopher's pallium (*Dialogue* 1), there was perhaps no clear distinction in practice between theology and philosophy.[52] There was for him but one true and perfect philosophy revealed in Jesus Christ. Barnard questions, however, whether Justin could be said to have come to terms with contemporary philosophy and culture, though not all scholars would agree. Edwards, for example, points to obvious affinities between Justin and his contemporary, Numenius of Apamea; to their Stoic-tinctured Platonism, their 'allegiance to a more spiritual doctrine' when discussing aspects of divinity, and their common use of 'dialogue as an instrument for the discovery of truth'. Both reflect the manner of Plato's dialogues and both privilege knowledge as a term of the highest praise. Justin is, like Numenius, an 'eclectic' only in the sense that he 'trusts no dogmas'. He 'knew something of the Stoic logos and the seeds that it implanted' (see below for a discussion of Justin's understanding of the logos) but the Platonist flavour and tendency of at least some of his thought is also clear. At *Dialogue* 127 where he says that

> 'the ineffable Father and Lord of all … remains in his own place. … He is not moved or confined to a spot in the whole world',

he appears to accept a version of the Aristotelian notion of God as the Unmoved Mover, as unknowable and transcendent cause.

In chapter 3 of the *Dialogue* Justin declares that 'God is discernible to the mind alone, as Plato says, and I believe him'. This is Tertullian's 'God of the philosophers' - utterly transcendent and separated from the world of sense - but it is not as far from the God of the Jews and Christians as that one of many of the other schools. From chapters 3 to 8, where Justin relates the manner of his conversion, he does first in relation to Plato's doctrine of the soul, a major point of contention between the Fathers and Plato: Justin argues initially, alongside Plato, that the pure soul which has an affinity to God can thereby see God (*Phaedo* 66a) - God as the 'pure, absolute essence of things' – to which his teacher replies that souls neither see God, nor for that matter transmigrate in other bodies (4). Justin then begins to accept that the soul is not in its nature immortal and, interestingly, employs Plato's argument at *Timaeus* 41a that God's will alone gives death and dissolution to created things (5). From the middle of the 5th chapter Justin himself argues that 'all things which exist apart from God, or will at any time exist, have the nature of decay and as such may be blotted out and cease to exist [should God so will]; for God alone is unbegotten and incorruptible [by nature], and therefore He is God while all other things beside him are created and corruptible'. His argument is of course that therefore souls both die and are punished as he goes on to say. For if, he continues, other entities were

52 At 1 *Apology* 3 Justin quotes Plato (*Rep.* 5.18) to the effect that rulers should rule in a manner consistent with piety and philosophy.

unbegotten they would be similar or equal to the Unbegotten (and thereby they would be themselves God). He then accepts the need to 'take your stand on one Unbegotten and [to] say that this is the Cause of all'. He then asks how this reality seems to have escaped the observation of philosophers like Plato and Pythagoras, 'those wise men who have been as a wall and fortress of philosophy to us'. By 'us' he probably means the Platonists (his pre-conversion persona). Osborn suggests that there may well be sarcasm in Justin's question but in my view such is unnecessary. His comment that the Christian view of God is more consistent with the notion of a transcendent first cause than the polytheism of the philosophers (even of Plato and Pythagoras) comes nearer to the mark. For Justin, Plato is close but not close enough; he is near the truth but cannot see the truth implications of his own teachings. Whether Plato or Pythagoras had a view of the sole transcendent first cause is of no interest to the old man; he simply wishes to demonstrate that whatever life the soul has is not innate to it but derives from God alone (6.1). And truth in any case, he says, comes from the prophets alone (7.1).

Justin is even more positive towards Plato and philosophy than is, for example, Minucius Felix and certainly in another world from Tertullian. In the *First Apology* he addresses the two emperors - the formal recipients of his treatise - as 'philosophers' (1), as truly pious and philosophical (2), and quotes Plato ('one of the ancients') to the effect that philosophising is critical to the health of the state (*Republic* 5.473d).

In chapter 5 he speaks approvingly of Socrates, who through true reason and examination sought to expose the demons and deliver men from their snare. For this they [sc. the demons] compassed his conviction and death (as an atheist and as one 'who introduced new divinities') and 'in our case they [sc. demons] display a similar activity'. In chapter 8 he cites Plato as support for the concept of the punishment of the wicked (which carries with it notions of responsibility and accountability) against the claims of those who advocate a notion of a governing fate. In chapter 18 his words,

> 'the death common to all, which, if it issued in insensibility, would be a godsend to the wicked. But since sensation remains to all who ever lived. ... ' (18,1),

look remarkably like those of Plato in the *Phaedo*,

> 'if death were an escape from everything, it would be a boon to the wicked. ... But now, since the soul is seen to be immortal....'(107c).

Justin then asks the emperors why, when the opinions of various of 'your authors' are raised in support of the Christian view of such matters - and these 'authors' include Pythagoras and Plato - they do not grant the same favours as they do to these also to the Christians 'who not less but more firmly than they believe in God?'

In chapter 20 Justin alludes to *Timaeus* 28c3-4 when he says that 'while we say that all things have been produced and arranged into a world by God, we shall seem to utter the doctrine of Plato'.. He argues also that the Christian belief that the souls of the wicked are endowed with sensation and are punished, while the good are sent to a blessed existence, is also that of the poets and philosophers (among whom Plato must have been to the forefront of his mind). At chapter 23, however, he makes the point that the truth of Christian teaching as delivered by Christ and the prophets is alone true, is older than all the writers who have ever existed, and is true not because Christians say the same things as do these other writers but because they are true in themselves. At 28,3-4 Justin declares that

> 'In the beginning [God] made the human race with the power of thought and of choosing the truth and doing right, so that all people are without excuse before God; for they have been born rational and contemplative'.

This notion is consistent with the Platonic notion of freewill and at chapter 44 Justin quotes Plato when he says that 'the blame is his who chooses, and God is blameless (*Republic* 617e) though he adds that the Athenian had taken this from Moses. He continues,

> 'And whatever both philosophers and poets have said concerning the immortality of the soul, or punishments after death, or contemplation of things heavenly, or doctrines of like kind, they have received such from the prophets as they have been enabled to understand and interpret these things'.

In chapter 46 he says that

> 'the Word of whom every race of men were partakers; and those who lived reasonably (*meta logou*) are Christians, even though they have been thought atheists; Socrates and Heraclitus and men like them … Abraham ….'.

At 59,1 he comments further, alluding again to *Timaeus* 28c, that

> 'from our teachers (the prophets) Plato borrowed his statement that God, having altered matter which was shapeless, made the world'.

Here, of course, there is a suggestion of a dualism on the part of Justin and the faint hint of the pre-existence of matter. Then, at 60.1, he refers to 'a physiological discussion concerning the Son of God' at *Timaeus* 36c - Justin simply assumes that Plato is speaking of the Second Person of the Trinity - where the philosopher says that '[God] placed him crosswise in the universe', which he borrowed from Moses' account in *Numbers* 21.8 of the bronze serpent. This reference, Justin says, Plato clearly misunderstood, confusing an obvious reference to a figure of the Cross with a crosswise placement. His reading of the *Timaeus* passage is clearly confused with that from the pseudo-Platonic *Epistle* 2.312e for he goes on to conclude that here - he means the latter reference - Plato also speaks of the 'third' power which, he says, is that Spirit which Moses said 'moved over the waters' (*Genesis* 1.2). Thus, Justin says, Plato assigns second place to the Logos (placed crosswise in the universe) which is with God, and the third to the Spirit. Finally, Justin comments that

> 'It is not, then, that we hold the same opinions as others, but that all speak in imitation of ours'.

Plato may be right, despite himself, but he scarcely could have known it and gained the truth in any case from the true believers.

In the *Second Apology* Justin again begins with a positive assessment of Socrates whose saying in the *Republic* that 'a man must in no wise be honoured before the truth' (595c) is a most admirable one (3). In chapter 10, the critical one for our purposes here, Justin compares Socrates (and thereby Plato) and Christ. He begins by pointing out that

> 'Our doctrines, then, appear to be greater than all human teaching' (10.1). This is so because Christ became (for us) 'the whole rational being, body, reason, and soul'. 'For whatever either lawgivers or philosophers uttered well, they elaborated by finding and contemplating some part of the Word. But since they did not know the whole of the Word, which is Christ, they often contradicted themselves'.

Those who lived before Christ and tried to speak of these things by reason were brought before the courts for impiety and troublemaking. Socrates in this was more zealous even than most and was accused of crimes not unlike those alleged against Christians, of introducing new gods and of official atheism. He (rather Plato!) cast out from the ideal state the poet Homer in his endeavours to urge people to reject demons and the poets who act as their mouthpieces (*Republic* 595a-b) and at 10.6, in reference to *Timaeus* 28c3-4,

> 'exhorted [his hearers] to become acquainted with the God who was to them Unknown [shades of Paul at *Acts* 17.22ff.], by means of the investigation of Reason, saying, "that it is neither easy to find the Father and Maker of all, nor having found him, is it safe[53] to declare to all"'.[54]

Yet, he goes on, 'these things our Christ did through his own power [as God]. For no-one would die for the teachings of Socrates as they did and do for those of Christ. For in Christ, whom even Socrates knew partially, philosophers, scholars, working men and the simply uneducated have come to believe the truth. For Christ is a 'power of the ineffable Father' and not, like Socrates, 'the mere instrument of human reason'. Thus while Socrates (read 'Plato') has some sense of the truth he does not have it all but can probably be said to come closer than any others outside of the faith. This is classic apologetic technique, whereby Justin articulates and defends the faith by showing that it is not contrary to the traditional teaching so much as it is both an improvement on it and, in fact, prior to it.

---

53 'Safe' rather than 'possible' as in the original of Plato.

54 Daniélou, *Gospel Message and Hellenistic Culture*, p. 108 suggests that this wording of *Timaeus* 28c3-4 is close to that of Albinus [Alcinous] at *Didask.* 27.1.

At 12,1 Justin makes clear that it was as a Platonist that he first became aware of the virtue of the Christians. But he is at pains to point out that he is one no longer, whatever his previous (and present?) affinity with them. At 13,1 he declares that

> 'I confess that I both boast and with all my strength strive to be found a Christian; not because the teachings of Plato are different from those of Christ, but because they are not in all respects similar, as neither are those of the others, Stoics, and poets, and historians. For each person spoke well in proportion to the share he had of the spermatic word ... whatever things were rightly said among all persons are the property of us Christians ... all the writers were able to see realities darkly through the sowing of the implanted word that was in them'.

Justin Martyr, at *First Apology* 60.6-7, quotes from the last part of *Epistle* 2.312e,

> '[and God gave] the third around the third',

following a discussion of *Timaeus* 36c and the concept of the Son being placed 'crosswise' in the universe – which Justin believes Plato misunderstood for the Cross – and of the Spirit. This third entity Plato identifies, says Justin, with the 'Spirit of God moving over the waters' spoken of by Moses.[55]

Justin is also clearly indebted to Stoicism. Although he does not fully embrace the Stoic distinction between the *logos endiathetos* and the *logos prophorikos* he comes close to so doing.[56] Justin understands, through the doctrine of the spermatic logos, many figures of the pre-Christian past to have been effectively Christians before Christ; in this category he includes Socrates (Justin's hero as a martyr to truth), Heraclitus, Abraham and Plato as those who partake of or live with the Word/reason (1 *Apology* 46). Yet of this doctrine the philosophers have merely the shadow - they did not have the whole of the Word - while Christians have, in Christ - 'the whole rational being' - the reality (2 *Apology* 10). Justin's notion that the human person lies at the centre of creation is both biblical and Stoic. The Stoic doctrine of the *pneuma*, as the principle of life in humankind and the universe, also exercises its influence on Justin. After Justin Greek philosophy could be seen by Christians as as much a preparation for the Gospel as Judaism had always been seen. He declares at 1 *Apology* 20,

> 'If, therefore, on some points we teach the same things as the poets and philosophers whom you honour, and on other points are fuller and more divine in our teaching, and if we alone afford proof of what we assert, why are we unjustly hated more than all others?'

He then goes to assert, as examples, the coherence of the Christian view of creation with that of Plato, and that of the end of the world with that of the Stoics. This

---

55 See N. Hyldahl, *Philosophie und Christentum: Eine Interpretation der Einleitung zum Dialog Justins*. (Kopenhagen, 1966), 276-7.

56 Rajak, 'Talking at Trypho', 65, argues that Justin's use of the term *logos* in the *Trypho* 'is in the Philonic or Johannine tradition, the word of God, and not Platonic'.

perhaps is Justin's greatest contribution to Christian thought and made possible the fuller entry of Christian thought into an engagement with the surrounding world than had been previously possible. Christianity was now intellectually equipped perhaps to take on the world.

At *1 Apology* 3 Justin employs Plato's *Republic* V.473d[57] to argue that justice should rule the Roman treatment of Christians. In chapter 11 Justin makes clear that Christian talk of a 'kingdom' is not of an earthly one but rather one which is 'with God'. Therefore, he implies, this hope does not equate necessarily with disloyalty to the Roman rule. At 17,1 Justin asserts that as good citizens Christians endeavour to pay their taxes both ordinary and extraordinary as required by Christ (*Matthew* 22, 17f.). At *2 Apology* 2, 1, passim, he speaks of the persecuting magistrates - with particular reference to the Urban Prefect (Lollius) Urbicus at Rome - as being incited against the Christians by evil spirits, this reference to the influence of demonic forces being a common theme in his writings. Justin, then, wishes to portray Christians as law-abiding citizens who will require even less of the state than the law allows as their right, will pay their taxes as required, and who view action taken against them not as emanating necessarily from the viciousness of the state but from evil spirits (and the emperor's subordinates?). At I *Apology* 12,1 Justin declares that in the promotion of peace Christians, more than other persons, are the 'natural helpers and allies of the emperor'. This is so because Christians believe that both the good and the wicked will face the judgement of God for their contribution or their failure to contribute to peace. Given the attachment of the Roman mind to the virtues of peace and concord in this period, these are not insignificant claims. It is not only that Justin claims that Christian are peaceful and law-abiding but that they actively and prayerfully uphold and promote, along with their God, these particular Roman virtues. At 1,17,3 he declares, after noting the willingness of Christians to pay any taxes properly due the government, that while they worship God alone, they do acknowledge the emperors as kings and rulers of men in all other matters. 'In all things otherwise', he declares, 'we will gladly serve you'. This is, however, followed by what can only be described as an implied yet none-too-subtle threat to the emperor at 17,4. Should the emperor, Justin declares, ignore the prayers and open posture (sc. transparency) of the Christians, the loss will not be theirs but, by implication, his. For God will inflict eternal punishment according to the acts committed by the individual and require account from each person according to the power they have received from God. As Christ has said, at *Luke* 12,48, 'to whom God has given much, of him shall more be required' which saying comes in the context of the parable of the faithful and the unfaithful servants (*Luke* 12,35-40). In his rule the emperor is the servant of God and will be judged accordingly. Justin's meaning could not be clearer nor his confrontational style more pronounced.

---

57 'Unless either philosophers become kings in our states or those whom we now call kings and rulers take to the pursuit of philosophy seriously and adequately, and there is conjunction of these two things, political power and philosophic intelligence....there can be no cessation of troubles...for our states.'

At *1 Apology* 55,1f. Justin sees all around him the symbol of the Cross, for him a sign of power and particularly of Christ's power. He sees it in the instruments of power and the means of advance in all aspects of life. He sees it in the masts of ships traversing the seas, in ploughs furrowing the fields, in machinery tools, and, above all, in the form - standing erect and hands outstretched - which sets humankind apart from the non-human world. He sees it also in the Romans' own military banners and in the trophies 'with which all your military advances are made, using these as the insignia of your power and government'. These words, says Chadwick, show that for Justin the Church 'now belongs to the gentile world and to the Roman empire in particular' and, in turn, the world and the Empire to the Gospel. We find here, he says, a pre-Constantinian example of the presupposition of a Christian Empire.[58] At *2 Apology* 2,19, having, by implication, himself strongly condemned the judicial actions of the Urban Prefect (Lollius) Urbicus - in condemning the Christian teacher Ptolemaeus and his fellow believer Lucius - as unworthy of both the emperor Antoninus Pius and the Roman Senate, he speaks of Christians being delivered from wicked rulers by martyrdom, with particular reference to the malign influence of demons in these condemnations. While this does not reflect a positive view of Roman rule as such - yet it does stop short of actually condemning the emperor, and indeed suggests that such acts of injustice are contrary to his wishes - it hardly constitutes the frontal assault on imperial power suggested by Pagels.[59] While 'Justin's deference', according to Guerra, 'to the *imperium* is never too pronounced'[60] - he appeals to a higher 'eschatological' court of appeal' - he nevertheless employs the Platonic ideal of the philosopher-king to whom one looks for wise and just rule.

At *1 Apology* 18,1 Justin declares that all previous emperors have died the death common to all humankind and thereby challenges their deification. At 21,3 he launches into what can only be described as a savage attack on the notion of the *apotheosis* of emperors who are then deemed as sons of Jupiter whose alleged immorality is a constantly revisited theme for Justin. Here Justin is drawing a comparison between the resurrection and ascension of Christ (1,21,1) and that of the emperor and those gods - other sons of Jupiter - listed earlier. At 21,6 he declares that only those persons who have lived near to God in holiness and virtue may be deified. Justin, then, has little to say of the cult of the living emperor but clearly will have no truck with any notion of deifying him when he is dead. He sees the practice at best as a poor imitation of the resurrection and ascension of Christ and at worst as a failure to recognise that genuine deification comes only to the followers of the God of the Christians.

---

58 H. Chadwick, 'Justin Martyr's Defence of Christianity', *BJRL* 47 (1964/65): 287.

59 E. Pagels, 'Christian Apologists and "the fall of angels": an attack on Roman Imperial Power', *HTR* 78 (1985): 304.

60 A.J.Guerra, 'The Conversion of Marcus Aurelius and Justin Martyr: the Purpose, Genre, and Content of the First Apology', *Second Century* 9 (1992): 178.

Tatian the Syrian: *ad Graecos*[61]

Tatian was apparently Syrian by birth - he describes himself as born in the land of the Assyrians (42) (though this may be a mere rhetorical flourish by way of identifying with the 'barbarians' and especially the new 'barbarians, the Christians) - and of pagan parents. He describes his own conversion at Rome having been drawn to the writings of the Old Testament after exploring other alternatives.[62] He was a pupil of Justin in Rome and in turn the teacher of the anti-Marcionite Rhodo.[63] Though initially regarded as quite orthodox in his doctrine - though this was of course a very fluid concept in the second century - he eventually left Rome and returned to the East around 172, possibly to Antioch - which may have been his birthplace - or perhaps to Edessa, and there established the Encratite sect. Eusebius describes Tatian as 'trained in the learning of the Greeks'[64] - Tatian himself says in chapter 1 that 'I was once a great proficient in [your learning]' - before moving into heresy. Tatian wrote a number of works, the best known the *ad Graecos* as well as the no longer-extant but highly influential Gospel harmony, the *Diatessaron*. It is not clear when or where the *ad Graecos* was written, whether before or after his alleged descent into heresy. I would suspect that the general orthodoxy of the treatise would suggest an earlier rather than a later date - though it must be dated after Justin's death and may indeed have been occasioned by it and explain in part at least Tatian's vehemence towards Greek thought. The work may have formed part of the Christian response to the persecutions of late 176 or early 177 or may be dated as early as 160.

Tatian presents himself as an unconditional foe of Greco-Roman culture in all its forms and aspects. Though the *ad Graecos* presents in an apologetic form it is primarily protreptic and intended to persuade its readers to embrace the Christian faith and Tatian's own teaching of it. In chapter 19, for example, Tatian urges his readers to 'follow the one God'. Its 'vituperative tone' is best explained by this classification, as is its lack of systematisation. Its failure to properly defend Christians against charges laid against them denies it the description of apology. Neither is it a theological treatise offered as exposition. It rather seeks out persons who will place themselves under Christian instruction (Tatian's in particular?) and his invitation to an examination of him at chapter 42 confirms this.

Tatian himself tells us that he was a student of rhetoric and the arts (35) and his work also shows the hallmarks of a grammarian's training. The work itself shows clear signs of rhetorical style but is lacking evidence of some of the traditional parts of rhetorical conventions. While the treatise comprises for the most part a set of *proofs* by which Tatian seeks to demonstrate the manifest superiority of Christian over pagan belief and ends with a *peroratio* of sorts (42), there is neither an *exordium* nor a *narratio* proper unless one counts the first three chapters in which he lambasts

61 All text references in this section, unless otherwise indicated, are to the *ad Graecos*.

62 Chapters 29 and 35: ' I embraced our barbaric philosophy'.

63 Eusebius, *EH* V.xiii.1.

64 Ibid., IV.xvi.7.

the beliefs of those whom he is seeking to convert. He is clearly aware of the Stoic distinction between the *logos endiathetos* and the *logos prophorikos* and his doctrine of the logos is related to that of Justin. In chapter 6, while promoting the Christian understanding of the resurrection of the body as once-for-all, he challenges the Stoic cyclical, repetitive view. Yet in his defence against claims that his teaching on the Logos is ditheist he is aided by philosophy both Stoic and Platonic. His thought is scarcely original but has affinities with much in contemporary thought. His thinking also reflects other aspects of Stoicism, particularly with respect to its views on wealth and treating material things with indifference. His pessimistic view of matter is, however, undeniably Platonist.

In the treatise Tatian launches what can only be described as a most vitriolic attack on Greek thought. He offers strident criticisms of the major philosophies of the day - in a way of which Justin himself would probably not have approved - accusing their practitioners not only of incompetence, intellectual contradiction and error, but also of blatant dishonesty and other personally undesirable qualities. His language is intemperate but he is a writer of passion. He claims to see nothing of lasting value in Greco-Roman culture and towards the end of the treatise goes to great lengths to demonstrate that Moses antedates Homer and his ilk by many years and is therefore the more ancient, the more divine in inspiration, and ultimately of greater value and reliability (cf. Justin).[65] This is not peculiar to Tatian, of course, but was in fact to become a patristic commonplace.

Tatian declares that the Greeks derived their institutions from the despised barbarians - from the Phrygians, Babylonians, Persians, Egyptians, and Phoenicians among others. The Greeks themselves do not speak a common language or dialect; 'I am at a loss', he says, 'whom to call a Greek' (1). 'Lay aside this conceit [that you have initiated significant discoveries]', he says to them. We have renounced your wisdom, for you have contrived the art of rhetoric to serve injustice and slander and put out the power of free speech for hire, he says. No major philosopher escapes his vitriol; not Plato, nor Aristotle (for allegedly limiting providence to the superlunar realm[66] and who is reckoned by Tatian as responsible for Alexander's shortcomings), Zeno or Diogenes (2). Socrates alone, perhaps in deference to Justin's characterisation of him as a 'Christian before Christ', is dealt some muted praise as a 'just person' (3). Philosophers 'vent…the crude fancies of the moment' and display conflicting opinions and arrogance (ibid.). In chapters 8 and 9 Tatian attacks the philosophers' notion of Fate as a 'flagrant injustice'. The notion of fate denies divine justice and righteousness and promotes a view of the course of life as irrational and leaves no-one personally accountable for their actions. He particularly attacks astrology and use of the Zodiac. In chapter 25 he condemns the foul appearance and displays of philosophers in public at Rome and their inharmonious disputes, Plato against Epicurus, Aristotle against Democritus, and so on. Here Tatian contrasts the

---

65 See chapters 31, and 36-41.

66 Probably based on a reading of the *de Mundo*.

disharmony produced by the philosophers' apparent squabbles with the harmony and concord of Christian unanimity. Why then condemn us?, he asks.

In chapter 3 Tatian attacks philosophers for paying court to kings unbidden and for flattering those at the head of civic affairs. In chapter 4 Tatian, like most Fathers of the period, declares his willingness to pay the taxes ordered by the emperor and to acknowledge his own position of subjection to the latter if required, but God alone, he says, is to be feared, and by implication, worshipped. Only if commanded (by the emperor or his officers?) to deny God, will Tatian decline to obey but rather die, thus pointing to the limits of his notion of acceptable civic obedience. With reference to the emperor Tatian says that 'man is to be honoured as a fellow-man'.[67] In chapter 23 Tatian appears to criticise the emperor - although it can hardly have applied to Marcus Aurelius himself who allegedly despised the amphitheatre - by claiming that he who is chief among you (the Greeks) collects a legion of blood-stained murderers (gladiators), engaging to maintain them for the bloodsport in which they are involved. In chapter 27 he declares that he 'does not conceal from the rulers that view of God which I hold in relation to his government of the universe'. Tatian can by implication acknowledge the legitimate authority of the emperor, but not, given its derivative nature, in any absolute sense. God alone rules absolutely. Tatian only once makes mention of the imperial cult. In chapter 10, after he has condemned the elevation by Hadrian of the dead Antinous to divine status, he condemns those who are paid to say that they have witnessed deceased emperors ascending from the funeral pyres to the heavens - the custom of *apotheosis*, an integral part of the cult. This practice, says Tatian, ridicules the gods and robs God of his proper due. Thus, it insults religion both pagan and Christian.

Tatian demonstrates his own conservative social views when he accepts the various stations of life in which people find themselves. 'My master commands me to act as bondsman and to serve; I acknowledge the serfdom', he says. He likewise accepts the given status of both slave and free in chapter 11 and in so doing may reflect a Stoic-like indifference to fortune and the acceptance of one's given 'place'. Rich and poor alike, he says, have a spiritual equality and enjoy the same limits to life. He is not as concerned as was Hermas, for example, with the issue of the pursuit, use and enjoyment of wealth in the Christian community. In chapter 19 he does speak of those who are made (presumably by the devil) fond of money, but in any case his accusation is laid at the feet of the Greeks. With a 'cynicism' not unlike that later of Tertullian in the *de Pallio* he speaks of the true believer declining kingship, wealth, military command, fornication, crowns and fame, of despising death and grief. 'Die to the world', Tatian says, 'and live to God'. In the Christian community, he suggests in chapter 32, and in apparent contrast to the surrounding culture, rich and poor live in harmony; the wealthy pursue their philosophic interests, the poor receive and enjoy, probably at the rich's expense, a free education. This is probably Tatian's

67 One is reminded of Terence's famous remark that '*homo sum: humani nihil a me alienum puto* (I am a man: I think that there is nothing human strange to me' (*Heauntontimor*, I,1.25).

ideal and little reflects the reality if we are to believe Hermas and others. He may also reflect in his writing something of a preference for the Roman virtue of order. In chapter 12 he draws on the analogy or model of the harmony of a concert of music for the arrangement of the constitution of a body, of that constitution as under one management or rule, and of the beauty and order of God's arrangement of unformed matter. In chapter 19 he speaks of the construction of the world as excellent in its perfect ordering by God (is there here a Stoic influence?) and declares that it is the life which men live in it which is bad.

Irenaeus of Lyons: *adversus Haereses* and *Epideixis*[68]

There was some human occupation at Lugdunum in 62/61 BCE by refugees fleeing Vienne but its formal establishment as a colony took place at the confluence of the rivers Rhône and Saone by Munatius Plancus in 43 BCE at the instigation of Julius Caesar. It became in time the nodal point of the Gallo-Roman road system. With Roman encouragement it became a major city, with magnificent buildings and an active mercantile community. Irenaeus was born between 140 and 160, and was a native of Asia Minor. His home town was probably Smyrna. He speaks of hearing Polycarp, whom he revered, when he was young.[69] He travelled in time to Gaul; he may well have been sent there by the church at Smyrna (by Polycarp?) and became a presbyter. He travelled to Rome in 177 as an emissary of the Gallic church to mediate in a dispute over Montanism.[70] While he was away a major persecution broke out in Lugdunum and many Christians, including the venerable bishop Pothinus, were massacred. Irenaeus succeeded him as bishop of Lyons and Vienne. He wrote the *adversus Haereses* (*Detection and Overthrow of Gnosis Falsely So-Called*) (hereinafter AH) as a description and attack on Gnostic doctrine, the *Epideixis* (*The Demonstration of Apostolic Preaching*) (hereinafter D), known to us only in Armenian (prior to its translation into English), and many other works which remain to us only in fragments if at all. A convinced chialist, Irenaeus had broad theological interests and was regarded as orthodox by Eusebius.[71] He also played a key role in the Easter-dating controversy, urging Victor of Rome to reconcile with the churches of Asia over the issue.[72] Irenaeus, given the length of his *adversus Haereses* in particular, does not appear at first glance to devote much time or energy

---

68 I have included Irenaeus in this section because he was a native of Asia Minor and stood very clearly in that Christian tradition and also wrote for a Greek-speaking Christian community; the city itself was also not a native Gallic one but very much a creation of the Roman state. It was no more Gallic than Roman London was British. Lugdunum was very much a cosmopolitan city; indeed it could properly be called an outpost of the East in Western Europe.

69 Eusebius, *EH* V.xx.5.

70 Ibid., V.iv.2.

71 Ibid., IV.xxi.1 and V.xx.1.

72 Ibid., V.xxiv.11f..

to an engagement with the society around him. But what he does say is of immense interest.

Irenaeus was a polemicist[73] whose approach were greatly influenced by his battles with the heretics he opposes. He is more concerned to combat Christian opponents than he is pagans. The *Epideixis* is a repetitious exposition of Christian doctrine, and, while catechetical in form,[74] was probably apologetical in intent.[75] Schoedel points to the influence of rhetorical forms on Irenaeus.[76] Even his disclaimer of rhetorical skill at AH 1. Praef. 3 is itself a traditional rhetorical device. There is an *exordium* (chapters 1-3 of Book 1), a *narration* (the remainder of Book 1), a *divisio* in Book 2, pr. 1.2 in which Irenaeus indicates the main lines of argument he intends pursuing,

> 'In the present book I will establish those points which fit in with my design, so far as time permits, and overthrow, by means of lengthened treatment under distinct heads, their [sc. the heretics'] whole system',

a *confirmatio* (of the Church's faith), and a *confutatio* (of Gnostic errors) (over Books 2 to 5), but no obvious *peroratio* unless one is inclined to view the recapitulations at the ends of Books 2 (35.4), 3 (24-25) and 4 (41.4) - but somewhat oddly not Book 5 - where Irenaeus claims to have proved his case as such. He employs rhetorical *enthymemes* and *topoi* and his use of examples from Homer testifies to the employment of these rhetorical forms.

Irenaeus clearly made use of handbooks of literary references, particularly that of Pseudo-Plutarch. His references to the learning and literature of the Greco-Roman world are, like those to pagan religious practices, principally concerned to discredit his heretical opponents. At AH 1.9.4 he compares the inappropriate use by some of passages from Homeric poems to the misuse by heretics of particular scriptural references and names. At 1.13.6-7 he connects the image of the Homeric helmet of Pluto, which renders its wearer invisible (*Iliad* v.844), to the deluding of women by heresy 'in our very own district of the Rhône'. At 2.14.1-4 he names the comic

---

73 This will apply, of course, to the *Epideixis*.

74 S.L.Graham, 'Structure and Purpose of Irenaeus' *Epideixis*', *SP* 36 (2001): 210-21, argues that the form of the *Epideixis* is that very popular, in both Stoic and Middle Platonist circles, introductory handbook or *eisagogē*. Intended for the non-specialist, the main body of these works were normally divided into two main parts treating the subject matter of the writing from two different perspectives. This is the case with the present work, says Graham, with chapters 8 to 42a and 42b to 97 comprising this 'kind of diptych' (214).

75 Graham, ibid., 218f., however, argues that this is a 'catechetical work...[offering an] elemental level of discourse'. 'It presents', she says, 'an early example of Christian adoption of a standard Hellenistic educational form and an early representative of systematic reflection on a particular problem for which Christian teaching was demanded' (220).

76 W.R.Schoedel, 'Philosophy and Rhetoric in the Adversus Haereses of Irenaeus', *Vigiliae Christianae* 13 (1959): 27ff.. See also P.Perkins, 'Ireneus and the Gnostics: rhetoric and composition in Adversus Haereses Book One', *VC* 30 (1976): 193-200 and T.C.K.Ferguson, 'The Rule of Truth and Irenaean Rhetoric in Book 1 of *Against Heresies*', *VC* 55 (2001): 356-375, for detailed studies of the influence of rhetorical conventions on Irenaeus' style.

poet Antiphanes - from whom the Valentinians allegedly 'shaped' their myth of the divine emanations in the Pleroma - Thales of Miletus, Homer again, the atheist Anaxagoras, Democritus, Epicurus, Plato (who at least speaks of God), Empedocles, and the Stoics as all ignorant of God, poets and historians alike, and declares that these are those from whom the Gnostics draw their beliefs. He quotes Homer to establish a parallel between the Olympian gods sitting with Zeus and the gnostic Aeons with Bythos at 2.22.6, and alludes to Horace and the 'hellebore' with respect to the alleged madness and vainglory of the Gnostics in their claim to be superior to the creator god at 2.30.1.

Schoedel suggests that Irenaeus' 'knowledge and use of philosophy is somewhat superficial' and his 'attitude towards philosophy is ambiguous'.[77] There are, however, some evidences of a positive attitude towards philosophy. He refers to Plato's *Laws* and the *Timaeus*, though not necessarily understanding them, but only at AH 3,25.5 could he be said, and then with little conviction, actually to commend him. Plato is still more religious, he says, than the heretics for, unlike Marcion, he teaches the same god to be good and just. Irenaeus here quotes from both *Laws* 4.715e[78] and *Timaeus* 29E,[79] the latter to demonstrate that the Creator is good. For the most part, however, he is highly critical of Plato and other philosophers. This criticism is largely informed by the alleged use of them by the Gnostics. If Irenaeus appears, even just once, to display some appreciation of Plato it is because for him philosophers are bad but Gnostics are worse! At AH 2.14.2 Irenaeus says that those who are ignorant of God are 'termed philosophers'. He attributes the Gnostic notion of the superiority of the model on which the Gnostic creator creates the world to Plato's theory of forms (2.14.3).[80] Yet, in his pointing to the difference between God and God's creation he draws upon the Platonic distinction between Being - God as absolute non-contingent - and Becoming (*Timaeus* 28a). The distinction between God and creation will never cease to be. There is, declares Osborn, Platonist influence behind Irenaeus' account of the ineffable One,[81] though in his account of the Logos, 'Irenaeus has a closer affinity with the Bible than with philosophers, for his sense of history ties him to the prophets, where "word" is always "word-event"'. Irenaeus found in Platonism 'arguments for free will and arguments about God'.

Meijering points to Irenaeus' view that the Gnostics trace their doctrines on the divine will to the Stoic doctrine of Fate (AH 2.14.4) and that of the Gnostics' notion of a limited salvation again to Stoicism (2.14.4). Osborn points to a possible influence

---

77 E.F.Osborn, 'Irenaeus on God – Argument and Parody', *SP* 36 (2001): 270-81, in concluding a discussion of what he calls Irenaeus' 'unacknowledged use of a fragment of Xenophanes' (270) of Colophon (570-475 BCE), notes that 'Irenaeus practices philosophy without quoting precedents' (281).

78 'According to the ancient story there is a god who holds in his hands the beginning and end and middle of all things, and straight he marches in the cycle of nature. Justice, who takes vengeance on those who abandon the divine law, never leaves his side'.

79 '[God] was good and in him that is good no envy arises ever concerning anything.'

80 See *Timaeus* 51b, the *Symposium*, the *Phaedo* and the *Republic*.

81 E.F. Osborn, *The Beginning of Christian Philosophy*. (Cambridge, 1981), p. 52.

on Irenaeus of the Stoic Chrysippus' notion of *he ton holon oikonomia* - that all is governed by immanent reason and fate - when the Father speaks of *verbum dei gubernans et disponens omnia* (AH 5.18.3) and maintains that there are similarities between Irenaeus' notion of cosmic reconciliation (AH 5.18.1) and the Stoic Zeno's *Hymn of Cleanthes*. Osborn also sees in Irenaeus the evident influence of Stoic natural theology - a cosmos permeated and ruled by one God - and that this scheme includes the Adam-Christ dialectic and the notion of the long-term education of the creature's free will. Löhr maintains that when Irenaeus argues that if the 'psychics' are either saved or condemned on account of the nature of their souls alone and that thus matters of personal faith and the descent of the Saviour would be 'superfluous' (AH 2.29.1)), this would seem to be a Christian version of a well-known philosophical argument. For thus did the Platonic Academy seek to refute the determinism of the Stoics. While Irenaeus does not directly compare Stoic and Valentinian determinism he does denounce 'the naturalistic imagery of Valentinian eschatology as Stoicism in disguise'. Schoedel suggests parallels in Irenaeus to Galen's treatise *On Medical Experience*, where the latter is prepared to limit his enquiry to the cataloguing of observed data and to refrain from causal explanation,[82] and to Diogenes Laertius' account of Pyrrho where he distinguishes Sceptic and Dogmatic approaches.[83]

At AH 2.6.2 Irenaeus, referring to the fact that the Supreme God is invisible and yet his supreme power is widely known and acknowledged, asks whether those who live under the empire of the Romans, although they have never seen the emperor, and are far separated from him both by land and sea, shall not nevertheless know very well, as they experience his rule, who it is that possesses the principal power in the state. Irenaeus is not here focused on the imperial power as such but on the usefulness of the illustration. The Gnostics argue that the very invisibility of the Supreme God means that he was unknown to the creator god and the angels. 'All creatures, through implanted reason, know that there is one God, Lord of all, even if they do not know him, as they only can through the Son' (2.6.1). They know at least of his existence (2.6.2). At 3.8.1 he makes reference to *Matthew* 22,21 - concerning the coin with Caesar's image - but employs it only to emphasise the theological point that God is indisputably God. At 4.21.3 he makes reference to *John* 19,15 - 'we have no king but Caesar' - but only to highlight the Jews' rejection of Christ imaged in Jacob, the first-born son. At 5.24. 1f. Irenaeus makes the point that it is God, and not the devil, who has appointed the kingdoms of this world. Quoting *Romans* 13,1, he declares that Paul spoke these words of actual human authorities. He includes also a reference to Jesus supporting the payment of tribute to the emperor at *Matthew* 17,27 as evidence of this. He asserts that God imposed human rule as a restraint to evil; that he instituted the fear of men because humankind did not sufficiently fear God. Such rulers are 'ministers of God' and magistrates who use

82 See AH 2.26.1 where Irenaeus prefers to believe in God simply than to need to have explanations of divine matters.

83 *Vit.* 9. 102-5. See also AH 2.28.2 where Irenaeus again shows his concern with undue attention being given to causal explanations beyond a simple trust in God.

their authority for just and legitimate ends act righteously, while those who act for injustice, impiety, illegality and tyranny are condemned before God. He repeats his view, and this is in fact the focus of his comments and not imperial authority *per se*, that earthly rule is appointed by God for the benefit of the nations, and not by the devil for his own. Laws are established for the restraint of an excess of wickedness, and kings are appointed, some for correction and preserving justice and some for fear, punishment and rebuke. Irenaeus acknowledges the legitimate authority of the emperor but it is always a derived authority and the supreme power of God must first be acknowledged before it. At AH 5.26.1, with reference to the 'ten kings' in *Daniel* 17,12f - and *Daniel* 7,8 in 5.25 - and *Revelation* 2,33f., Irenaeus declares that the present ruling empire (presumably that of Rome) will dissolve into the foretold ten kingdoms, which event will precede the end of the world and the advent of the eternal kingdom. The kingdom, the city and the house will themselves be divided into ten, he says. The city is undoubtedly Rome and the house may well be the imperial *domus*. Again, these references should not be seen as anti-Roman. They speak merely of the provisional and derived nature of human authority and rule. For Irenaeus, whatever the shortcomings of Roman rule, it contributes to the well-being of God's realm. Irenaeus makes no recognisable reference to the imperial cult.

Irenaeus has next to nothing to say about Roman or Gallic society but his treatises do address a marked concern for order and harmony in life. At AH 1.10.2 he compares the perfect harmony of the church's tradition with the discordant opinions of the heretics. Difference for Irenaeus, whose motto was supposedly *semper eadem*, is indicative of disorder and error. At 2.15.3 he declares that the account which the Christians give of creation is of one harmonious with that regular order of things prevailing in the world. In another sphere he employs the image of a rich man depositing his money in a bank as an image for the orderly transmission of true doctrine by the first apostles to the church. His lists of episcopal succession and much else that he says of the church and its teaching reflect this desire for and appreciation of order and due process. At AH 4.26.3 he criticises presbyters who show pride at their office and thereby conform to the pride, ambition and seeking after glory of the secular world.

Select Bibliography

Antioch:

G. Downey, *A History of Antioch in Syria: from Seleucus to the Arab Conquest*. (Princeton, 1961).

Ignatius:

W. Schoedel, *Ignatius of Antioch: a commentary on the Letters of Ignatius of Antioch*. (Philadelphia, 1985).

C.Trevett, *A study of Ignatius of Antioch in Syria and Asia*. (Lewiston, 1992).

Theophilus:

R.M.Grant (ed.), *Theophilus of Antioch Ad Autolycum*. (Oxford, 1970).

Asia Minor:

D.Magie, *Roman Rule in Asia Minor to the end of the third century after Christ*. (Princeton, 1950).

S.R.F. Price, *Rituals and Power: the Roman Imperial Cult in Asia Minor*. (Cambridge, 1984).

Polycarp:

H.O.Maier, 'Purity and Danger in Polycarp's Epistle to the Philippians: The Sin of Valens in Social perspective', *Journal of Early Christian Studies* 1 (1993): 229-47.

Melito of Sardis:

L.H.Cohick, *The Peri Pascha attributed to Melito of Sardis: setting, purpose, and Sources*. (Providence, 2000).

A.Stewart-Sykes, 'Melito's Anti-Judaism', *Journal of Early Christian Studies* 5 (1997): 271-83.

Justin Martyr:

L.W.Barnard, *Justin Martyr: his life and thought*. (Cambridge, 1966).

A.J.Guerra, 'The Conversion of Marcus Aurelius and Justin Martyr: the Purpose, Genre, and Content of the First Apology', *Second century* 9 (1992): 171-87.

E.F.Osborn, *Justin Martyr*. (Tübingen, 1973).

Tatian:

G.F.Hawthorn, 'Tatian and his Discourse to the Greeks', *Harvard Theological Review* 57 (1964): 161-88.

Irenaeus:

R.M.Grant, *Irenaeus of Lyons*. (London and New York, 1997).

E.F.Osborn, *Irenaeus of Lyons*. (Cambridge, 2001).

W.R.Schoedel, 'Theological Method in Irenaeus (Adversus Haereses 2, 25-28)', *Journal of Theological Studies* ns35 (1984): 31-49.

Chapter 5

Alexandria and the Fathers

> 'The first city of the civilised world, certainly far ahead of all the rest in elegance and extent and riches and luxury.' (Diodorus Siculus, 17.52.5)
>
> 'The city is prosperous, rich and productive ... [the Alexandrians'] only god is money, and this the Christians, the Jews, and in fact, all nations adore.'
>
> (the Emperor Hadrian)

Alexandria was founded by Alexander the Great in 331 BCE near the Egyptian village of Rhakotis. Its founder was buried there and his tomb became a major pilgrimage site, visited particularly by rulers who saw themselves as latter-day Alexanders. It was an utterly Greek city and culturally other than the native Egyptian. From the time of Alexander's foundation of the city to beyond the Roman period it was the most important commercial city in the Mediterranean world. A marvellously cosmopolitan city, and one prone to communal upheaval and mob violence throughout its history, it possessed world-famous avenues and an array of magnificent buildings: the great lighthouse, the Pharos, two superb harbours to exploit its outstanding commercial potential and a series of canals linking these and Lake Mareotis, the temple of the Imperial Cult, the famous Museon - perhaps the major centre of intellectual endeavour in antiquity but sadly destroyed in the 270s during civil conflict - and the Serapeum which in time became under the Romans the greatest centre of pagan worship in all of Egypt. Diplomatic relations were established in 273 BCE between Rome and Ptolemy II and over time Egypt became a protectorate of sorts and client state of Rome. From around 80 BCE, from the time of Sulla, the shadow of potential Roman intervention in the affairs of Egypt was ever-present. The kingdom itself - and the city with it - only became officially Roman property in 30 BCE with the suicide of Cleopatra Thea Philopator, the last of the Ptolemaic rulers. Octavian's policy was to preserve with only little modification the administrative system established by the Ptolemies. Alexandrian society, like elsewhere in the empire, was divided between *honestiores* and *humiliores*.

A Jewish uprising in 115-117, initially anti-Greek, in Alexandria saw the virtual destruction of the Jewish community after a brief but violent struggle. Said Appian, Trajan 'destroyed the Jewish race in Egypt'. Haas, however, calls it only a 'near-fatal blow'. Only two years after the alleged disappearance of the community a Jewish delegation travelled from the city to Hadrian to combat Greek accusations. Alexandrian Jews did not, however, participate in the Bar Kochba rebellion in the 130s and none took part in the disturbances of 215 during Caracalla's visit to the city. It maintained this low profile during the third century and its recovery can be dated to the end of that century. Clearly, between 117 and the late third century the community was quiet but not non-existent. Many Jews in 117 emigrated to Palestine and those remaining in Alexandria were relocated outside the walls away from the Greek community.

Under the Severans, significant changes took place. There is no indication that the Alexandrians supported the imperial claims of Didius Julianus but they did support Pescennius Niger who had served previously as a popular army officer in Egypt. The late second/early third century saw increasing tax assessments and much hardship caused thereby. Resentment and violence were two widespread consequences. In 202/3 there was a major persecution of Christians in both Alexandria - Origen's father was one of the martyrs - and in Carthage; there are clear indications of imperial support for these actions. The grant by Caracalla in 212 of universal Roman citizenship, whatever its intention, had the effect of making irrelevant all at once the much treasured Alexandrian citizenship. In 215 a visit by Caracalla saw demonstrations against the murder of Geta, the brother of the emperor killed on the instructions of the latter, and a measure of ridicule of the emperor's preceived pretensions to model himself on both Alexander the Great and Achilles. On the emperor's orders thousands of Alexandrians were massacred or expelled. Many, including Origen, fled the city.

Trigg calls Alexandria in antiquity 'the spiritual centre of an aggressive Hellenism'.[1] In the first century BCE - through Eudorus of Alexandria, whom Dillon calls a 'founding father' of Middle Platonism - and the first century CE - through Philo of Alexandria - the city was regarded as a major centre of Middle Platonist thought. Then, in the second century, the major loci of this particular 'school' moved to the Greek mainland, to Athens itself, and to Smyrna, North Africa and elsewhere. Middle Platonism did not return to centre-stage in Alexandria until the early third century and even then its major exponent, Ammonius, the teacher of Origen, was not part of the city's recognised philosophical establishment. Yet the fact that Alexandria may not have produced many first-rate original thinkers in the second century does not mean that the city did not remain a major centre of learning and culture. The opposite is in fact the case. Alexandria remained a place in which ideas flourished and the very air, it is said, was filled with vigorous debate. It was in this city, therefore, that questions about Christian identity - particularly against the background of Christian-Jewish hostility - those related to the Christian life in the context of contemporary debates about the proper life for the philosophically-trained, matters having to do with contemporary debates concerning first principles, the relation of the divine to matter, of the intelligible sphere to the sensible, the relation between entities within the intelligible (in Christian thinking in terms of the relationship of Father and Son); and the debate within the Christian community itself about the Christian's engagement with the philosophical tradition generally came particularly, though not exclusively here, to the fore.

---

1 J.W.Trigg, *Origen: the Bible and Philosophy in the Third-Century Church.* (London, 1983), p. 3.

Epistle of Barnabas

This treatise has no explicit recipient - though it was probably addressed to a particular Christian community in Egypt - and no named author. It was attributed by tradition to the Apostle Barnabas but this was discounted long ago. The dating of the work has been a matter of much debate and is placed variously between the early part of the second century and 135. Paget argues that it belongs to a period bracketed by the destruction of the Second Temple and the beginnings of the second Jewish Revolt (which latter event it does not mention) and therefore has a *terminus ad quem* of around 130 CE. Its preference for allegory, the unmistakable influence of Philo, and the regard in which it was held by Alexandrian theologians all suggest to a number of commentators an Alexandrian provenance. The earliest writer to witness to the existence of the work was Clement of Alexandria. While the assignation of the work to Syria or Palestine is possible - it evidences some knowledge of rabbinic traditions and some points of similarity with Justin - this is ultimately unconvincing. The epistle was held in high esteem in Alexandria, the apostle Barnabas, though not the author of the work, is traditionally associated with Alexandria, and there are clear parallels between Barnabas and Jewish-Alexandrian literature, especially with Philo and the *Letter of Aristeas*. Paget sees significant parallels between Barnabas and the *Preaching of Peter*, an Egyptian work of the early second century quoted by Clement, and suggests that both are products of a similar anti-Jewish theological environment.

The *Epistle* has an epistolary form but this is probably a mere literary convention. It observes and incorporates many of the features of conventional rhetoric. The first part of chapter 1 is an *exordium* designed to earn the goodwill of its recipients whom it addresses as 'sons and daughters' in whom he says there are evidences of the outpouring of the Spirit. The latter part of this opening section resembles a Hellenistic *partitio* in which the author lays out three primary doctrines concerning hope, righteousness and love of joy and gladness as the fruits of righteousness. Yet these do not actually shape the substance of what he ultimately argues. Chapters 2 to 16 comprises the *proofs* and include elements of both *refutatio* in which he condemns a variety of Jewish practices and observances - sacrifices, fasts, food laws, sabbath, and Temple among them - and *confirmatio* in which he interprets much of the Old Testament in a way favourable to Christian claims. He argues that the covenant[2] is the possession of Christians and not of Jews, the latter having lost all claim to it through their idolatry (4). He draws as his witnesses the scriptures, particularly from the Pentateuch, the Prophets (especially Isaiah), the Psalms, and various New Testament writings. He offers a *peroratio* in chapters 17 and 21, with the former comprising a *recapitulatio* of his arguments and the latter an exhortation. Chapters

2 R.Hvalvik, *The Struggle for Scripture and Covenant: the purpose of the Epistle of Barnabas and Jewish-Christian Competition in the Second Century* (Tübingen, 1996), pp. 92f., argues that our author had a one covenant theology rather that the two-covenant one more common among Christian writers of the time.

18 to 20 concern the notion of the Two Ways, those of light and darkness, and while consistent with his overall theme, appear awkwardly placed.

Barnard argues that the Epistle was in fact a paschal homily intended for delivery at Easter, though not by the author himself, before a Christian congregation.[3] He points to the emphasis in the work on suffering - an appropriate paschal motif - frequent allusions to baptism - practice, catechesis, and credal formulas - references to the Exodus setting, to the Eucharist, and to the theme of Darkness and Light, the Two Ways. Paget, however, finds this description of the letter 'too precise'. It lacks the specificity of a genuine letter but there are some epistolary features, shared with Ignatius, in it. The exegesis of scripture is a significant, perhaps the primary, element of the author's purpose. Its anti-Jewish atmosphere is not merely formalistic and its probable dating prior to 115 CE makes sense when the Jewish community in the city was still considerable. Our author takes Jewish opinions seriously and this only makes sense if they were a significance presence in the city. There are similarities with the *adversus Iudaeos* literature and Barnabas' failure to call the Jews to conversion suggests a polemic rather than a protreptic purpose (see below for a brief discussion of Hvalvik's views). His purpose was undoubtedly to help establish a clear and well-defined identity for the small Christian community over against the larger and more influential Jewish one in Alexandria. Paget challenges any suggestion that Barnabas was an 'inept regurgitator of pre-existent material' and declares that he was rather a 'redactor who adds significantly to his sources'. The work certainly does not appear to be a unified document - there are many contradictions and inconsistencies, for example - but it does have a 'stylistic unity'. Barnabas 'cannot be explained as the representative of a single, unified tradition' but of a series of traditions. Hvalvik argues that the audience for the letter was a Christian one, that its purpose was essentially to dissuade Christians tempted to either involve themselves in Jewish practices or even to convert to Judaism outright,[4] and that the letter itself is of the protreptic type.[5] He suggests the last on the basis that a protreptic writing can seek either to persuade or to dissuade, in this case to dissuade Christians tempted to engage in Jewish practices or to defect outright. In my view Hvalvik is wrong in this. A protreptic writing, as an instrument of conversion, will both dissuade and persuade, to convince the would-be convert of the error of their present position in order to clear the way for them to be persuaded to change allegiances. The *Epistle* is not a conversionary vehicle. It is, as an exhortatory piece intended to keep the faithful as such, better regarded as a paraenetic piece intended to encourage the faithfulness and allegiance of existing Christians.

Barnabas has virtually nothing to say about the wider culture or society in which he lived and worked and nothing of substance to say about Roman rule. His sole reference to the emperors in chapter 4 concerns the coming end and provides no

3 L.W.Barnard, 'The Epistle of Barnabas - a Paschal Homily?', *Vigiliae Christianae* 15 (1961): 8-22.

4 Hvalvik, *The Struggle for Scripture and Covenant*, pp. 82-101.

5 Ibid., pp. 158-165.

particular commentary on the imperial office nor, for example, the imperial cult. He makes no genuine, direct reference to pagan religion or practice. These are not his concern here. His only immediate and direct concern is that of the Christian community and of their relationship, or in his view non-relationship, to the then dominant Jewish community. His purpose is polemical exegesis. His purpose is not to see only limited value in Jewish opinion and practice but no value at all. The Jewish dispensation is neither provisional nor preparatory for the Christian. It is non-existent and even demonic. For Barnabas the Old Testament has only one meaning and that coincides entirely with the Christian. And this Christianisation took place not in the realm of the theoretical but in the context of actual conflict between Jew and Christian and led to some of the most vitriolic anti-Judaism seen to this point in the brief history of the church.

Epistle to Diognetus

This work, a protreptic apology in the form of a letter 'written in elegant Greek'[6] suggests itself as an answer to a query from a well-placed friend of the author about Christianity. That this work is of the protreptic genre is evident in a number of passages;[7] our author does not simply seek to explain but to convert. For example, at 1.1 he declares that Diognetus is 'exceedingly zealous to learn the religion of the Christians'. At 2.1 he urges his friend to 'clear yourself of all the prejudice which occupies your mind, and throw aside the custom which deceives you, and become as it were a new man from the beginning'. This is not mere apologetics. At 10.1 he asks '[i]f you desire this faith, and receive the complete knowledge of the Father' and at 12.1 '[i]f you consider and listen with zeal to these truths you will know what things God bestows on those that love him rightly'. At 12.7, with the tell-tale hortatory subjunctive of the protreptic genre, he pleads that Diognetus will 'Let your heart be knowledge and your life the true and comprehended word'. The author is not named in the work but its provenance is by general consent agreed to be Alexandrian, though the work suggests a possible Athenian provenance with allusions to the Eleusinian mysteries and Athenian numismatic images. The author's knowledge of Irenaeus and Hippolytus suggests an early third century date. Quasten declares that 'the epistle deserves to rank among the most brilliant and beautiful

---

6 M. Heintz, 'Μιμητης θεου in the Epistle to Diognetus', *JECS* 12 (2004): 107.

7 That the work is protreptic is attested by Aune in 'Romans as a *Logos Protreptikos*', in K.Donfried (ed.), *The Romans Debate* 2nd ed., (Peabody, 1991), p. 285, by F.Young, 'Greek Apologists of the Second Century', in Edwards, *Apologetics in the Roman Empire*, p. 88 - '[the *Epistle*] presents itself as an explanation which becomes increasingly an exhortation to joyful acceptance of these truths' - and by Heintz, 'Μιμητης θεου in the Epistle to Diognetus', 107. The latter's claim, however, that chapter 10 is 'clearly paraenetic' (108) is incorrect, given that exhortation-as-paraenesis as opposed to exhortation-as-protreptic is normally directed to the already faithful which Diognetus clearly is not. Chapter 10 is simply further evidence of the protreptic nature of the work.

works of Christian Greek literature'. It displays some of the marks of a rhetorical convention. Its opening chapter comprises both an *exordium* in which the author seeks the goodwill of Diognetus and a *narratio* in which he provides the background to the letter in an enquiry from Diognetus about God, Christian worship, contempt for the world and for death, refusal to believe in the traditional deities, repudiation of Jewish beliefs, the nature of Christian love, and the perennial of why the Christian Gospel has appeared now and not formerly. Our writer then proceeds in his *proofs* to deal with most of these issues though not in the order given at the beginning. He offers a *refutatio* by way of dismissing the claims of traditional religion (2). In chapters 2 and 3 he explains why Christians have separated from the Jews and in chapter 5 offers an overview of the distinct Christian *ethos*. He speaks of Christians and the world in chapter 6, of revelation in 7 and about human knowledge of God in 8. In all of these he draws on the scriptures as witness. In chapters 9 and 10 he outlines the divine economy of salvation and enumerates the benefits of conversion. In chapter 11 he begins his *peroratio* with a recapitulation of his arguments focused on the person of Christ and in 12 concludes with an exhortation to conversion.

The work reflects a Stoic-like cosmology and generally suggests a fusion of later Stoic thought and Middle Platonism common in the late second and early third centuries. With respect to 6,2, for example,

> 'the soul is spread through all members of the body, and Christians throughout the cities of the world',

some argue for the influence of Plutarch's *de Anima* and Plato's *Phaedo* 65c-d.[8] Heintz also points to the affinity of what is for him a major theme of the *Epistle* - the concept of the 'imitation of God' - with thought contemporary with the work. He points to the famous *Theaetetus* 176b of Plato - where the end of man is named as a 'likeness to God' - and *Phaedrus* 252c-253b[9] - where similar sentiments are displayed.[10] Heintz also points to similar thinking in Pythagorean teaching, in the Stoic tradition, and in Philo. Yet all of this reflects not necessarily dependence on the part of our *Epistle* or even influence on it but rather a context in which common religious sentiments appears. Yet, as Heintz properly points out, for the writer of the *Epistle* the 'imitation of God' is not, as for the philosophers, the product of personal discipline and moral effort, but a possibility mediated only through God's Son.[11]

---

8 'Surely the soul can best reflect when it is free of all distractions…when it ignores the body and becomes…independent.'

9 See 252e, for example, where Socrates declares that 'the followers of Zeus desire that the soul of him whom they love be like Zeus'.

10 Heintz, 'Μμιμητης θεου in the Epistle to Diognetus', 108f.

11 Ibid., 117f..

Athenagoras: *Legatio*

Athenagoras was a contemporary of Tatian but far more positive towards the learning and culture of the Greeks than him. He was, also, more able in language and style and in the arrangement of his material and probably the most articulate of the early Christian apologists.[12] His style evidences schooling in rhetoric (see below) but little else can be known about him since he is mentioned only by Methodius. He wrote the *Legatio pro Christianis*, formally addressed to the emperors Marcus Aurelius and Commodus and intended to refute charges against Christians of atheism, cannibalism and incest - Athenagoras addresses the issue of atheism at some length from chapters 4 to 30 and the other charges from chapters 31 to 36 - and possibly (see below) the *De Resurrectione* though some challenge his authorship of the latter. Grant was one who offered a challenge to the notion of Athenagoras having penned the latter work.[13] Schoedel, Lona, Zeegers-Vander Vorst and Runia support Grant while Barnard, Malherbe and Pouderon argue the contrary. Zeegers-Vander Vorst, in what could be described as the most exhaustive consideration of the question - whereby she critiques the arguments of the principal players in the debate and then offers her own magisterial examination of issues such as vocabulary, modalities of expression, methods of refutation, appeals to scripture and classical authors, stylistic habits and concepts - comes down clearly in favour of those who argue for Athenagoras not having written the *de Resurrectione*, arguing that the similarities urged by supporters of authenticity are almost invariably to do with matters which are 'non-existent or commonplace … [or sometimes] trivial'. There perhaps the matter should lie and one should not then place too much reliance on the evidence of the *de Resurrectione* in establishing the engagement of Athenagoras with the society and culture of Alexandria in the second century.

A connection of Athenagoras with Alexandria is found in Philip of Side's account of his life and there the Athenian is declared as Head of the famous Catechetical School. Schoedel, however, finds Philip a less than encouraging witness. The argument for Alexandria is carried by Pouderon, while those ranged against him include Schoedel, Barnes, Ruprecht and Runia. Yet to reject out of hand all of the information provided by Philip of Side because he is wrong on some details is unnecessary. His witness can remain as evidence for an Alexandrian 'period' for Athenagoras and there is no other evidence which directly or indirectly contradicts this. We may note also that at *Legatio* 14,2 Athenagoras seems to display first-hand knowledge of contemporary Egyptian religious practices and not to have drawn his information from a handbook. Most scholars place the writing of the *Legatio* in the mid-to-late 170s.

---

12 L.W.Barnard, *Athenagoras: a study in second century Christian apologetics* (Paris, 1972), p. 55, calls him 'the most logical of the Greek Christian apologists'.

13 R.M.Grant, 'Athenagoras or Pseudo-Athenagoras', *Harvard Theological Review* 47 (1954): 121-9.

Schoedel points to the fact the *Legatio* is often read as apologetic literature in the mould of the epideictic strategies known to us from Menander's third century writings. Yet he says that the work is actually a petition 'for the intervention of the emperors on behalf of the Christians by seeing to it that imperial officials follow proper procedures in dealing with Christians and that they not yield to extralegal pressures'. Schoedel argues that Athenagoras' 'treatment of the emperors reflects standard rhetorical prescriptions for orations in praise of the king' and suggests that parallels can be found in Menander's rhetorical handbook for the writer of panegyrics and in Pliny's *Panegyricus* for Trajan.[14] Athenagoras himself says at 11.3 that he 'is making his defence (*apologoumenon*) before philosopher-kings'. The form arose as a 'significant literary vehicle' out of the particular circumstances of both Christian and Jewish communities of the time against the background of a particular imperial petitionary system.[15] Buck challenges this view. The *Legatio* is simply too long for an ambassadorial delivery before the emperors. Such a notion rests on a rather tenuous assumption that one can draw parallels between Jewish and Christian situations of the time. Schoedel's conclusions, she says, are 'too complex and unwieldly to be viable'. But it was not only the form of the *Legatio* which precluded its delivery before the emperors but its very content. It 'is simply too vague' for such a purpose. 'Athenagoras is singularly unclear as to what he is requesting from the emperors', and notwithstanding his comments at 2,1, his petition is simply 'imprecise'. Buck concludes that the work was never presented before the emperors and was not intended to be. Should she be right, however, about the shortcomings of the work as an actual petitionary offering then even as a model for such it cannot be well-regarded.

It is, however, whatever its actual use, in form a rhetorical piece 'composed in the style of an ambassadorial speech'. It evidences the contemporary conventions of Hellenistic rhetorical style and structure. The preface and first chapter combine an *exordium* in which Athenagoras seeks the goodwill of the emperors by reference to them as the 'greatest of kings', as 'philosophers', as peaceable and humane. This opening chapter also contains the beginnings of a *narratio* in which the author points to the manifest injustice of the treatment of Christians by the state. In chapter 2 he continues this *narratio*. Then he offers a *partitio* in which he outlines the three main allegations or charges laid against Christians, those of atheism, cannibalism, and promiscuity and incest. At chapter 4 he begins his *probatio* with a lengthy defence against the charge of atheism and this occupies the bulk of the treatise (4-25). He employs scripture as witness for his case and points to the evident good character of Christians (*ethos*) as proof of their piety. From chapter 14 he begins an attack on pagan religion (a *refutatio*) which continues until chapter 30. At chapter 31 he begins a brief dismissal of the charges of cannibalism, incest and promiscuity and

---

14 W.R.Schoedel, 'In Praise of the King: a rhetorical pattern in Athenagoras', in D.F.Winslow (ed.), *Disciplina Nostra*. (Philadelphia, 1979), pp. 70f..

15 Many scholars support Schoedel's notion of a petition intended for presentation in person before the imperial presence, Barnes, Grant, Barnard and Millar among them.

offers a more detailed defence against these from chapters 32 to 36. In the final chapter (37) he concludes with a *peroratio* in which he summarises his central thesis that Christians, far from being atheist and promiscuous, are indeed 'godly, mild and chastened in soul' and exhorts the emperors to treat them the more appropriately.

While Malherbe argues that at first glance Athenagoras' treatment of ethics in the *Legatio* chapters 11 and 12 might appear anti-philosophical, he actually uses particular philosophical traditions in the discussion and even his anti-sophistic approach is standard usage. Malherbe compares the *Legatio* - with supporting references from the *de Resurrectione* - with Alcinous' *Didaskalikos*, with particular reference to the latter's tripartite structure - Physics, Ethics and Dialectic/Logic. Athenagoras is generally positive towards Plato in particular. His opening account of the Christian view of God at 4.2,

> 'we teach that there is one God, the Maker of all, and that He is not created (since it is not Being (*to on*) that is Created, but non-being)',

is consistent with Plato at *Timaeus* 28c3-4 on God as Creator and Father of all and at 27b on the distinction between being and becoming – although the notion of matter as created is not – though neither of Plato's texts is referred to specifically. As part of a series of maxims pointing to the uncreated nature of God at 6.2, Athenagoras quotes *Timaeus* 28c3-4 (with no variation from the original wording) to demonstrate that God is both uncreated and eternal and then follows this with reflections on *Timaeus* 41a. He introduces this latter passage, comprising God's address to the inferior gods, 'Gods that are the sons of gods, I am their creator. I am the father of works', with the assertion that 'if Plato recognizes other gods – the sun, the moon, the stars - he recognizes them as created', then he must consider the one, uncreated maker of the universe to be God. The point which Athenagoras goes on to make, and this is his sole reason for introducing Plato here, is that if Plato is not an atheist then neither can Christians be. This usage of the text demonstrates that the author's intention is apologetic in that he seeks a bridge to comprehension and not at all to conversion.

At 7,1, after Athenagoras has brought Plato and others as witnesses to the notion of the unity of God he writes,

> 'Seeing, then, that by and large all admit, though reluctantly, when they get down to the first principles of everything, that the divine being is one, and since we insist that he who ordered our universe is God, why is it that they enjoy the licence to speak and write what they want concerning the divine being, whereas a law has been imposed upon us who can establish with compelling proofs and arguments the correctness of what we think and believe - that God is one?'

Here Athenagoras makes a similar complaint to that made by Justin at *First Apology* 18. These philosophers, however, continues our author, 'were able to gain no more than a peripheral understanding [about God] (7,2), but 'we, however, have prophets as witnesses of what we think and believe' (7,3). This reflects similar views expressed, again by Justin, in both the *First Apology* and the *Dialogue*. At 8,2 he declares that

> 'created things are similar to their exemplars, whereas uncreated things are dissimilar, deriving their existence from no-one and without reference to models'.

The 'exemplars' or 'paradigms' are almost certainly the Platonic Ideas. At 10,1 Athenagoras' description of God as 'uncreated, invisible, impassible, incomprehensible, and infinite [and] apprehended by mind and reason alone' and so on, is also consistent with Plato and with Tertullian's 'God of the Philosophers'. He concludes,

> 'I have given sufficient evidence that we are not atheists on the basis of arguments presenting this God as one.'

At 10,2, while discussing the Son of God, Athenagoras speaks of the Son as 'the Word of the Father in Ideal Form (*en idea*) and energizing power (*energeia*)' and declares that 'the Son of God is the *nous* and *logos* of the Father'. These are clearly drawn from Platonic terminology. At 10.3 Athenagoras speaks of God as 'eternal Mind (*nous aidios*)'; as we saw earlier, after Antiochus, Alexandrian Platonism understood the highest god as a transcendent *nous* who creates indirectly through a second god (and thereby splits the Demiurge of the *Timaeus* in two). Eudorus, although reflecting a very strict monism, seems to reflect the *Philebus* (26e-30e) which sees the God/One as Mind while Philo in the *Creation* posits an active causal principle as 'perfectly pure and unsullied Mind of the Universe' (7-9). While Plutarch separates the supreme Monad from the second-placed Mind (the Mind of the Demiurge of *Timaeus* 28c), Atticus describes the supreme God as Mind, *inter alia*. We might also note at 10.4 the influence of Middle Platonism on Athenagoras' doctrine of the Holy Spirit, which appears at first glance emanationist,

> 'an effluence of God flowing from [God] and returning back again like a beam of the sun'.[16]

This notion of procession and return is perhaps the single most significant contribution of Neopythagoreanism to Middle Platonism. The activity of the Spirit is described by him in Platonic terms - perhaps in the sense of that World Soul common to both Middle Platonist and Stoic thought - and while it is argued by some that our author has a Stoic conception of the Spirit's activity (the Stoic *pneuma* as the principle of life in humankind and the universe, the active principle which holds each material object together, the cohesive element in all life) in the universe Middle Platonic influence is also possible.[17] At 10.5 Athenagoras declares that

---

16 See also 24,2.

17 At *Legatio* 5,3 Athenagoras refers to the Spirit as that by whom all things created by God are governed, at 6,3 as that who holds all things in being, the Spirit who pervades the whole world, at 24,4 as the one entrusted with the control of matter, while at 22,3 he explicitly

> 'we also say that there is a host of angels and ministers whom God, the Maker and Creator of the world, set in their places through the Word that issues from him and whom he commanded to be concerned with the elements, the heavens, and the world with all that is in it and the good order of all that is'

and in this reflects an affinity with certain Middle Platonist interpretations of *Timaeus* 41a f.

At 12,1f. Athenagoras employs Plato's reference to Minos and Rhadamanthus as the judges and punishers of evil persons (*Gorgias* 523c-524a) to support the Christian notion of sinners being held accountable by God for their sin. At 13.2 Athenagoras refers to 'the Creator and Father of the Universe' - employing language close to that of *Timaeus* 28c and certainly the order of descriptors. At 15,1[18] he speaks of Christians, in language reminiscent of *Timaeus* 27d, as

> 'we who do distinguish and divide the uncreated from the created, being from non-being, the intelligible from the perceptible, and who give each of them its proper name'.

At 16,3 he alludes again to *Timaeus* 28c3-4 when he cites Plato as saying that the world is God's craftsmanship and at 16,4 draws on his support for the notion that that which has a bodily nature cannot be free from change (that is, it is perishable) (*Politics* 269d). On the distinction again between 'becoming' and 'being' he claims no disagreement between himself and the philosophers at 19,2 and cites *Timaeus* 27d on the notion of the intelligible as uncreated and the perceptible as created, that is, having both beginning and end. At 23,5-6 he cites *Timaeus* 40a-b on the distinction between God (and the planets and fixed stars produced by the Uncreated One) and the demons, and also quotes *Timaeus* 40d-e in full on the origin of the demons and deities. He then (at 23,7) refers to Plato as one who understands the eternal God as apprehended by mind and reason, as true being, as one in nature, as good, as the first power, and then at 23.7 *Epistle* 2.312e (see below) and asks whether one who understands all this can fail to grasp or comprehend the truth of the beings who have come into being from the realm of perception (again the criticism of Plato's 'uncertainty' principle). At 23,9 he refers to *Phaedrus* 246e and the account of Zeus the charioteer crossing the heavens and declares that this 'Zeus' is not the son of Cronus but merely a name which refers to the Maker of all things, the true God.[19] His reference at 24,3 to the angels called into being by God to exercise providence over the things set in order by him is reminiscent of *Timaeus* 41a, and at 36,3, when speaking of the resurrection, declares that there is

---

recognises this affinity between the Stoic and Christian concepts of the Spirit as the one which pervades matter. At 5,3 there is an implied allusion to the myth of the charioteer from Plato's *Phaedrus* 246a-b which figures in much Middle Platonist discussion of the World Soul.

18 See also 19.1.

19 See the suggestion that Harpocration of Argos made the same claim, at Dillon, *The Middle Platonists*, p. 260.

> 'nothing in the teachings of Pythagoras or Plato [which] stands in the way of bodies' being reconstituted from the same elements once their dissolution to that from which they arose has taken place'.

While there is much of Stoic thought in the *Legatio* and he cites Homer 21 times, Herodotus 12 and Euripides eight times against Plato ten, Athenagoras is a Platonist within the Christian camp. He takes Plato seriously and much of what he has to say is shaped by his engagement with his Athenian predecessor. Athenagoras presents Christian doctrine within a framework principally provided by Middle Platonism. Yet he remains the apologist and polemicist. He is a Platonist but at most a Christian Platonist.

Though Platonism remains the prime source for his ontology and he yet employs the outline of a Middle Platonic theological system, he remains committed to the notion of revelation as the ultimate source of truth. He modifies Platonic metaphysics from the biblical point of view, absorbs aspects of Stoic monotheism, his notion of the harmony of the cosmos,

> 'if the world is an instrument in tune, and moving in well-measured time' (16.3),[20]

reflects Stoic language, while that of the cosmos as an enclosed sphere moving in rhythm (16,3) is Neopythagorean. Yet Christian notions of providence, for example, are sharply distinguished from Stoic and other Hellenistic notions of *pronoia* (19 and 36-37). Athenagoras sought to overthrow 'the equation of providence (*pronoia*) with [notions of] destiny, fate, or chance/necessity (*heimarmenē, moira, tuchē*)' associated with Aristotelians - at 25.2 he attacks Aristotle's failure to allow for divine providence in the sublunar world – Epicureans – at 12.2 he implicitly attacks those who have no place for divine providence in this realm, referring to them as those 'who reckon the present life of very small worth indeed' - and others. The Christian notion of providence had nothing to with the Greek one of irrational accident or of blind chance (8.8). Yet at 19.2 he acknowledges the Stoic belief in divine providence as one in a God both active and governing. He wants above all, however, to make use of the most significant elements of Greek learning and sees no fundamental conflict in this between the Gospel and Hellenistic culture.

Athenagoras' distinction between power and order in his trinitarian exposition has clear parallels in pagan treatments of both divine and earthly monarchies. At *Legatio* 18, 2 he even, like Maximus of Tyre who compares the one God and his many gods to a king who parcels out responsibilities to subordinates, compares the rule of Marcus and son with the divine Father and Son. Athenagoras thus exploits a pluralist strain in Christian thought as a response to charges of a Christian atheism in the context of pagan concerns with monotheism, concerns both philosophical and political. Athenagoras speaks at 4,2 of the order and harmony of the universe produced by the existence of the one, supreme God - although he does not use the usual word employed by other Fathers for this, viz. *homonoia* - and at 15,3 and

20 Also at *Legatio* 4.

25,3-4 of a Stoic-like order in the arrangement of the world and of the creation of individual persons and of everything in its assigned place,

> 'of those things which belong to the constitution of the whole world there is nothing out of order or neglected, but each one of them has been produced by reason, and, therefore, they do not transgress the order prescribed to them; and man, too, so far as He that made him is concerned, is well ordered ... ' (25, 3-4).

Athenagoras is, like virtually all the Fathers, highly critical of Greco-Roman religious practices and beliefs and this forms a large part of his attack on the allegations against the Christians of atheism. He argues at 34 for the superiority of Christian moral teaching and practice over the pagan. At 36.4f. he makes clear that Christians will have nothing to do with the amphitheatre and other popular spectacles. At no point, even when he is attacking religious sacrifices, however, does he make mention of the imperial cult. This is not surprising given that his intention is to persuade the emperors to support the lessening of attacks on Christians. At 37.2 he offers prayers for the emperors and for the expansion of their rule, so that all may become subject to them. He makes no specific mention of Jewish beliefs and practices. This is probably to be explained by the fact that it is not his particular concern in this work and that by the third quarter of the second century the Jewish community hardly posed a threat, physical or theological, to the Christian.

Clement of Alexandria

Titus Flavius Clemens was born around 150 CE to pagan parents and probably in Athens. After his conversion he travelled extensively through southern Italy, Syria and Palestine, seeking out Christian teachers (*Stromateis* 1,1,11). He then moved on to Alexandria where he sat at the feet of Pantaenus, the alleged head of a school for catechumens whom Clement succeeded around 200.[21] In 202 or 203 he fled the persecution of Septimius Severus with his pupil Alexander (later bishop of Jerusalem) and took refuge in Cappadocia. Clement probably moved to Jerusalem about 205 and certainly died before 221. Eusebius[22] lists ten works by Clement, of which four are extant: the *Stromateis*, the *Paedagogus*, the *Protreptikos*, and the *Who is the Rich Man that is being saved?* The *Stromateis* is a largely apologetic writing with no strict ordering of topics. Dawson describes it as 'a lengthy, rambling series of obscurely arranged ruminations on Christianity as the true *gnosis*'. Yet it clearly has, in my view, a definite purpose and direction. In it Clement seeks to teach or to explicate the faith to mature Christians by defending the use of pagan wisdom to interpret true *gnosis*. The work is intended by him to encourage such Christians to see in pagan learning a

---

21 D.Dawson, *Allegorical Readers and Cultural Revision in Ancient Alexandria.* (Berkeley, 1992), p. 222, claims that Clement was not the head of an official catechetical school but 'an independent teacher in loose relation to the Christian church in Alexandria'.

22 *EH* 6.13.1-3.

possible set of tools for understanding the Gospel against the backdrop of a prejudice on the part of many traditional, conservative Christians towards such learning. The *Paedagogus*, for its part, was primarily instructional and perhaps best understood as a handbook for catechumens and other new Christians.[23] His *Protreptikos* belongs to the same genre of the protreptic pieces - those urging conversion to philosophy - by Aristotle, Cicero, Epicurus, and the Stoics Cleanthes, Chrysippus and Poseidonius. It is an exhortation to pagans to embrace the new philosophy and is appropriately full of hortatory subjunctives. It may have been intended originally as a refutation of Celsus' *Discourse* to which latter work later Origen made his celebrated response. The *Rich Man* is a homily on *Mark* 10, 17-31.

The influence of the classic conventions of contemporary rhetoric on Clement's arrangement of his material is obvious. The *Protreptikos* is clearly rhetorical in style. It begins with a *narratio* rather than an *exordium*, certainly not one intended to win the goodwill of his hearers. This should not surprise us, however, given that Clement's primary intention was not to win applause but, in his exhortation for pagans to abandon idolatry for God, souls for Christ. Chapters 2 to 10 comprise the *probatio*: 2 to 5 a *refutatio* of pagan beliefs and practices, 6 to 9 a *confirmatio* of the Christian faith, 10 a further *refutatio* of the objection that it is wrong to abandon custom. Chapters 11 and 12 comprise the *peroratio* with the first a recapitulation of argument and the second an emotional appeal to conversion. The *Paedagogus* likewise begins with a *narratio* in which Clement deals with the different forms of discourse, the *hortatory* intended to bring to piety, the *preceptive* to action consistent with piety, and the *persuasive* to heal the passions. Chapters 2 to 7 of Book I comprise a *confirmatio*, 8 a *refutatio* of the notion that the good cannot be also just, and 9 to II.12 a further series of *confirmationes*. Book 2, chapter 13 is a *refutatio* while chapters 1 to 11 include both *confirmatio* and *refutatio*. Chapter 12 begins as part of the preceding set of *confirmationes* but concludes as the *peroratio* comprising both recapitulation and emotional appeal and exhortation to piety. Each of the first seven books of the *Stromateis* - the relationship of the eighth to the rest of the work is unclear - begins with a *narratio* and include elements of both a *confirmatio* of the Christian faith and a *refutatio* of paganism. The only exception perhaps is book three which is almost in its entirety a refutation of heresy, in particular that of the Basilideans, the Marcionites, the Carpocrations and Tatian. In chapter 18 of the seventh book Clement takes a predictable (almost traditional) swipe at contemporary rhetorical practice. There he comments,

> 'Now the Miscellanies are not like parts laid out, planted in regular order for the delight of the eye, but rather … The Miscellanies, then, study neither arrangement not diction; since there are even cases in which the Greeks on purpose wish that ornate diction should be absent, and imperceptibly cast in the seed of dogmas, not according to the truth, rendering such as may read laborious and quick at discovery. For many and various are the baits for the various kinds of fishes.'

---

23 Dawson, *Allegorical Readers and Cultural Revision*, p. 183, calls it a handbook of social and personal ethics.

Clement is certainly eclectic in his use of philosophy; while he demonstrates a not unusual preference for Plato, whom he quotes constantly (see below), much of his effort is directed towards seeking to find in pre-Christian thought elements or traces of evangelical truth. He desired above all to make Christianity more accessible for educated people prepared to listen. In the first book of the *Stromateis* Clement declares that 'philosophy … was a preparation [sc. for the Greeks] paving the way for him who is perfected in Christ' (*Stromateis* 1,5,11) and that this 'is shown to have come down from God to men, not with a definite direction, but in the way in which showers fall down on the good land, and on the dunghill, and on the houses' (1,7,1).

At 1,5,28.1 he declares that philosophy 'is a kind of propaedeutic for those who reap the faith through proof'. It is of value primarily for those who seek to become Christians and require proof but not quite so much for those who are already Christians. In his sixth book of the same work he speaks of ordinary Christians being 'frightened at the Hellenic philosophy, as children are at masks, being afraid lest it lead them astray' (6,10,81.2). 'But if', he continues, 'the faith (for I cannot call it knowledge) which they possess be such as to be dissolved by plausible speech, let it be by all means dissolved, and let them confess that they will not retain the truth. For truth is immoveable; but false opinion dissolves' (ibid.). And later in the same chapter he maintains that truth, though partial, 'appears in Hellenic philosophy'. At 1,1,17.4 Clement declares that, like a farmer irrigating his land in advance of sowing, he will 'prepare the land of the Hellenes with things from their own works that are drinkable, so that they can receive the spiritual seed that is sown and cultivate it with ease'. 'Our book', he declares, 'will not shrink from making use of what is best in philosophy and other preparatory instruction' (1,1.15.3).

Clement openly acknowledges, as did Plato himself, the esoteric and enigmatic character of the higher *gnosis*.[24] *Stromateis* 5.3.17.4 ('Wise souls, pure as virgins, understanding themselves to be situated amid the ignorance of the world') (see Plato's *Republic* 6.494a[25]), 5.6.33.5 ('for almost the whole Scripture gives its utterances in this [sc. enigmatic] way') (*Theaet.* 155e[26]), and 5.7.6 ('The Egyptians

---

24 Clement, in his use of both *gnosis* and (true) *Gnostic*, makes clear that he differentiates these from the usage by those regarded as heretics like Valentinus and Basilides. It is a regrettably common mistake, made by both undergraduates and even some scholars, that Clement's use of both terms should see him ranked with the heretics!

25 'Philosophy, then, the love of wisdom, is impossible for the multitude (plēthos adunaton einai)'. Clement simply quotes from the *Republic* here but also quotes *Matthew* 22,14, *1 Corinthians* 8,7, *2 Thessalonians* 3,1-2, and Cleanthes the Stoic in support of his position.

26 Socrates: 'You will be grateful to me if I help you discover the veiled truth in the thought of a great man'. Theaetetus: 'Of course I shall be, Socrates, very grateful'. Socrates: 'Then you have a look round, and see that none of the uninitiated are listening to us - I mean the people who think that nothing exists but what they can grasp with both hands; people who refuse to admit that actions and processes and the invisible world in general have any place in reality'.

did not entrust the mysteries they possessed to all and sundry, and did not divulge the knowledge of divine things to the profane') (*Epinom.* 973e[27]) clearly evidence Clement's understanding of this higher *gnosis* as consisting of the contemplative life. Clement's ideal of this contemplative life is connected particularly with the Platonic tradition and with Philo. Rizzerio, discussing the notion of *gnostike physiologia* in Clement,[28] declares that Clement is 'conscient' with two meanings given to the term *physiologia* by his contemporaries, that of a science which seeks the causes of natural phenomena and also that, which notion is more 'religious', of a science capable of discovering the true principles behind these phenomena in the light of revelation. Recognising properly that, for Clement, the term *gnostike* is the equivalent of the 'truly Christian', Rizzerio argues that his notion of *physiologia* differs from the Greek notion of the term and that it therefore 'conforms to Christian teaching'.

For Clement Greek philosophy, prior to the Incarnation and the coming of faith, provided a preparation for the Greeks for the Gospel's coming (*praeparatio evangelica*); while inferior to the Jewish law (*Strom.* 6.6:44,4), for example, philosophy was, as we have seen, providential and as such came from God. Indeed Clement employed philosophical argument against those Christians who protested against the Christian use of or engagement with philosophy. Yet his employment of pagan authors is not undiscriminating. He cannot, for example, in order not to concede something to the Gnostics, accept that 'preconceptions are innate'. The 'prophets' of Greek philosophy were Homer, Plato, Pythagoras and others. Yet even earlier 'barbarian' sages were, for Clement, the sources for these 'prophets'. These ancient sages - pre-Socratics, Egyptians, Indians and Jews - were for him the true philosophers (see *Stromateis* 1.15). God, says Clement, communicated through the mediation of angels - which idea is a 'fundamental view of Clement's' - the doctrines which God chose to impart, the sages taught these to their people, and the Greeks 'plundered' them wholesale. And thus when Clement speaks of philosophy as a providential preparation for the coming of faith, it is not the actual schools of Greek philosophy to which he is referring, but primarily the ancient 'barbarian' philosophies. Yet in all of this the 'Word of revelation [remains]', for Clement, 'the fountainhead of all philosophy' (*Strom.* 6,7:57,2-58,1). 'True philosophy derives from God' (*Strom.* 6,7:58,3). For Clement (see *Stromateis* 1,7,37 above), 'Pythagoras and Plato, listening to the inner voice and with the help of God, have reached the truth'.

Clement employs the 'stock texts' of his day from Plato and I provide here some samples of this usage. At *Protreptikos* 6,68,1 and *Stromateis* 5,12,78,1 and 5,14:92,1-4, for example, he makes use of *Timaeus* 28c3-4.[29] In the *Protreptikos*

27 'My [sc. the Athenian's] thesis is that attainment of bliss and felicity is impossible for mankind, with the exception of a chosen few.'

28 L. Rizzerio, 'La notion de γνωστικη φυσιολογια chez Clément d'Alexandrie', *Studia Patristica* 26 (1993): 318-23.

29 'It is a hard task to find the Father and Maker of this universe, and when you have found him, it is impossible to declare him at all.'

reading Clement has just finished attacking the philosophers for making an idol of matter (as a first principle) and for being ignorant of the great First cause, the Maker of all things and Creator of first principles, the unbeginning God. In this he primarily targets the Stoa, Aristotle and Epicurus and declares (in 6) that 'I seek after God and not the works of God. He then quotes the *Timaeus* reading declaring that he has not wholly disowned Plato who 'has touched on the truth' through the inspiration of the spirit ('an effluence') who has led him to a confession of the one God. In the first *Stromateis* passage he again quotes from the *Timaeus,* calling Plato the 'truth-loving' to emphasise the fact that God cannot be comprehended in words or by human thought, that God is beyond expression in words, the divine unutterable by human power; in the second passage he has attacked the plagiarism of the Greeks from the 'barbarians', again targeting the Stoics, Aristotle and Pythagoras (and at times Plato himself) for including matter among the first principles but quotes from the *Timaeus* again to demonstrate that for Plato the universe itself is created, springing from non-existence. At *Protreptikos* 6,68,5 (in part) and *Stromateis* 5,14:103, 1 and 7,2:9,3 (perhaps by allusion) Clement refers to Plato's *Epistle* II,312e.[30] In the first he demonstrates by reference to this Platonic text that philosophers can sometimes get it right, on this occasion with respect to the notion of God as cause of all good things. In the second, in a manner not inconsistent with its Plotinian usage, he says that by this text he 'understand[s] nothing else than the Holy Trinity to be meant; for the third is the Holy Spirit, and the Son is the second, by whom all things were made according to the will of the Father'. (Note that at *Stromateis* 5.14.5 Clement quotes *Epistle* 6.323d[31] to demonstrate that here Plato 'exhibits the Father and the Son'.) In the third he speaks of the Father as the cause of all good things, as the efficient cause of motion, and declares from one original principle, which acts according to the Father's will, the first and second and third depend. *Laws* IV,715e-716a[32] is cited by Clement at *Protreptikos* 6,69,6 and *Stromateis* 2,22:132,2 (in part) and 7,16:106, 3 (by allusion). In the *Protreptikos* passage, having already praised Plato for touching on the truth by inspiration of a divine effluence, he quotes from the *Laws* to the effect that God is alone the measure of the truth of all existence, that the only just measure is the only true God. In the first *Stromateis* passage, when speaking of the chief virtue and the highest perfection as assimilation to the Good and likeness to God he employs this piece to connect the fear of God with the divine law and the inspiration to the likeness to God; in the second he alludes to such a passage when he speaks of Scripture as the criterion by which truth and heresy, knowledge and rash opinion, may be distinguished. Clement uses *Epistle* VII, 341c[33] - in conjunction

30 'All things are around the king of all things, and all things exist because of him, and that is the cause of everything good, and a second [cause] is around the second things, and a third around the third.'

31 'You must swear by the Lord and Father of the Ruler and Cause.'

32 'Now God, as the ancient saying has it, holding the beginning and end and middle of all existence, … keeps an unswerving path, revolving according to nature; but ever there follows along with him Right, to take vengeance on those who forsake the divine law.'

33 '[God] can in no way be described.'

with *Timaeus* 28c - at *Stromateis* 5,12:78,1. Clement employs it to underscore the point that the idea of God, like the idea of the Platonic Idea, cannot be explained by human thought. *Timaeus* 41a[34] is cited by Clement at *Stromateis* 5,14:102,5 as yet an another example of Greek plagiarism from the barbarians and follows it with an explanation of *Epistle* II.312e (see above) as pointing to the Holy Trinity. Clement implicitly applies *Phaedrus* 246e[35] to the Logos at *Stromateis* 7,2:5,1 when he speaks of the paternal Word as that which orders all things according to the Father's will.[36] Clement also makes use of the Myth of the Cave (see *Republic* 514a-517a) to express the descent of the Word and his resurrection at *Stromateis* 5,14:105,2-4. There is also the obvious linkage in Clement at *Stromateis* 5.14 between *Genesis* 1,26 and Plato's *Theaetetus* 176b[37] with respect to the latter's notion of the *homoiōsis theō.* Clement sought as a Christian Platonist to give the notion of the reconciliation of all things in Christ a rational and ethical coherence. He is also indebted to Aristotle, quotes thirty-three fragments of Heraclitus, though the latter probably does not directly influence him (his references are probably drawn from other sources), and his ethics are clearly influenced by the Stoic.[38] Clement regarded philosophy as useful but as secondary to faith (*Stromateis* 1,5:28,2) but was also probably the first Christian author to champion the cause of the heritage of ancient culture within a Christian context. It had its place even for those who oppose its claims. For Clement, to prove philosophy useless one must philosophise (*Stromateis* 1,2:19,1),[39] to refute it one needs first to understand it. For the notion of the quest (*Stromateis* 8, passim) Clement employed the language and spirit of philosophical knowledge.

Osborn observes three distinct stages in Clement's account of the Logos and the influence on these by Philo and other philosophers: the mind of God, the totality of ideas, and the world-soul.[40] The first (*Stromateis* 4.25.155; 5.11.73) comes from

---

34 'Gods that are sons of gods, I am their Creator. I am the father of works which are indissoluble only so far as I will it, for all things which are composite are corruptible.'

35 'Zeus, the great sovereign in heaven, driving his winged chariot, is the first to go forth, setting in order all things and attending to them. There follows him a host of gods and demons.'

36 See G.W.Butterworth, 'Clement of Alexandria's *Protrepticus* and the *Phaedrus* of Plato', *Classical Quarterly* 10 (1916): 198-205.

37 'That is why a man should make all haste to escape from earth to heaven; and escape means becoming as like God as possible (*homoiōsis theō kata to dunaton*); and a man becomes like God when he becomes just and pure, with understanding'. See Dillon, *The Middle Platonists*, p. 44, on the Platonic ideal *telos* of the 'likeness to God'.

38 See also L.Emmett, 'Clement of Alexandria's *Protrepticus* and Dio Chrysostom's *Alexandrian Oration*, *SP* 36 (2001): 409-14, for the argument for an affinity between Clement and Dio's work, U.Neymeyr, 'Der Protreptikos des Clemens und des Galen', *SP* 36 (2001): 445-8, for that between protreptic writings of Clement and Galen, and K.Parel, 'The Disease of the Passions in Clement of Alexandria', *SP* 36 (2001): 449-55, for the claimed use by Clement of a traditional analogy between the medical art of healing the body and the relieving of the soul's distress through philosophy.

39 This was the argument of Aristotle in his *Protrepticus*.

40 Osborn, *The Beginnings of Christian Philosophy*, p. 241.

Philo but is also found in Aristotle, Alcinous, Plutarch and others. The second, the Logos as the first principle of created things (*Stromateis* 4.25.156) is found in Philo but also in Plotinus and Plato's *Parmenides*. The third, the Logos as an immanent world-soul is found in Philo, Alcinous, Plutarch, Atticus and Numenius and may have a Stoic origin.[41]

Stählin[42] lists from Clement's extant works - though one should not take the figures too precisely - 1273 borrowings from Paul, 618 from Plato, 243 from Homer, 117 from Euripides, and 279 from Philo, though the last is only mentioned four times by name - a low proportion when compared to the others listed - but this may mean, in Clement's arguments against the Gnostics who made much of their immediate teachers, that he regarded Philo as a 'direct mentor'. This is certainly the case with Pantaenus whom Clement never mentions at all directly by name in the *Stromateis*.

Runia argues that Clement's writings 'reveal surprisingly little contact with the Jewish community of his day (which may not yet have recovered from the terrible events earlier in the century) and certainly very little inclination to engage in open and direct discussion with them'. Van den Hoek suggests that both Clement and Origen's links with Philo and other Jewish Hellenistic and Jewish Christian sources was primarily a literary one: 'Clement does not reflect living contacts with Jewish scholars'. Carleton Paget likewise is doubtful that the available evidence from Clement's writings suggest *viva voce* contact with Jews. There is no evidence of a desire to convert Jews in Clement's works, and certainly not in the *Protreptikos*, and where there are signs of an anti-Jewish polemic in the *Stromateis* it has no sense of immediacy. That there was no significant Jewish population in the city in Clement's time is confirmed by the available historical evidence of the low profile of the Alexandrian Jewish community after 117 CE.

Origen of Alexandria

More is known of the life of Origen than of many of the other Fathers. This is due mainly to Eusbeius of Caesarea who in his *Ecclesiastical History* devotes much of the sixth book to him. We have also the evidence of Gregory the Wonderworker's 'Farewell Oration' to Origen, as well as mentions by both Jerome and Photius. Origen was born around 185 CE to a Christian home in which he was the eldest son. His father, Leonidas, was a Christian martyr during the persecution of the emperor Septimius Severus in Alexandria in 202. It is even said that had not Origen's mother hidden his clothes the somewhat impetuous youth may well have joined his father in a martyr's death. But this was not to happen for another 50 years. In any event, the famous Catechetical School at Alexandria suffered a severe reverse during the

---

41 See R.Mortley, *Connaissance religieuse et herménetique chez Clément d'Alexandrie*. (Leiden, 1973), p. 113, note 2, who states that 'Clément accepte la doctrine stoïcienne du Logos, en l'assimilant avec la personne du Pédagogue, comme le directeur de la nature et de la morale humaine'.

42 O.Stählin, *Clemens Alexandrinus*. Text. (Leipzig, 1905-36).

persecution and Demetrius, bishop of Alexandria at the time, secured the headship of the school for the young Origen. Reports that during this early period the zealous (even fanatical) young Origen castrated himself, in literal obedience to the demands of *Matthew* 19,12 ('those made eunuchs for the sake of the kingdom'), are now largely discounted. His tenure of the headship of the School, in which he possibly succeeded such luminaries as Pantaenus and Clement (who probably influenced Origen considerably), lasted until 231. While there he taught principally philosophy, theology and biblical studies, while his subordinates took responsibility for the traditional subjects of dialectics, physics, mathematics, geometry and astronomy. During the period of his tenure, he travelled much, venturing as far afield as Rome (in 212), Arabia, Antioch and Palestine (in 216). While in the latter place he so impressed the bishops of Jerusalem and Caesarea that they asked him to preach - unusual for a layperson - and in 231, when he again visited the region, they ordained him as priest. Both incidents enraged Demetrius, both because it appeared that his own rights as Origen's bishop had been infringed and also because he probably envied his brighter and younger subordinate. In 231, then, soon after his ordination in Palestine, Origen was excommunicated and deprived of his priesthood at successive synods in Alexandria. He departed immediately for Caesarea in Palestine where the bishop ignored the Alexandrian decisions and appointed Origen to head a new school of theology where he remained for over 20 years. It was here that Gregory delivered his famous farewell discourse. Origen left for Arabia around 244 where he was also well received. During the Decian persecution of 251/2 Origen was horribly tortured and died of his wounds at Tyre in 253. The controversies over his memory and teachings began not long after his death and continued for a number of centuries.

The sheer volume of his writings was prodigious. His corpus of letters - numbering over a hundred but now unfortunately lost to us - were known to Eusebius who quotes from them frequently. His most lasting contributions to Christian thought were his extensive biblical commentaries, of which that on the Gospel of John is arguably the most famous. His exegetical approach was primarily allegorical and it may properly be said that he is regarded widely as the founder of the Christian allegorical tradition which prevailed mainly at Alexandria and also in parts of the West. He saw at least three levels of meaning in scripture, that for the elite, the 'spiritual', that for the simple, the 'carnal', and, in the middle, that for the ordinary, reasonably educated Christian, the 'psychic' or 'soul-ish' (*animalis* in Latin). He was essentially a man of the Bible - the Bible was his sole source of revelation, though he was more profoundly influenced by Greek philosophy than he himself may have appreciated or acknowledged - and his approach was consistently christocentric. He saw biblical exposition as his primary task. He sought, in the cultural context of cosmopolitan Alexandria, to interpret Christianity in a language familiar to the Platonic tradition (particularly in his early writings), but remained intensely biblical. He was, unlike Clement, sternly austere and less sympathetic towards pagan philosophy; Plato was true at times, despite himself. He sought, too, to meet Jewish controversialists on their own ground and compiled the *Hexapla*, with the Hebrew text of the Old Testament set alongside columns of a number of Greek versions. He was willing to argue for the Christian point of view from the Hebrew text but argued consistently for the ultimate authority of the Septuagint.

He wrote a number of treatises, foremost among them the *Peri Archōn* (or *De Principiis*) (*On First Principles*) - a piece of speculative theology containing, *inter alia*, his understanding of both cosmogony and cosmology - and the *Contra Celsum* (*Against Celsus*) - an apologetic rebuttal of the claims of Christianity's alleged irrationality by a second century pagan critic,[43] and written at the insistence of his patron Ambrose for educated Christians seeking resources to combat the type of intellectual objections raised against the faith by Celsus.[44] He also wrote *Peri Euches* (*On Prayer*) in 233 or 234, while in Caesarea, at the insistence of Ambrose and a friend Tatiana: it is by general regard one of the greatest works on Christian prayer. He wrote against the Gnostics, on education, ambition, apostasy, the Empire and the involvement of Christians in government service. He was later accused of subordinationism (i.e., of the Son to the Father, the Son being described as a 'Second God' and the Spirit a 'Third') [45] and of teaching the possibility of Satan's ultimate salvation and restoration to grace. Eusebius regarded him as the supreme saint, the great teacher persecuted from within and without the church. Origen dealt also with a number of other issues in his writings. He sought to address Gnosticism by addressing their particular questions: evil, the place of matter, freewill. He argued that the Fall, a thereby pre-mundane event, led to the creation of the material world (and that the various spiritual beings, depending on the degree of their revolt against God became angels, humans or daemons), but that this creation was the act of a loving God (and not an accident). It was intended for the retraining of the creature (although Origen does speak of the experience as a form of punishment). The wrath of God, he declares, has a remedial purpose. He saw the material world as temporary and provisional and therefore as not the ultimate end of humankind.

Origen's engagement with Greek philosophy was hardly uncritical.[46] 'Do not covet the deceptive food philosophy provides; it may turn you away from the truth' (*Hom. Lev.* 10,2). At *Contra Celsum* praef. 5 Origen refers to the Apostle's claim in *Colossians* that while Greek philosophy has many impressive doctrines it yet 'presents as truth what is untrue'. And yet, notwithstanding that he did not share the

---

43 Celsus, a Platonist, wrote an attack on Christianity, titled *True Religion*, sometime in the early part of the second half of the second century.

44 See M.Frede, 'Origen's Treatise *Against Celsus*', in Edwards, *Apologetics in the Roman Empire*, pp. 131-55 and S-P.Bergjan, 'Celsus the Epicurean? The Interpretation of an Argument in Origen, *Contra Celsum*', *HTR* 94 (2001): 179-204.

45 See J.Dillon, 'Origen and Plotinus: The Platonic Influence on Early Christianity', in T.Finan and V.Twomey (eds), *The Relationship between Neoplatonism and Christianity.* (Blackrock, 1992), where the author attributes this position of Origen to borrowing from Numenius.

46 I am conscious that more has probably been written on Origen's engagement with ancient thought than for any other pre-Nicene Father. I cannot hope to do justice even to the scholarship in this area of recent times. I seek only here to provide an extended summary of current thinking.

apparent optimism of Clement, he recognised the need to explore issues and problems theologically which were central to contemporary philosophical discourse. In his *Letter to Gregory*, written in the 240s to Gregory Thaumaturgus, Origen portrays philosophy as an 'adjunct' to Christianity, as a useful introduction to the proper study of Christianity, but not as the 'main game' (1). Philosophy, he maintains, is subordinate to the Bible and cautions against its misuse. At *Contra Celsum* 4.30 Origen acknowledges that some of the philosophers did know God, since God made himself plain to them, but they did not either 'glorify' or 'give thanks' to God but rather 'professed themselves to be wise'. It is generally agreed that his own teacher was the Platonist philosopher Ammonius Saccas (c. 175-242) who was also later the teacher of Plotinus.[47] Except for the *Contra Celsum* there are few direct quotations from the philosophers or even direct references to them in his writings.[48] He clearly knew Plato as well as Aristotle and Chrysippus. The great Platonic themes - a God distinct from creation, the immortality and pre-existence of the soul,[49] and the power of contemplation to achieve a likeness to God - are present in his writings.[50] His Platonism, however, is drawn from only a few works of Plato (the *Timaeus*, the *Theaetetus*, the *Phaedrus*, the *Laws* and the *Epistles*), while his psychological vocabulary is Stoic and his dialectic Aristotelian. His Platonism is the contemporary eclectic Middle Platonism and not the Neoplatonism which emerges in his own time. Origen learnt his allegorical method in large part from the Stoics and their interpretation of the Homeric poems, though we know from Plutarch that Middle Platonism also demonstrates an allegorical temper. What Origen does learn from the philosophers is this allegorical exegesis and it is in this above all that Origen sees something which can be salvaged from them (*Hom. Gen.* 6, 2-3; *Hom. Lev.* 7,6).

Crouzel argues that Origen 'possesses a sound training in philology and dialectic and is acquainted with all the subjects studied in his day' and these he employs in his literal interpretation of Scripture, in teaching generally and specifically in his writing against Celsus. He does not, however, unlike Clement, regard philosophy as a preparation for the Gospel for the Greeks quite as the prophets were for the Jews. Origen is critical of philosophy but is clearly learned in it. Like Clement Origen often points to the alleged 'insufficiency' of philosophy even if it is, from time to time, found to be agreement with the Christian faith. He will have nothing to do, however, with the 'pernicious sophistry' of the Greeks nor with the 'rhetoric prevalent in the law-courts' (*CC* 3.39). Yet it must be said that the style of some at least of his treatises has been shaped in part at least by the conventions of contemporary

47 For a contrary view see M.J. Edwards, 'Ammonius, Teacher of Origen', *Journal of Ecclesiastical History* 44 (1993): 169-181.

48 Note the allusions only to Plato at *De Principiis* 2.1.3; 1.4; 3.4.1; 6.1.

49 At *Contra Celsum* 3.22 and elsewhere he commends those philosophers who teach the immortality of the soul.

50 E.F.Osborn, 'Causality in Plato and Origen' in L.Lies (ed.), *Origeniana Quarta*. (Innsbruck, 1987), p. 367, declares that 'Origen so integrates Platonic and Christian thought that the denial of the existence of a Christian Platonism is only possible to those who do not understand how definitions work'.

rhetorical theory. The preface to the *De Principiis* comprises both an *exordium* (1-3) and a *narratio* (4-10). Most of Book one comprises a *confirmatio* of the Christian faith and at 1.8.4 he refers to the arguments which have gone before as 'proofs'. In the same section he refers to books which are to follow as containing refutations of his opponents' arguments. Books 2 and 3 each begins with a *narratio* and include both *confirmatio* and *refutatio*. Book 4 comprises a *confirmatio* in its argument for the divine inspiration of the scriptures and includes a recapitulation of his arguments towards the end. The *Contra Celsum* begins with a *narratio* and for the most part comprises a *refutatio* of his opponent. Book 8 moves from *refutatio* to *confirmatio* and section 76 of the book comprises a brief *peroratio* by way of a brief summary of his purpose accomplished.[51]

For Origen many truths have been manifested to the philosophical schools by God but some who have learned there have turned this truth 'into a lie and worshipped and served the creature rather than the Creator' in the words of the Apostle in *Romans* 1, 25 (*CC* 7.47). Origen can see some measure of common ground between Christianity and philosophy - particularly in the latter's Platonist form - but believes that this seeming community of thought ultimately founders on the apparent self-love implicit in the philosophical view which contrasts so much with the Christian love for God. The philosopher has no sense of authentic grace and none of a personal relationship with God. Origen comments, with particular reference to Plato, that while the philosopher said many things which were actually true this 'did not help his readers towards a pure religion at all, nor even Plato himself, in spite of the fact that he taught such profound philosophy about the highest good' (*CC* 6.5).[52] His religious life does not inform his moral life and cannot provide a 'true saving knowledge of God'. It cannot, above all, cure sin. Origen calls the famous passage of the *Timaeus* 28c3-4, loved by Christian Father and pagan alike (see above), 'noble and impressive' (*CC* 7.42) and Plato a 'more effective teacher of theological truth' (*CC* 7.42.1). But he also acknowledges that God in his pure state may only be known with divine aid and thus the fact that Plato is technically correct does not bring his readers any closer to actually knowing the truth. Plato and other philosophers also predominantly teach only the elite, while the prophets and the disciples of Jesus teach the multitude (*CC* 7.60). Plato, unlike Jesus, is simply inaccessible to both the unlearned and even the moderately learned (*CC* 7.61). What Celsus sees as a weakness for Christianity, Origen understands only as its greatest strength, its very accessibility.

Like other Christian commentators he ranks the philosophical schools in order of merit. Epicureanism, with its pleasure-driven morality, its denial of Providence, and other anti-Gospel attributes, comes a distant last. Origen declares that in many

51 See P.O'Cleirigh, '*Topoi* of Invention in Origen's *Homilies*', in G.Dorival and A.Le Boulluec (eds), *Origeniana Sexta*. (Leuven, 1995), pp. 277-87, for a discussion of a particular aspect of Origen's debt to rhetorical methodology.

52 Indeed, says Origen in the same passage, the very mean style of the divine scriptures 'has made honest readers inspired by it'.

of his writings Celsus is 'found to be an Epicurean' (*CC* 1.8; see also 1.10 and 2.35). Aristotle, while Origen will make some use of his language and method, is not highly regarded by him. The former's denial of the reach of Providence to this sublunar realm counts very much against him and has him accounted an atheist like the Epicureans, though Aristotle is 'less irreverent about providence' than Epicurus (*CC* 1.21). Origen endorses Stoic morality - indeed he commends the Stoic doctrine that as 'one lie is not more untrue than any other lie, and is not a lie in any greater degree, so a truth is not more true than any other truth in a greater degree' (*CC* 2.7)[53] and approves that which maintains that 'the virtue of both man and God is the same' (*CC* 4.29) as supportive of the concept of absolute moral categories - but condemns their cosmology and theology as materialist (*CC* 4.14) and their cyclical view of time as incompatible with the biblical (*CC* 4. 67f.). For the last mentioned Origen also fails to mark the Pythagoreans as highly as he might on other grounds. Yet he often includes them favourably in the same breath and sentence as the Platonists (see *CC* 1.32) and speaks with particular favour of the neo-Pythagorean Numenius whom he calls 'learned' (*CC* 1.15). Of all the schools Origen admires most that of the Middle Platonists (that is, their version of Plato). At *Contra Celsum* 6.2 Origen denies that he is criticising Plato when he demonstrates that admiration by the masses does not equate with profound learning (he notes that Plato, while reflecting such learning, is not widely read by ordinary people). Rather, he describes Plato as one from whom 'the great world of mankind has derived help'. In his debate with Celsus Origen both approves and condemns different Platonist positions, is informed by Plato's exemplarist view of the world and his notion of the immortality of the soul (see the *Phaedo*), but rejects his tripartite view of the human soul. Origen's understanding of the absolute transcendence of God is also given greater focus by Platonism although it also leads him in some ways into his subordinationism.[54]

Crouzel argues that 'the context of Origen's exegesis is a vision of the world dominated by the relation of the model and the image, which makes it akin to the exemplarism of Plato'[55] and that Origen's 'divine world of the mysteries' is 'analogous to Plato's ideas, [and] possesses perfect existence and intelligibility'.[56] In other areas, however, the influence of Platonism is not as obvious as it might seem to others. Crouzel declares, for example, that 'it is not possible to assimilate Origen's trichotomy [sc. man as spirit, soul and body] to Plato's:[57] the latter is about the soul alone [sc. intelligence (*nous*), anger (*thumos*) and covetousness (*epithumia*)], the

53 Diogenes Laertius declares that 'it is [the Stoics'] doctrine that nothing is in between virtue and vice. ... For as a stick must be either straight or crooked, so a man must be either just or unjust, but not either more just or more unjust' (7.127).

54 J.W.Trigg, *Origen*. (London and New York, 1998), p. 23, however, points out that Origen did not need Platonism to point him towards subordinationism. It was the common position of pre-Nicene theologians.

55 H. Crouzel, *Origen*. (Edinburgh, 1989), p. 78.

56 Ibid.

57 See the allusions to Plato's *Republic* 4.436a-441c and *Timaeus* 42a (on the twofold nature of humankind) in *De Principiis* 3.4.1.

former about the whole man [sc. spirit (*pneuma*), soul (*psychē*), body (*soma*)]'.[58] When Origen speaks of God revealing something of Godself when he created humankind in his image 'Origen reproduces a principle of Greek philosophy which is a common-sense affirmation: only the like knows the like'. Origen also 'recognises the value of the Platonist dialectic which takes the creatures up to God' but condemns both Plato and Socrates, notwithstanding their 'lofty thoughts on God,' for not practising this themselves. One might also note Origen's positive use of Plato's *Letter VII* on the recognition of the five elements on which knowledge depends: name (*onoma*), definition (*logos*), image (*eidōlon*), science (*epistēmē*) and that object which is both 'knowable and true', the Platonic 'idea' (CC 6,9). Crouzel points also to the possible influence of Plato's employment of the analogy of light for the 'graces of knowledge' in *Republic* 6, 506-509 (*CC* 7,45) whereby God 'is the Light that makes it possible to know the intelligible realities'.

Origen sees in Plato's *Epistle* VI. 323d[59] a reference to the Christian doctrine of the Father and Son much as Clement did at *Stromateis* 5.14.102 (*CC* 6.8). Yet, while Justin (*1 Apol.* 60.7) and Clement (*Strom.* 5.14.103,1) draw a trinitarian inferences from Plato's *Epistle* II.312e,[60] Origen does not when he cites it at *Contra Celsum* 6.18f.[61] Indeed, he goes to make clear that he does not have a need for such a Platonic reference when he has the witness of the prophets, *Isaiah* 6,2 and *Ezekiel* 1,5-27 and 10, 1-21 among them. Again, he declares that Plato himself actually took many things from the Jews and uses *Phaedrus* 247c[62] as an example. Origen also commends Plato's distinction between being and becoming in *Timaeus* 28a and the notion of contemplation as a way to knowing God (*CC* 7.45).

Origen's ascetical and ethical doctrine, while primarily biblical, are also to be found in Stoicism, Platonism, and to a lesser degree Aristotelianism. Likewise Origen's teaching on ethics was based on the four cardinal virtues as defined by Plato[63] - prudence, temperance, justice, and courage. We note also the allusion by Origen at *De Principiis* III.6.1 to the famous passage from Plato's *Theaetetus* 176b on the highest good for man being a likeness to God but declares also that this was not original to him but first said by Moses at *Genesis* 1,26. He commends the decision by Plato to exclude from his Republic Homer and the poets on the grounds that they do harm to the young (*CC* 4.48-50). In relation to Origen's use of philosophy as a handmaid to theological enquiry it has been long established that he had a thorough knowledge of Stoic logic. This notion has traditionally been based upon the *Contra Celsum*. It is also, however, evident in Origen's best-known biblical commentary, that

---

58 Crouzel, *Origen*, p. 87.

59 'Swear by the God that is Ruler of all that is and that shall be, and swear by the Lord and Father of the Ruler (*hēgemonos*) and Cause (*aitiou*).'

60 See Clement of Alexandria for the employment of this text from Plato.

61 Here Origen merely reports Christian use of this text as an example of what Celsus claims as misunderstandings by Christians of Plato.

62 A reference to the 'heaven which is above the heavens'?

63 We must note, of course, that these virtues were also held as primary by Zeno (according to Plutarch), Aristotle and Pythagoras.

on the Gospel of John. He sees this with respect to the relationship of God and the Word (92-100), of the Gnostic doctrine of natures (100-110), and on the glorification of the Son and the Father in the Economy of Suffering (110-117). Says Heine, 'In his use of Stoic logic, Origen has employed some of the most sophisticated tools of his day for the analysis of thought. The unobtrusive way in which he uses it shows that he has internalized the subject so thoroughly that it shapes the way he thinks about texts and about the way others have interpreted those texts'.[64]

In his *Homily on Leviticus* Origen urges his readers to use philosophy as an auxiliary to Christian learning, the 'divine philosophy' (7,6). The educated Christian must know philosophy in order to use it appropriately and, in the end, to refute it. Yet an undiscerning Christian who seeks to apply philosophy to the scriptures will only end in heresy and idolatry. Origen does not, then, forbid its use but merely urges caution and a primary focus on the Word and Wisdom of God. Grace is needed to support the Christian seeking to remain faithful to Christ in the midst of secular learning. Christians must 'rebuild' this learning as Christian learning, as the true philosophy (*Hom. Num.* 20,3). Philosophy may aid but the mysteries taught by scripture are the final arbiter. Reason, for example, comes into play only to divulge what the scriptures do not say clearly. He found in Platonism ammunition to use against the Gnostics, in its affirmation of the innate goodness of the created order, on the activity of divine providence, and the emphasis on human freedom and moral accountability.

And yet the question must be asked to what extent Origen was aware of the profound influence of Platonist (and other philosophical) thought on his own and thus to what extent he is as self-critical as he might have been. It may be that notwithstanding the apparently more positive view that Clement had of philosophy in the construction and ownership of his own theology Origen was in fact less aware of this in his own case than Clement was in his and thus less self-critical. Trigg even suggests that the ideal of what he calls Platonist 'intellectual holiness' may in fact only be more evident in Plotinus than it is in Origen himself.[65] Trigg also points to the as yet not fully explored use by Origen of medical knowledge and principles. At *Contra Celsum* 3.12, for example, he refers favourably to the practice of medicine.[66]

At *Contra Celsum* 1.3 Origen speaks of the 'Roman Senate, the emperors, the army, the people, and the relatives of believers' fighting against the Gospel and declares that only the divine power prevented its destruction and allowed it to conquer 'the whole world that was conspiring against it'. At 2.79 he refers likewise to 'kings, governors, the Roman Senate, rulers everywhere, and the common people' as opposed to the spread of Jesus' teaching. Caspary argues that there is a theology of

---

64 R.E.Heine, 'Stoic Logic as Handmaid to Exegesis and Theology in Origen's Commentary on the Gospel of John', *JTS* 44 (1993): 117.

65 Trigg, *Origen*, pp. 74f.

66 See the unnamed article 'Medical Theory and Theology in Origen', in R.Hanson and H.Crouzel (eds), *Origeniana Tertia*. (Rome, 1985), pp. 191-9.

politics implicit in Origen's *Contra Celsum* and that it is based around his exegesis of two key biblical passages, *Romans* 13,1 - 'Let every person be subject to the higher powers' - and *Matthew* 22,21 - 'render unto Caesar etc.'.[67] Origen himself argues for a form of Christian pacifism, whereby Christians 'keep their hands unstained' so that their prayers for those who fight in just wars and the emperor who rules 'righteously' might be heard in heaven (CC 8.73). It is, says Origen, that Christians avoid civic service only because they seek to serve the higher good of man's salvation (*CC* 8.75). It is Christian piety which most aids the emperor's rule. For Origen the Roman Empire is not simply the fourth and last empire of *Daniel* 2,40 nor the power that holds back the Antichrist of *2 Thessalonians* 2,7, but rather the very expansion of the Empire is connected to that of the Church. Even the victory of monotheism over polytheism may be reflected in the triumph of Augustine's monarchy over that polyarchy which saw war and violence and insecurity on the frontiers of the empire. 'God was preparing the nations for his teaching', Origen declares, 'that they might be under one Roman emperor, so that the proclamation and the spread of the Gospel might be facilitated by the security of the sole emperor's rule' (*CC* 2.30). Origen even implies that it was part of the divine providence that Jesus was born during the early principate under Augustus. The *Pax Romana* may then be seen as a 'special feature' of the interim arrangement between the First and Second Comings. Origen even considers the hypothetical possibility of Christian leaders acting as civil magistrates 'in a city which is God's, if there is such a city anywhere in the universe' (*CC* 3.30). And yet, while Origen comes close to the Eusebeian view of a Christian Empire, he ultimately avoids the implication of this tendency. Origen may assign to the Roman Empire a providential and eschatological purpose but he can also do so for the Devil, and therefore his assigning of such a role to the state does not imply a particular view of that Empire's innate qualities. When Origen, in the *Contra Celsum*, is playing the role of the anti-pagan polemicist, his view of Church and Empire is antithetical but when that of an apologist he places more emphasis on a rapprochement between them. Thus what appear at times as contradictions in his thought are actually reflective of different contexts and purposes. Indeed, says Caspary, Origen actually offers even a third view of the Empire which is fundamentally 'secular', as paralleling the function of the Church (see Origen's exegesis of *Romans* and of other commentaries) and which, along with the polemical-demonic and the apologetic-reconciliatory viewpoints, is largely informed by his trichotomous view of the nature of man and his consequent understanding of the three levels of spiritual meaning.[68] Origen's view of the Empire, therefore, is positive but only in terms of the providence of God and not in terms of any particular intrinsic value he assigns to that Empire *per se*. For even when he stresses the demonic aspects of the state he yet acknowledges that it has a providential purpose as an instrument of a divine *paideia*. 'The state', declares Caspary, has for Origen 'a redemptive function, but

---

67 G.E.Caspary, *Politics and Exegesis: Origen and the Two Swords*. (Berkeley, 1979), p. 125.

68 Ibid., p. 180.

that redemptive function is purely external'. It merely provides the peace which is necessary to the redemptive process:

> 'Origen could hold at one and the same time a theology of politics that saw the Roman Empire as having a christological dimension, as being a purely secular good established by God essentially for the sake of non-Christians, and yet as also an instrument of the Devil'.[69]

Trigg points in the *Contra Celsum* to Origen's defence of the Christians' refusal to honour the emperor's genius. Either the genius does not exist and such worship would be dishonest, or it does exist and is thereby a daemon, and such worship would be 'wicked' (*CC* 8.75). God's law, or the philosophers' natural law, must take priority over the emperor's law.

Origen's contact with Jews is more likely to have come during his period in Caesarea than in Alexandria. The Jewish community in the latter place had probably recovered somewhat from the disaster of 115 but even in 215, during the protests against the emperor Caracalla, it did not raise its head. That Origen's major 'Hebrew' influence in the Alexandrian period also came from a convert from Judaism to Christianity - the ex-rabbi who taught him Hebrew and whom Origen calls 'the Hebrew' (*Comm. on Jeremiah* 20,7) - testifies to the probable low profile of the Jewish community at Alexandria. Caesarea, on the other hand, was a major centre of Jewish learning. For Origen Judaism was the most serious threat to Christianity; in Palestine, rather more than in third century Alexandria, Jews and Christians competed for the allegiance of pagans. At *De Principiis* 4.2 Origen criticises Jewish legalism and its failure thereby to recognise the Messiah. He refers to a debate with rabbis - almost certainly in Caesarea - over the Suffering Servant of *Isaiah* 52 and speaks of making enquiries among Jewish scholars (*Comm. on Matt.* 11.9). He allegorises the Old Testament in order to demonstrate against the Jews that it pointed to Christ and the individual soul (*Hom. on Leviticus* 7.5). In his *Homily on Jeremiah* (12.13) and the *Contra Celsum* (8.69) he contributes to the sad history of Jewish-Christian relations and to anti-Semitism when he declares that Jews have lost land and home and the favour of God because they are the killers of Christ. Yet Origen's anti-Jewish stance is not particularly vitriolic for its time and is largely shaped by his perceived need to claim the Old Testament for the new faith and to combat the arguments of Celsus.

Select Bibliography

Alexandria:

J.Dillon, *The Middle Platonists*. (London, 1996).

C.Haas, *Alexandria in Late Antiquity. Topography and Social Conflict*. (Baltimore, 1997).

69 Ibid., p.189.

G.L.Steen (ed.), *Alexandria: the Site and the History*. (New York and London, 1993).

Epistle of Barnabas:

R.Hvalvik, *The Struggle for Scripture and Covenant: the purpose of the Epistle of Barnabas and Jewish-Christian Competition in the Second Century*. (Tübingen, 1996).

J.C.Paget, *The Epistle of Barnabas: Outlook and Background*. (Tübingen, 1994).

Epistle to Diognetus:

R.G.Tanner, 'The Epistle to Diognetus and Contemporary Greek Thought', *Studia Patristica* 15 (1984): 495-508.

Athenagoras:

P.L.Buck, 'Athenagoras's *Embassy*: a literary fiction', *Harvard Theological Review* 89 (1996): 209-26.

W.R.Schoedel, *Athenagoras: Legatio and De Resurrectione*. Text, translation and notes. (Oxford, 1972).

W.R.Schoedel, 'Apologetic Literature and Ambassadorial Activities', *Harvard Theological Review* 82 (1989): 55-78.

Clement:

J.Behr, *Asceticism and Anthropology in Irenaeus and Clement*. (Oxford, 2000).

D.Dawson, *Allegorical Readers and Cultural Revision in Ancient Alexandria*. (Berkeley, 1992).

P.Karavites, *Evil, Freedom, and the Road to Perfection in Clement of Alexandria*. (Leiden, 1999).

S.R.C.Lilla, *Clement of Alexandria: a study in Christian Platonism and Gnosticism*. (Oxford, 1971).

R.Mortley, *Connaissance religieuse et herménetique chez Clément d'Alexandrie*. (Leiden, 1973)

Origen:

H.Crouzel, *Origen*. (Edinburgh, 1989).

J.Daniélou, *Origen* (tr. W.Mitchell). (London and New York, 1955).

J.W.Trigg, *Origen: the Bible and Philosophy in the Third-century Church*. (London, 1983).

Chapter 6

Conclusions

There is no doubt that Church Fathers before Nicaea, in both East and West, in the development and articulation of their own theologies were influenced by their interaction with the culture or cultures which surrounded them. We would not have assumed otherwise. But how they were influenced by these cultures and how they engaged and/or interacted with them is sometimes something of a surprise. In terms of the definitions of the notion of 'culture' referred to in this work, particularly those of Malinowski and Tanner, it can be easily seen that the Fathers surveyed did engage with and were clearly influenced by the recognised elements of these cultures. The Fathers freely and openly, though also often perhaps unconsciously (for that is so with all of us), employed language forms, linguistic and other symbols, habits and practices of thought, ideas and beliefs (or at least the frameworks for these) drawn from the societies and communities in which they lived and worked. In the area of custom and social organisation - in matters such as civic and domestic concord and harmony, class structures and divisions, patronage rights and even the role of the *paterfamilias* - many of the Fathers were profoundly influenced by the attitudes and even the values of the world around them, to the extent of translating these naturally into the life and witness of the church as easily as they breathed in the very air. They drank from the well of ancient and contemporary learning and often acknowledged the divine source of aspects of this, the expression of their thought was shaped very much by the genres of the day, and they were content to give the state and the emperor some measure of respect and even obedience. It is perhaps only in the matter of fundamental and ultimate values that the Fathers dissociated themselves from the culture of the communities in which they lived. For in the matter of the Christians' ultimate value of a belief in the one, true God and in his Son and the Spirit there could be no compromise with community, family, state, emperor, cult or the very heights of ancient learning.

It is not my intention to reproduce in detail the results of the investigations of each of the Fathers discussed but rather to offer a brief summary of their cultural interaction in terms of the areas outlined in the introductory chapter. Almost without exception those Fathers who speak of the emperor or imperial office, or of Roman rule generally, accept the reality and the legitimacy, under God, of such rule. Most would seem to endorse, at least implicitly, the notion of Tertullian that obedience towards the emperor and imperial rule is acceptable, subject to the claims of such rule operating strictly within the 'limits of Christian discipline'; that is, where the claims of obedience towards the emperor and his subordinates can never overrule that owed towards God and the Christian's worship of him. Indeed, in line with contemporary understandings of the emperor as the 'elect of God [Zeus]', a number of Fathers - Tertullian, Theophilus, and Irenaeus among them - speak quite easily of the emperor as appointed by God. With respect to the imperial cult, however, the Fathers are universally clear. They will, for the most part, pray for the emperor and his family but they will have no truck with any cult attached to the emperor's person and the idolatry implied therein. A number of Fathers specifically attack the claimed deification of deceased emperors by the Senate.

A number of Fathers clearly share the contemporary Greco-Roman horror at civic discord and schism - particularly the Rome-based ones (see Clement and Hermas in particular) although Ignatius also must be included here - and thereby embrace the concomitant high valuation of the qualities of civic and ecclesiastical harmony and concord as reflecting the world arranged in an orderly manner by God. A number also embrace, by way of translation into the ordering of the church, notions of class and other social distinction. Tertullian is a notable representative of this practice. The distinction of *honestior* and *humilior* is not made explicit in any Father but it is present implicitly. The translation of the system of patronage, practised in both East and West, is also evident in the writings of a number of Fathers, and Hermas, Cyprian and Hippolytus are notable in this regard. Attitudes towards wealth creation and engagement in commercial activities on the part of Christians vary but while some, like Cyprian, see personal wealth and Christian commitment as utterly incompatible, most merely recognise the potential distractions of wealth and business for those seeking to live out their Christian obligations.

In the area of education and learning many, though not all, of the Fathers discussed evidence a high quality education in rhetoric and philosophy, even where the latter is largely sourced from the available doxographies of the time. The 'Greeks' know their Homer and the 'Latins' their Virgil and Cicero. Virtually all of the Fathers, even those who do not evidence a first-rate education, demonstrate a working knowledge of the rules of rhetorical structure and argument. They employ the normative genres of the day with a marked preference for exhortation, either paraenetic (internal to the church) or protreptic (external), with a number of others penning apologetics of note. A number, of course, cover a variety of genres in their corpus. Many Fathers, including those like Tatian and Theophilus who display a great deal of antipathy towards pagan learning and fear to appear to compromise with non-Christian learning, demonstrate clear evidences of their reading of pagan literature - particularly of philosophical treatises either in the original or by way of doxographies - and the influence of this, negatively or positively, on their thought is readily obvious. Tertullian, Justin, Clement of Alexandria, and Origen, by way of example, are clearly immersed in philosophical enquiry, while Justin and Clement clearly understand Greek philosophy as provided by God for the Greeks as a preparation for the coming of the Gospel. Origen will not, at least not explicitly, go this far but he will speak of the 'auxiliary' value of the study of philosophy for that of the scriptures. In the West Stoicism is perhaps the philosophy of choice - with Clement of Rome, Hermas, Minucius Felix, Hippolytus, Tertullian and Cyprian deeply influenced by aspects of it - although Greeks like Theophilus, Justin, Athenagoras and Irenaeus also display its marks on their thought. In the East it is, of course, Plato and the Middle Platonists (including some Neopythagoreans) who lead the way. Theophilus is critical but respectful, Justin is steeped in Plato but recognises the limits, Irenaeus finds it hard to see beyond the thought of philosophy (even Plato) as the source of heresy, Athenagoras and Clement of Alexandria are full of Plato, while Origen rarely, outside of the *Contra Celsum*, quotes philosophers and has to deal with the Platonism of Celsus himself, which colours his otherwise admiring approach to the Athenian giant. Among the Latin Fathers Minucius Felix employs the witness of Platonic metaphysics, and Tertullian, while wary, is profoundly respectful of Plato and takes conversation with his thought with the utmost seriousness. Philo is, of course, also profoundly influential, particularly on the Alexandrians. Aristotle registers on the scale from time to time - although as much negatively as positively - but has to wait until the Middle Ages to make his true impact on Christian theologising. Epicureanism registers on the early patristic radar only to be attacked for its alleged atheism and denial of providence.

The placement of Tanner's notion of cultural engagement over the thought of the Fathers is revealing. The notion that it is how the Fathers use the materials available to them and not especially what materials they use, that they might use 'in odd ways' whatever 'language-games they already happen to speak', that their theologising is essentially a 'hybrid formation', and that the distinctiveness of this theologising is 'not formed *by* the boundary [with other belief systems] as *at* it' - Tanner's notions applied to the circumstances of the pre-Nicene Fathers - fits surprisingly well. These Fathers do not, for the most part, repudiate the office of the emperor, or contemporary education and learning - rhetoric, issues of genre, philosophy, to name but aspects of this - or class structures, or systems of patronage. They simply view and employ them differently than most of their contemporaries in their own 'odd ways'. Some repudiate the accumulation of personal wealth but only because it is likely to get in the way of Christian discipleship, while all reject outright pagan religion (as contrary to the demands of the Gospel), the imperial cult (and most especially the notion of the *apotheosis* of deceased emperors) as potentially idolatrous - though they will pray for the safety of the emperor and the imperial house - and the immoralities observed in company with many aspects of pagan life. They live in the world in which they live; they can only express themselves in the language of that world much as the Incarnation is the expression of God's own self in the language of the world. There is no Christian culture here utterly separate from the surrounding culture; at best such Christian 'culture', if it exists, is merely a sub-set of the dominant 'culture' of the day. It cannot be otherwise. The author of the *Epistle to Diognetus* is right in seeing Christians as aliens but they are aliens who live here and breathe the very air where they live.

> '[Christians] dwell in their own fatherlands, but as if sojourners in them; they share all things as citizens, and suffer all things as strangers. Every foreign country is their fatherland, and every fatherland is a foreign country .... They pass their time upon the earth, but they have their citizenship in heaven'.. (*Epistle to Diognetus* 5,5f.)

Bibliography

Texts and Translations

Athenagoras, *Legatio*: Coxe, A.C., Translation. The Ante-Nicene Fathers II. (Edinburgh: T&T Clark,, 1994).

———: Schoedel, W.R., *Athenagoras: Legatio and De Resurrectione*. Text, translation and notes. (Oxford: Clarendon, 1972).

1 Clement: Joubert, A., *Clément de Rome, Épître aux Corinthiens*. Introduction, texte et traduction, notes et index. SC 167. (Paris: Cerf, 1971).

———: Lake, K., *The Apostolic Fathers I*. Text and translation. Loeb Classical Library. (Cambridge, MA: Harvard University Press, 1977).

Clement of Alexandria: *Clément d'Alexandria, Le Pédagogue I*. Texte grec. Introduction et notes (Marro, H-I.) et traduction (Harl, M.). SC 70. (Paris: Cerf, 1960).

———: *II*. Texte grec. Traduction (Mondésert, C.) et notes (Marrou, H-I.), SC 108. (Paris: Cerf, 1965).

———: *III*. Texte grec. Traduction (Mondésert, C. et Matray, C.) et notes (Marrou, H-I.). SC 158. (Paris: Cerf, 1970).

———: *Le Protreptique*. Texte grec. Introduction, texte, traduction et notes (Mondésert, C.). SC (number unknown), (Paris: Cerf, 1976).

———: Marcovich, M. (ed.), *Clementis Alexandrini Protrepticus*. Supplement to *Vigiliae Christianae* 34. (Leiden: Brill, 1995).

———: *Works*: Coxe, A.C., Translation. The Ante-Nicene Fathers II. (Edinburgh: T&T Clark, 1994).

Cyprian, *Letters*: *The Letters of St. Cyprian*. 3 volumes. Translation and notes. ACW 43, 44 and 46. (New York: Newman Press, 1984-6).

———: *Works*: Coxe, A.C., The Ante-Nicene Fathers V. Translation. (Edinburgh: T&T Clark, 1990).

———: Weber, R., and Bévenot, M., *Sancti Cypriani Episcopi Opera*. Corpus Chistianorum. Series Latina III. (Turnhout: Brepols, 1972).

———: Simonetti, M., and Moreschini, C., *Sancti Cypriani Episcopi Opera*. CCL IIIA, (Turnhout: Brepols, 1976.

———: Diercks, G., *Epistularium*. CCL IIIB, (Turnhout: Brepols, 1994).

———: Diercks, G., *Epistularium*. CCL IIIC, (Turnhout: Brepols, 1996).

Epistle of Barnabas: Lake, K., *The Apostolic Fathers I*. Text and translation. Loeb Classical Library. (Cambridge, MA: Harvard University Press, 1977).

———: Kleist, J.A., ACW 6. (Westminster, MD: Newman Press, 1948).

Epistle to Diognetus: Marrou, H-I., *A Diognète*. Introduction, édition critique, traduction et commentaire. SC 33, (Paris: Cerf, 1965).

———: Lake, K., *The Apostolic Fathers II.* Text and translation. Loeb Classical Library. (Cambridge, MA: Harvard University Press, 1976).

Hermas, *The Shepherd*: Lake, K., *The Apostolic Fathers II.* Text and translation. Loeb Classical Library. (Cambridge, MA: Harvard University Press, 1976).

———: Coxe, A.C., Text. The Ante-Nicene Fathers II. (Edinburgh: T&T Clark, 1994).

———: Osiek, C., *Shepherd of Hermas: a commentary.* (Minneapolis: Fortress, 1999).

Hippolytus: *Contra Noetum*: Butterworth, R., *Hippolytus of Rome, Contra Noetum.* Text introduced, edited, and translated (*Heythrop Monographs* 1977), pp. 122-31.

———: Marcovich, M. (ed.). *Refutatio omnium haeresium.* (New York: W. De Gruyter, 1986).

———: *Works:* Coxe, A.C., The Ante-Nicene Fathers V. (Edinburgh: T&T Clark, 1990).

Ignatius, *Letters*: Camelot, P., *Ignace d'Antioche. Lettres.* Texte grec. Introduction, traduction et notes. SC 10, (Paris: Cerf, 1969).

———: Schoedel, W.R., *Ignatius of Antioch: a commentary on the Letters of Ignatius of Antioch.* (Philadelphia: Fortress, 1985).

Irenaeus, *Adversus Haereses*: Rousseau, A., *et al.*, *Irénée de Lyon, Contre les Hérésies.* Texte et traduction. SC 263, Paris, 1979; 264, Paris, 1979; 293, Paris, 1982; 294, Paris, 1982; 210, Paris, 1974; 211, Paris, 1974; 100, Paris, 1965; 152, Paris, 1969; 153, Paris, 1969 (Paris: Cerf).

———: Coxe, A.C., Translation. *The Ante-Nicene Fathers* II. (Edinburgh: T&T Clark, 1993).

———: *Proof of Apostolic Preaching*: Smith, J.P., *St. Irenaeus. Proof of Apostolic Preaching.* Translated and annotated. ACW 16. (New York: Paulist Press, 1952).

Justin Martyr, *First Apology*: Hardy, E.R., Library of Christian Classics 1, (London: SCM, 1953).

———: Coxe, A.C., Translation. The Ante-Nicene Fathers I. (Edinburgh: T&T Clark, 1993).

———: Marcovich, M. (ed.), *Iustini Martyris Apologiae pro Christianis.* (Patristische Texte und Studien 38). (Berlin-New York: W. De Gruyter, 1994).

———: *Dialogue with Trypho*: Coxe, A.C., The Ante-Nicene Fathers I. (Edinburgh: T&T Clark, 1993).

———: Marcovich, M. (ed.), *Iustini Martyris Dialogus cum Tryphone.* (New York: W. de Gruyter, 1997).

Melito of Sardis, *On Pascha*: Hall, S.G. (ed.), *On Pascha and fragments.* Text and translation. (Oxford: Clarendon, 1979).

Minucius Felix, *Octavius*: Beaujeu, J., *Octavius.* Texte et traduction. (Paris: Belles Lettres, 1964).

———: Rendall, G.H., Text and translation. LCL. (Cambridge, MA: Harvard

University Press, 1977).

Origen: Chadwick, H., *Origen: Contra Celsum*. (Cambridge: CUP, 1953).

———: Borrer, M., *Origène, Contre Celsum I*. SC 132, Paris, 1967; *II*. SC 136, Paris, 1968; *III*. SC 147, Paris, 1969; *IV*. SC 150, Paris, 1969; *V*. SC 227, Paris, 1976. Introduction, texte critique, traduction et notes (Paris: cerf).

———: Butterworth, G.W., *Origen: On First Principles*. Translation and notes. (Peter Smith, 1973).

———: Crouzel, H., and Simonetti, M., *Origène, Traité des Principes I*. SC 252, Paris, 1978; *II*. SC 253, Paris, 1978; *III*. SC 268, Paris, 1980. Introduction, texte critique et traduction (Paris: Cerf).

———: Works: *GCS*, 12 volumes, (Leipzig, 1941).

Polycarp, *to the Philippians*: Camelot, P., *Polycarpe de Smyrne, Lettres au Philippiens*. Texte grec. Introduction, traduction et notes. SC 10, (Paris: Cerf, 1969).

———: Lake, K., *The Apostolic Fathers I*. Text and translation. LCL. (Cambridge, MA: Havard University Press, 1977).

Tatian, *Ad Graecos*: Coxe, A.C., Translation. The Ante-Nicene Fathers II. (Edinburgh: T&T Clark, 1994).

———: Marcovich, M., *Tatiani Oratio ad Graecos*. TU 4,1. (Berlin and New York: W. de Gruyter).

Tertullian, *Works*: *Quinti Septimi Florentis Tertulliani Opera*. CCL I: *Opera Catholica* and *Adversus Marcionem*. (Turnhout: Brepols, 1954).

———II: *Opera Montanistica*. (Turnhout: Brepols, 1954).

———: Glover, T.R., *Apology* and *de Spectaculis*: LCL, (Cambridge, MA: Harvard University Press, 1977).

Theophilus, *Ad Autolycum*: Grant, R.M. (ed.) *Theophilus of Antioch Ad Autolycum*. (Oxford: Clarendon, 1970).

———: Coxe, A.C., The Ante-Nicene Fathers II. (Edinburgh: T&T Clark, 1994).

Reference Works

Africa, T., *Rome of the Caesars*. (New York: Wiley, 1965).

Alföldy, G., 'The Crisis of the Third Century as seen by Contemporaries', *Greek, Roman and Byzantine Studies* 15 (1974): 89-111.

Aune, D., 'Romans as a Logos Protreptikos in the context of Ancient Religious and Philosophical Propaganda', in Hengel, M. and Heckel, U., *Paulus und das antike Judentum*. Tübingen, 1991, 91-124.

Bakke, O.M., *Concord and Peace*. (Tübingen: Mohr, 2001).

Bammel, C., 'The state of play with regard to Hippolytus and the *Contra Noetum*', *Heythrop Journal* 31 (1990): 195-9.

Barnard, L.W., 'The Epistle of Barnabas - a Paschal Homily?', *VC* 15 (1961): 8-22.

———,'Clement of Rome and the Persecution of Domitian', *New Testament Studies*

10 (1964): 251-60.

———, *Justin Martyr: his life and thought*. (Cambridge: CUP, 1966).

———, 'The Embassy of Athenagoras', *VC* 21 (1967): 88-92.

———, 'The Heresy of Tatian - Once Again', *JEH* 19 (1968): 1-10.

Barnes, T.D., 'The Family and Career of Septimius Severus', *Historia* 16 (1967): 87-107.

———, 'Legislation Against the Christians', *JRS* 58 (1968): 32-50.

———, 'The Embassy of Athenagoras', *JTS* ns26 (1975): 111-4.

———, *Tertullian: a historical and literary study*. 2nd edition. (Oxford: Clarendon, 1985).

Bauckham, R.J., 'The Great Tribulation in the Shepherd of Hermas', *JTS* 25 (1964): 27-40.

Bauer, J.B., 'An Diognetus VI', *VC* 17 (1963): 207-10

Beard, M. *et al*, *Religions of Rome*. 2 volumes. (Cambridge: CUP, 1998). I: *A History*. II: *A Sourcebook*.

Beaujeu, J., 'Les apologètes et le culte du soverain', in den Boer, W., *Le Culte des Souverains dans l'Empire Romain*. (Genève: Fondations Hardt, 1972), 103-42.

Bergian, S-P., 'How to speak about early Christian apologetic literature? Comments on the recent debate', *SP* 36 (2001): 179-204.

Beyschlag, K., *Clemens Romanus und der FrühKatholizimus*. (Tübingen: Mohr Siebeck, 1966).

Birley, A.R., 'The Coups d'État of the Year 193', *Bonner Jahrbuch* 169 (1969): 246-80.

———, *Septimius Severus: the African emperor*. Rev. ed. (London: Eyre and Spottiswoode, 1988).

———, *Hadrian: the restless emperor*. (London: Routledge, 1997).

Bobertz, C.A., 'The Role of Patron in the *Cena Dominica* of Hippolytus' *Apostolic Tradition*', *JTS* 44 (1993): 170-84.

———, 'Patronage Networks and the Study of Ancient Christianity', *SP* 24 (1993): 20-17.

———, 'Patronal Letters of Commendation: Cyprian's *Epistulae* 38-40', *SP* 31 (1997): 252-9.

Bouchier, E.S., *Life and Letters in Roman Africa*. (Oxford: Blackwell, 1913).

———, *Syria as a Roman Province*. (Oxford: Blackwell, 1916).

Bowe, B.E., *A Church in Crisis: Ecclesiology and Paraenesis in Clement of Rome*. (Minneapolis: Fotress, 1988).

Brent, A., *Hippolytus and the Roman Church in the Third Century*. (Leiden: Brill, 1995).

———, 'Ignatius of Antioch and the Imperial Cult', *VC* 52 (1998): 30-58.

Brown, P., 'Approaches to the Religious Crisis of the Third Century AD', in Brown, P., (ed.), *Religion and Society in the Age of Augustine*. (London: Faber and Faber, 1972), pp. 74-93.

———, *The Body and Society: Men, Women and Sexual Renunciation in Early*

Christianity. (New York: Columbia University Press, 1988).
Buck, P.L., 'Athenagoras's *Embassy*: a literary fiction', *HTR* 89 (1996): 209-26.
Burns, J. Patout, 'Social Context in the Controversy between Cyprian and Stephen', *SP* 24 (1993): 38-44.
———, 'The Role of Social Structures in Cyprian's Response to the Decian Persecution', *SP* 31 (1997): 260-7.
Burrows, M.S., 'Christianity in the Roman Forum: Tertullian and the apologetic use of history', *VC* 42 (1988): 209-35.
Cadoux, C.J., *Ancient Smyrna*. (Oxford: Blackwell, 1938).
Carcopino, J., *Daily Life in Ancient Rome*. (London: Routledge and Keegan Paul, 1973).
Caspary, G.E., *Politics and Exegesis: Origen and the Two Swords*. (Berkeley: University of California Press, 1979).
Casson, L., *Everyday Life in Ancient Rome*. (Baltimore: The Johns Hopkins University Press, 1998).
Chadwick, H., 'Justin Martyr's Defence of Christianity', *BJRL* 47 (1964/65): 275-97.
———, *Early Christian Thought and the Classical Tradition*. (Oxford: Clarendon, 1966).
Champlin, E., *Fronto and Antonine Rome*. (Cambridge, MA: Harvard University Press, 1980).
Charlesworth, M.P., 'The Refusal of Divine Honours: an Augustan Formula', *PBSR* 15 (1939): 1-10.
Clark, E.A., *Clement's Use of Aristotle*. (New York: E.Mellen Press, 1977).
Clarke, G.W., 'The Historical Setting of the *Octavius* of Minucius Felix', *JRH* 4 (1967): 267-86.
———, 'The Date of the Oration of Tatian', *HTR* 60 (1967): 123-6.
Cohick, L., 'Melito of Sardis's PERI PASCHA and its "Israel"', *HTR* 91 (1998): 351-72.
———, *The Peri Pascha attributed to Melito of Sardis*: *setting, purpose and sources.* (Providence: Brown Judaic Studies, 2000).
Coleborne, W., 'The *Shepherd* of Hermas: a case for Multiple Authorship and Some Implications', *SP* 10 (1970): 65-70.
Collins, J.J., 'Introduction: Towards the Morphology of a Genre', *Semeia* 14 (1979): 1-20.
Crouzel, H., *Origen*. (Edinburgh: T&T Clark, 1989).
Daniélou, J., *Origen*. (trans. W. Mitchell) (London and New York: Sheed and Ward, 1955).
———, *Theology of Jewish Christianity.* (London: Darton, Longman and Todd, 1963).
———, *Gospel Message and Hellenistic Culture*. (London: DLT, 1973).
Dawson, D., *Allegorical Readers and Cultural Revision in Ancient Alexandria.* (Berkeley: University of California Press, 1992).
De Ste, Croix, G.E.M., 'Suffragium: from Vote to Patronage', *British Journal of*

Sociology 5 (1954): 33-48.

Derry, K., 'One Stone on Another: Towards an Understanding of Symbolism in The Epistle of Barnabas', *JECS* 4 (1996): 515-28.

Dillon, J., *The Middle Platonists*. (London: Duckworth, 1996).

———, *Alcinous: The Handbook of Platonism*. (Oxford: OUP, 2002).

Dix, G., and Chadwick, H. (eds), *The Treatise on The Apostolic Tradition of St. Hippolytus of Rome*. 2nd revised edition. (London: Alban, 1992).

Dodds, E.R., *Pagan and Christian in an Age of Anxiety*. (Cambridge: CUP, 1968).

Downey, G., *A history of Antioch in Syria: from Seleucus to the Arab Conquest*. (Princeton: Princeton University Press, 1961).

Drijvers, H.J.W., 'The Persistence of Pagan Cults and Practices in Christian Syria', in Drijvers, H.J.W. (ed.), *East of Antioch. Studies in Early Syrian Christianity*. (London: Variorum, 1984), pp. 35-43.

Duncan-Jones, R., 'Wealth and Munificence in Roman Africa', *PBSR* 31 (1963): 159-77.

———,*The Economy of the Roman Empire*. 2nd edition. (Cambridge: CUP, 1984).

Dunn, G.D., 'Rhetorical Structure in Tertullian's *Ad Scapulam*', *VC* 56 (2002): 47-55.

Düring, I., *Aristotle's Protrepticus: An Attempt at Reconstruction*. (Göteborg: Acta Universitatis Gothoburgensis, 1961).

Edwards, M.J., 'On the Platonic Schooling of Justin Martyr', *JTS* ns42 (1991): 17-34.

———, 'Justin's Logos and the Word of God', *JECS* 3 (1995): 261-80.

———, *Origen against Plato*. (Aldershot: Ashgate, 2002).

Edwards, M.J., Goodman, M., and Price, S., *Apologetics in the Roman Empire: Pagans, Jews, and Christians*. (Oxford: OUP, 1999).

Emmett, L., 'Clement of Alexandria's *Protrepticus* and Dio Chrysostom's *Alexandrian Oration*', *SP* 36 (2001): 409-14.

Fears, J.R., *Princeps a Diis Electus: the Divine Election of the Emperor as a political concept at Rome*. (Rome: American Academy, 1977).

Fishwick, D., 'The Imperial Cult in Roman Britain', *Phoenix* 15 (1961): 213-29.

———, 'The Development of Provincial Ruler Worship in the Western Roman Empire', in Haase, W., (ed.), *Principat*, ANRW, XVI, II, (London and New York: W. de Gruyter, 1978), pp. 1201-53.

———, *The Imperial Cult in the Latin West: Studies in the Ruler Cult of the Western Provinces of the Roman Empire*. 2 vols. (Leiden: Brill, 1987).

Fishwick, D., and Shaw, B.D., 'The Formation of Africa Proconsularis', *Hermes* 105 (1977): 369-80.

Frend, W.H.C., 'Open Questions concerning the Christians and the Roman Empire in the Age of the Severi', *JTS* 25 (1974): 333-51.

Fuellenbach, J., *Ecclesiastical Office and the Primacy of Rome*. (Washington: CUA Press, 1980).

Garnsey, P., *Social Status and Legal Privilege in the Roman Empire*. (Oxford:

Clarendon, 1970).

———, 'Rome's African Empire under the Principate', in Garnsey, P. and Whittaker, C.R., (eds.) *Imperialism in the Ancient World*. (Cambridge: CUP, 1978), pp. 223-54, 343-54.

Garnsey, P., and Saller, R., *The Roman Empire: Economy, Society and Culture*. (London: Duckworth, 1994).

Giet, S., *Hermas et les pasteurs: les trois auteurs du Pasteur d'Hermas*. (Paris: Presses universitaires de France, 1963).

Good, D., 'Rhetoric and Wisdom in Theophilus of Antioch', *ATR* 73 (1991): 323-30.

Goodman, R., 'Nerva, the *Fiscus Judaicus* and Jewish Identity', *Journal of Roman Studies* 79 (1989): 40-44.

———, *The Roman World: 44BC - AD180*. (London and New York: Routledge, 1997).

Graham, S.L., 'Structure and Purpose of Irenaeus' *Epideixis*', *SP* 36 (2001): 210-21.

Grant, R.M., 'Irenaeus and Hellenistic Culture', *HTR* 42 (1949): 41-51.

———, 'The Problem of Theophilus', *HTR* 43 (1950): 179-96.

———, 'The Date of Tatian's Oration', *HTR* 46 (1953): 99-101.

———, 'The heresy of Tatian', *JTS* ns5 (1954): 62-8.

———, 'Athenagoras or Pseudo-Athenagoras', *HTR* 47 (1954): 121-9.

———, 'Studies in the Apologists', *HTR* 51 (1958): 123-34.

———, 'Some errors in the Legatio of Athenagoras', *VC* 12 (1958): 145-6.

———, 'Scripture, Rhetoric and Theology in Theophilus', *VC* 13 (1959): 33-45.

———, 'Tatian (*OR*. 30) and the Gnostics', *JTS* ns 15 (1964): 65-9.

———, 'Five Apologists and Marcus Aurelius', *VC* 42 (1988): 1-17.

———, *Greek Apologists of the Second Century*. (Philadelphia: Westminster, 1988).

———, *Irenaeus of Lyons*. (London and New York: Routledge, 1997).

Guerra, A.J., 'The Conversion of Marcus Aurelius and Justin Martyr: the Purpose, Genre, and Content of the First Apology', *Second Century* 9 (1992): 171-87.

Haas, C., *Alexandria in Late Antiquity. Topography and Social Conflict*. (Baltimore: The Johns Hopkins University Press, 1997).

Hanfmann, G.M., *Sardis: from Prehistoric to Roman Times*. (London: Harvard University Press, 1983).

Hahneman, G.M., *The Muratorian Fragment and the Development of the Canon*. (Oxford: Clarendon, 1992).

Harding, S.F., 'Christ as Greater than Moses in Clement of Alexandria's *Stromateis* I-II', *SP* 31 (1997): 397-400.

Harrill, J.A., 'Ignatius, Ad Polycarp 4.3 and the Corporate Manumission of Slaves', *JECS* 1 (1993): 107-42.

Hawthorne, G.F., 'Tatian and His Discourse to the Greeks', *HTR* 57 (1964): 161-88.

Heine, R.E., 'Stoic Logic as Handmaid to Exegesis and Theology in Origen's

Commentary on the Gospel of John', *JTS* ns44 (1993): 90-117.
Heintz, M., 'Μιμητης θεου in the Epistle to Diognetus', *JECS* 12 (2004): 107-19.
Henne, P., *L'Unité du Pasteur d'Hermas*. (Paris: J.Gabalda, 1992).
———, 'Hermas, un pseudonyme', *SP* 24 (1993): 136-9.
Herron, T.J., 'The Most Probable Date of the First Epistle of Clement to the Corinthians', *SP* 21 (1989): 106-21.
Hilhorst, A., 'Hermas', *RAC* 14 (1988): 682-702.
Hinchliff, P., *Cyprian of Carthage and the unity of the Christian Church*. (London: Chapman, 1974).
Hull, R.F., Review of Hvalvik, R., *The Struggle for Scripture and Covenant: the Purpose of the Epistle of Barnabas and Jewish-Christian Competition*. Tübingen, 1996 in *JECS* 6 (1998): 325-7
Hvalvik, R., *The Struggle for Scripture and Covenant: the purpose of the Epistle of Barnabas and Jewish-Christian Competition in the Second Century*. (Tübingen: Mohr Siebeck, 1996).
Hyldahl, N., *Philosophie und Christentum: Eine Interpretation der Einleitung zum Dialog Justins*. (Kopenhagen: Munksgaard, 1966).
Jaeger, W., *Early Christianity and Greek Paideia*. (Cambridge, MA: BIC, 1961).
Jeffers, J.S., *Conflict at Rome: Social Order and Hierarchy in Early Christianity*. (Minneapolis:Fortress, 1991).
Jones, A.H.M., *The Roman economy: studies in ancient economic and administrative history* (edited by P.A. Brunt). (Oxford: Blackwell, 1974).
Jones, C.P., *The Roman World of Dio Chrysostom*. (Cambridge, MA: Harvard University Press, 1978).
Jordan, M.D., 'Ancient Philosophic Protreptic and the Problem of Persuasive Genres', *Rhetorica* 4 (1986): 309-33.
Karavites, P., *Evil, Freedom, and the Road to Perfection in Clement of Alexandria*. (Leiden: Brill, 1999).
Kennedy, G., *The art of persuasion in Greece*. (Princeton: Routledge and Keegan Paul, 1963).
———, *The art of rhetoric in the Roman world, 300B.C. – A.D.300*. (Princeton: Princeton University Press, 1972).
Kenney, J.P., 'Divinity and the Intelligible World in Clement of Alexandria', *SP* 21 (1987): 308-15
Keresztes, P., 'The literary genre of Justin's First Apology', *VC* 19 (1965): 99-110
Kraeling, C.H., 'The Jewish Community at Antioch', *Journal of Biblical Literature* 51 (1932): 130-60.
Lennox Manton, E., *Roman North Africa*. (London: Seaby, 1988).
Lewis, N., *Life in Egypt under Roman Rule*. (Oxford: Clarendon, 1983).
Lilla, S.R.C., *Clement of Alexandria: a study in Christian Platonism and Gnosticism*. (Oxford: OUP, 1971).
Lindemann, A., *Die Clemensbriefe*. (Tübingen: Mohr, 1992).
Long, A.A., *Stoic Studies*. (Cambridge: CUP, 1996).
Long, A.A., and Sedley, D.N., *The Hellenistic Philosophers*. 2 vols. (Cambridge:

CUP, 1987).

Magie, D., *Roman Rule in Asia Minor to the end of the third century after Christ*. 2 vols. (Princeton: Princeton University Press, 1950).

Maier, H.O., 'Purity and Danger in Polycarp's Epistle to the Philippians: The Sin of Valens in Social perspective', *JECS* 1 (1993): 229-47.

Malherbe, A.J., 'The Structure of Athenagoras, "Supplicatio pro Christianis"', *VC* 23 (1969): 1-20.

———, 'Athenagoras on Christian Ethics', *JEH* 20 (1969): 1-5.

———, 'The Holy Spirit in Athenagoras', *JTS* ns20 (1969): 538-42.

Mansfeld, J., 'Resurrection added: the Interpretatio Christiana of a Stoic doctrine', *VC* 37 (191983), 227-8.

Marcovich, M., 'Clement of Alexandria, *Protrepticus*', *SP* 31 (1997): 452-63.

Marrou, H.I., *A History of Education in Antiquity*. (trans. Y.G.Lamb). (New York: Sheed and Ward, 1956).

Meeks, W.A., and Wilken, R.L., *Jews and Christians in Antioch in the First Four Centuries of the Common Era*. (Missoula: Scholars Press, 1978).

Mellink, O., *Death as eschaton: a study of Ignatius of Antioch's Desire for Death*. (Amsterdam: University of Amsterdam, 2000).

Millar, F., *The Emperor in the Roman World*. (London: Duckworth, 1977).

———, *The Roman Empire and its Neighbours*. 2nd edition. (London: Duckworth, 1981).

Minns, D., *Irenaeus*. (London: Geoffrey Chapman, 1984).

Mortley, R., 'The Theme of Silence in Clement of Alexandria', *JTS* ns24 (1973): 197-202.

———, *Connaissance religieuse et herménetique chez Clément d'Alexandrie*. (Leiden: Brill, 1973).

McGehee, M., 'Why Tatian never "Apologized" to the Greeks', *JECS* 1 (1993): 143-58.

MacMullen, R., *Enemies of the Roman Order: Treason, Unrest and Alienation in the Empire*. (Cambridge, MA: Harvard University Pres, 1966).

McVey, K.E., 'The use of Stoic Cosmogony in Theophilus of Antioch's Hexaemeron', in Burrows, M.S. and Rorem, P., (eds), *Biblical Hermeneutics in Historical Perspective: Studies in Honor of Karlfried Froelich on His Sixtieth Birthday*. (Grand Rapids: Eerdmans, 1991), pp. 32-58.

Nahm, C., 'The Debate on the "Platonism" of Justin Martyr', *Second Century* 9 (1992): 129-51.

Nautin, P., 'Notes Critiques sur Théophile d'Antioche, Ad Autolycum Lib. II', *VC* 11 (1957): 212-25.

———, *Origène: Sa vie et son oeuvre*. (Paris: Beauchesne, 1977).

Niebuhr, R., *Christ and Culture*. (New York: Harper, 1951).

Nilson, J., 'To whom is Justin's *Dialogue with Trypho* addressed?', *Theological Studies* 38 (1977): 538-46.

Noakes, K.W., 'Melito of Sardis and the Jews', *SP* 13 (1975): 244-9.

O'Hagan, A.P., 'The Great Tribulation to Come in the Pastor of Hermas', *SP* 4

(1961): 305-11.

O'Rourke, J.J., 'Roman Law and the Early Church', in Benko, S., and O'Rourke, J.J., (eds), *Early Church History: The Roman Empire in the Setting of Primitive Christianity*. (London: Oliphants, 1972), pp. 165-86.

Osborn, E.F., *Justin Martyr*. (Tübingen: Mohr, 1973).

———, *The beginning of Christian philosophy*. (Cambridge: CUP, 1981).

———, 'Clement of Alexandria: A Review of Research, 1958-1982', *Second Century* 3 (1983): 219-43.

———, *The Emergence of Christian Theology*. (Cambridge: CUP, 1993).

———, 'Arguments for Faith in Clement of Alexandria', *VC* 48 (1994): 1-24.

———, *Tertullian: First Theologian of the West*. (Cambridge: CUP, 1997).

———, 'Irenaeus on God – Argument and Parody', *SP* 36 (2001): 270-81.

———, *Irenaeus*. (Cambridge, CUP, 2001).

Osiek, C., *Rich and Poor in the Shepherd of Hermas*. (Washington: Catholic Biblical Association of America, 1983).

———, 'The Genre and Function of the *Shepherd of Hermas*', *Semeia* 36 (1986): 113-21.

———, 'The early second century through the eyes of Hermas: continuity and change', *Biblical Theology Bulletin* 20 (1990): 116-22.

———, 'The Oral World of early Christianity in Rome: the case of Hermas', in Donfried, K.P., and Richardson, P., (eds), *Judaism and Christianity in first-century Rome.* (Grand Rapids: Eerdmans, 1998), pp. 151-172.

———, *Shepherd of Hermas: a commentary*. (Minneapolis: Fortress, 1999).

Paget, J.C., *The Epistle of Barnabas: Outlook and Background*. (Tübingen: Mohr, 1994).

———, 'Clement of Alexandria and the Jews', *Scottish Journal of Theology* 51 (1998): 86-97.

Patterson, J.R., 'The City of Rome: from Republic to Empire', *JRS* 82 (1992): 186-215.

Perkins, J., 'The "Self" as Sufferer', *HTR* 85 (1992): 245-72.

Poirier, P-H., 'Éléments de Polémique Anti-Juive dans L'Ad Diognetum', *VC* 40 (1986): 218-25.

Porter, S.E. (ed.), *Handbook of Classical Rhetoric in the Hellenistic Period 330BC-AD400.* (Leiden: Brill, 1997).

Pouderon, B., *Athénagore d'Athènes: philosophe Chrétien*. (Paris: Beauchesne, 1989).

———,'Athénagore chef d'école. À propos du témoignage du Philippe de Sidé', *SP* 26 (1993): 167-76.

Price, R.M., 'Are there "Holy Pagans" in Justin Martyr?', *SP* 31 (1997): 167-71.

Price, S.R.F., *Rituals and Power: the Roman Imperial Cult in Asia Minor*. (Cambridge: CUP, 1984).

Procopé, J.F., 'Morality and Manners in Clement's *Paidagogos*', *SP* 26 (1993): 313-

7.

Quasten, J., *Patrology*. 4 volumes, (Westminster: Newman Press, 1983):
Vol. I: *The Beginnings of Patristic Literature – From the Apostles Creed to Irenaeus.*
Vol. II: *The Ante-Nicene Literature After Irenaeus.*
Vol. III: *The Golden Age of Greek Patristic Literature.*
Vol. IV: *The Golden Age of Latin Patristic Literature From the Council of Nicaea to the Council of Chalcedon.*

Rankin, D.I., 'Was Tertullian a schismatic?', *Prudentia* 18 (1986): 73-80.

———, 'Tertullian's Consistency of thought on ministry', *SP* 21 (1989): 271-6.

———, *Tertullian and the Church*. (Cambridge: CUP, 1995).

———, 'Was Tertullian a Jurist?', *SP* 31 (1997): 335-42.

———, 'Tertullian's Vocabulary of the Divine "Individuals" in *adversus Praxean*', *Sacris Erudiri* 40 (2001): 5-46.

———, 'Class Distinction as a Way of Doing Church: The Early Fathers and the Christian *plebs*', *VC* 58 (2004): 298-315.

Raven, S., *Rome in Africa*. 3rd edition. (London and New York: Routledge, 1993).

Ridings, D., 'Clement of Alexandria and the Intended Audience of the *Stromateis*', *SP* 31 (1997): 517-21.

Rist, J.M., *Stoic Philosophy*. (Cambridge: CUP, 1969).

Rives, J.B., *Religion and Authority in Roman Carthage from Augustus to Constantine*. (Oxford: Clarendon, 1995).

Roberts, L., 'The Literary Form of the *Stromateis*', *Second Century* 1 (1981): 211-22.

Robillard, E., 'L'Êpître de Barnabé: trois époques, trois théologies, trois rédacteurs', *Revue Biblique* 78 (1971): 184-209.

Runia, D.T., *Philo of Alexandria and the Timaeus of Plato*. (Leiden: Brill, 1986).

Saller, R.P., *Personal Patronage under the Early Empire*. (Cambridge, CUP, 1982).

———,'Patronage and friendship in early Imperial Rome: drawing the distinction', in Wallace-Hadrill, A. (ed.), *Patronage in Ancient Society*. (London and New York: Routledge, 1989), pp. 49-62.

Sandbach, F.H., *The Stoics*. 2nd edition. (Bristol: Bristol Press, 1989).

Schoedel, W.R., 'Philosophy and Rhetoric in the Adversus Haereses of Irenaeus', *VC* 13 (1959): 22-32.

———, 'Christian "Atheism" and the Peace of the Roman Empire', *Church History* 42 (1973): 309-19.

———, 'Theological Norms and Social Perspectives in Ignatius of Antioch' in Sanders, E.P. (ed.), *Jewish and Christian Self-Definition*. Vol. 1: *The Shaping of Christianity in the Second and Third Centuries*. (London: SCM, 1980), pp. 30-56.

———, 'Theological Method in Irenaeus (Adversus Haereses 2. 25-28)', *JTS* ns 35 (1984): 31-49.

———, 'Apologetic Literature and Ambassadorial Activities', *HTR* 82 (1989): 55-

78.

Sherwin-White, A.N., *The Roman Citizenship*. (Oxford: Clarendon, 1973).

Sibinga, J. Smit, 'Melito of Sardis. The Artist and his Text', *VC* 24 (1970): 81-104.

Sider, R.D., *Ancient Rhetoric and the art of Tertullian*. (Oxford: OUP, 1971).

Simpson, A.D., 'Epicureans, Christians and Atheists in the second century', *TAPhA* 72 (1941): 372-81.

Southern, P., *Domitian - Tragic Tyrant*. (London and New York: Routledge, 1997).

Stark, R., *The Rise of Christianity. A Sociologist Reconsiders History*. (Princeton: Princeton University Press, 1996).

Steen, G.L., (ed.), *Alexandria: the Site and the History*. (New York and London: New York University Press, 1993).

Stewart-Sykes, A., 'Melito's Anti-Judaism', *JECS* 5 (1997): 271-83.

———, *Preacher and Audience: Studies in Early Christian and Byzantine Homiletics*. (Leiden: Brill, 1998).

Talbert, R.J.A., *The Senate of Imperial Rome*. (Princeton: Princeton University Press, 1984).

Tanner, K., *Theories of Culture: A New Agenda for Theology*. (Minneapolis: Fortress, 1997).

Tanner, R.G., 'The Epistle to Diognetus and Contemporary Greek Thought', *SP* 15 (1984): 495-508.

Torchia, N.J., 'Theories of Creation in the Second Century Apologists and their Middle Platonist Background', *SP* 26 (1993): 192-9.

Trevett, C., 'Ignatius "To the Romans" and 1 Clement LIV-LVI', *VC* 43 (1989): 35-52.

———, *A study of Ignatius of Antioch in Syria and Asia*. (Lewiston: Edwin Mellen, 1992).

Trigg, J.W., *Origen: the Bible and Philosophy in the Third-Century Church*. (London: SCM, 1983).

———, *Origen*. (London and New York: Routledge, 1998).

Ullmann, W., 'The cosmic theme of the *Prima Clementis* and its significance for the concept of Roman Rulership', *SP* 11 (1972): 85-91.

Van den Hoek, A., 'The "Catechetical" School of Early Christian Alexandria and its Philonic Heritage', *HTR* 90 (1997): 59-87.

Van Unnik, W.C., 'Is 1 Clement 20 purely Stoic?', *VC* 4 (1950): 181-9.

Veyne, P., *Bread and Circuses: Historical Sociology and Political Pluralism*. (London: Penguin, 1990).

Vogel, C.J. de, 'Platonism and Christianity: a mere antagonism or a profound common ground?', *VC* 39 (1985): 1-62.

Wallace-Hadrill, D.S., *Christian Antioch: a study of early Christian thought in the East*. (Cambridge: CUP, 1982).

Wells, C., *The Roman Empire*. 2nd edition (Cambridge, Mass: Harvard University

Press, 1984).

Whittaker, M., 'Tatian's Educational Background', *SP* 13 (1975): 57-9.

Winden, J.C.M., 'Minucius Felix, Octavius 19, 9', *VC* 8 (1954): 72-9.

Yamauchi, E.M., *The Archaeology of New Testament Cities in Western Asia Minor*. (London: Pickering and Inglis, 1980).

Young, M.O., 'Justin, Socrates and the Middle-Platonists', *SP* 18 (1989): 161-6.

Young, S., 'Being a Man: The Pursuit of manliness in the Shepherd of Hermas', *JECS* 2 (1994): 237-55.

Zeegers-Vander Vorst, N., 'Les citations poétiques chez Théophile d'Antioche', *SP* 10 (1970): 168-74.

———, *Les citations des poètes grecs chez les apologistes chrétiens du IIe siècle.* Recueil de Travaux d'Histoire et de Philologie. 4th series, vol. 47. (Louvain: Bibliothèque de l'Université, 1972).

———, 'La Création de l'Homme (GN 1,26) chez Théophile d'Antioche', *VC* 30 (1976): 258-67.

Zuntz, G., 'Melito - Syriac?', *VC* 6 (1952): 193-201.

Citations from the Fathers

Subject Index